Rethinking
White-Collar Crime

Rethinking
White-Collar Crime

TONY G. POVEDA

Praeger Series in Criminology and Crime Control Policy
Steven A. Egger, Series Editor

Westport, Connecticut
London

Library of Congress Cataloging-in-Publication Data

Poveda, Tony G.
    Rethinking white-collar crime / Tony G. Poveda.
        p.   cm.—(Praeger series in criminology and crime control policy, ISSN 1060–3212)
    Includes bibliographical references (p.   ) and index.
    ISBN 0–275–94586–3 (alk. paper)
    1. White-collar crimes—United States.   I. Title.   II. Series.
HV6769.P67   1994
    364.1'68'0973—dc20   94–1143

British Library Cataloguing in Publication Data is available.

Library of Congress Catalog Card Number: 94–1143
ISBN: 0–275–94586–3
ISSN: 1060–3212

First published in 1994

Praeger Publishers, 88 Post Road West, Westport, CT 06881
An imprint of Greenwood Publishing Group, Inc.

Printed in the United States of America

The paper used in this book complies with the
Permanent Paper Standard issued by the National
Information Standards Organization (Z39.48–1984).

10 9 8 7 6 5 4 3 2

Copyright Acknowledgment

Extracts from Tony G. Poveda, "White-Collar Crime and the Justice Department," *Crime, Law, and Social Change* 17 (May 1992): 235–252, were used and cited in Chapter 8. Reprinted by permission of Kluwer Academic Publishers.

For my wife, Maria

Contents

Preface

As I write this brief introduction in the fall of 1993, the Mollen Commission has just completed two weeks of hearings on police corruption in New York City, where it disclosed how rogue officers were dealing drugs and brutalizing dealers and innocent citizens alike, especially in minority neighborhoods. Prudential Securities, the nation's fourth largest brokerage firm, has agreed to pay restitution and fines totaling more than $371 million for defrauding hundreds of thousands of customers over the last decade. A federal judge in Philadelphia is considering whether a proposed settlement involving 6.3 million General Motors (GM) pickup trucks is adequate. GM still denies the trucks, with side-mounted gasoline tanks, are defective and refuses to recall them, but it has offered owners a $1,000 coupon toward future purchases of GM trucks. After seven years of defying a presidential order that barred government contracts with companies that defraud the federal government, the U.S. Agriculture Department has agreed to comply with the directive. The case in question involved 52 U.S. dairies, including some of the largest in the country, which had been convicted of price-fixing and bid-rigging on federal contracts for the school lunch program in the late 1980s. Contrary to presidential directive, the Agriculture Department continued to do business with these convicted corporate offenders. Finally, Michael Milken, who recently served nearly two years in federal prison for securities fraud, is teaching a management course for future M.B.A.s at UCLA this semester and is also working on developing an educational television network.

These seemingly disparate events underscore some of the ideas and themes I will pursue in this book. They highlight not only the diversity of white-collar crime, but also the distinctive manner in which society responds to white-collar offenders—what some regard as a double standard of justice. Additionally, these events reveal the relative absence of shaming in association with much of white-collar crime, where white-collar offenses are handled as administrative or civil matters and ex-offenders are sometimes viewed as folk heroes.

More subtle is the impact such events have on the social fabric, particularly our sense of trust and confidence in the institutions around us. A February 1993 national poll showed that the public's trust in government is at an all-time low since such surveys have been conducted (1958), even lower than it was in the mid-1970s when President Richard Nixon resigned in the wake of the Watergate scandal. White-collar crime is, at its core, a violation of public trust. Lawlessness in government and business threatens the very integrity of these institutions. For society to function with a spirit of order and legitimacy, there must be a modicum of trust, whether it be trust in our police or elected representatives, the financial institutions in which we deposit our money, or the myriad of consumer products we purchase each year.

One of the major themes of this volume is this linkage between the public's trust and confidence in social institutions and white-collar crime. The ongoing disclosures of wrongdoing in our political and financial institutions, especially in the last 20 years, have seriously eroded the public's confidence in these institutions. Traditionally, the conventional wisdom regarding white-collar crime has served to conceal or minimize these violations in contrast to the alarm that accompanies the exposés of conventional crime. The disclosures and the growing recognition of crime among the wealthy and powerful have begun to take their toll in declining levels of social trust and rising cynicism about our justice system.

On the surface, this is a book about a type of crime, white-collar crime. But it is much more than that. Another major theme of this volume is that we cannot separate our thinking about white-collar crime from conventional crime. There is an ongoing invidious comparison between the two, with the implication that when we learn something about white-collar crime, we are simultaneously learning something about conventional crime and criminal justice. In this respect, this book's main idea of rethinking white-collar crime is a heuristic device to encourage critical thought about the nature of all crime, law, and criminal justice.

PLAN OF THE BOOK

This book is organized into three major parts. Part One, which includes the first four chapters, focuses on the definitional and conceptual issues that must be considered in our rethinking of white-collar crime. The first task (Chapter 1) is to explore the dualism in our thinking between white-collar and conventional crime, particularly two myths that permeate much popular and criminological thought: the myth of the criminal type and the myth of the law-abiding citizen. Besides making explicit these two myths, it is also necessary to compare the harms that derive from the two groups encompassed by these myths: the elite (the law-abiding) and the economic underclass. By demonstrating that crime exists among the privileged, and that it is comparable in harm to that of the crimes of the poor and powerless, we begin the process of demystifying the crimes of the powerful. In Chapter 2, the conventional wisdom of white-collar crime is further explored, with the aim of showing how our myths about white-collar crime reduce its visibility as well as the seriousness with which it is regarded by the public. Chapter 3 traces the evolution of the idea of white-collar crime from Edwin H. Sutherland to the Justice Department; it considers the definitional controversy as well as the conceptual challenge that white-collar crime poses for the field of criminology. In the final chapter of Part One (Chapter 4), the double-standard issue is examined in relation to the differential official handling of white-collar and conventional crime by the justice system. Why is white-collar crime largely handled by one type of public law and conventional crime by another? This chapter gives special attention to the "war on drugs" and why society responds to some drugs as a "criminal" problem and to others as a "regulatory" matter. This rounds out the scope of definitional and conceptual issues that inform the rest of the book.

Part Two addresses the problem of explaining white-collar crime, especially crime committed by those at the top of the social and opportunity structures of society. It considers first (Chapter 5) the "facts" of white-collar crime: What do we know about the patterns and distribution of white-collar crime in society? What types of white-collar offenses can be delineated, and what differences exist between conventional and white-collar offenders? What are some of the distinctive research problems raised in the study of white-collar crime? The challenge posed for theory, including the problem of explaining criminal conduct that stems from the normally law-abiding segments of the population, is examined in Chapter 6. The major theories that have been applied to white-collar crime are reviewed as are recent attempts to integrate some of the traditional theories. Overall, this section assesses the state of theory in white-collar crime.

In the final part of the book (Part Three), the questions and issues raised in the social control of white-collar crime are confronted. Chapter 7 reviews the traditional approaches to the control of white-collar crime. Included is a history of white-collar crime legislation that surveys the early changes in the law of theft, the embezzlement statutes, antitrust laws, and laws that were passed during the Progressive, New Deal, and consumer eras of this century. Throughout the twentieth century, the administrative and civil laws have comprised the major mechanisms for the social control of white-collar crime, with the criminal law (and the criminal justice system) an avenue of last resort. The last two chapters (Chapters 8 and 9) consider the limitations of these traditional approaches and what that implies for our rethinking of white-collar crime. Can white-collar crime enforcement ever be more than a symbolic gesture, particularly when the targets of enforcement are the wealthy and powerful? Can solutions to the white-collar crime problem transcend the ideological and political obstacles that have limited traditional regulatory approaches? These questions are explored in the closing chapters.

ACKNOWLEDGMENTS

One incurs a debt of gratitude to many along the way in completing a project such as this. I shall begin with the several generations of students who have now passed through my white-collar crime classes at the State University of New York at Plattsburgh. Over the years they have provided a useful sounding board, allowing me to develop and refine my ideas; needless to say, this has been a learning process for all.

I am grateful to my department colleagues at SUNY Plattsburgh for their support and encouragement, particularly Robert Weiss who made sure that no current events pertaining to white-collar crime escaped my attention. The librarians at the University were always generous with their time in seeking out hard-to-find materials, especially documents librarian Tim Hartnett.

Often, it seems, when you have a book idea or insight that you believe to be brilliant and profound, it is difficult to find others who share in that wisdom. Fortunately for me, Steven Egger, Series Editor at Praeger, believed in my book idea from the beginning. I thank him for his confidence and for the sponsorship of my work. I am also grateful to James Ice, Sociology Editor, and to Sasha Kintzler, Production Editor, for shepherding this project through its various phases at Greenwood Publishing.

Finally, I wish to thank my wife and family for their support and patience, allowing me to escape periodically into the world of libraries, word processing, and reflection. I hope the product of all of this will be a contribution to our knowledge of white-collar crime, useful to students and colleagues alike.

Part One

DEFINITIONAL AND CONCEPTUAL ISSUES

■ CHAPTER ONE ■

Demystifying the Crimes of the Powerful

One of the major themes of this book is that when we think about white-collar crime,[1] we are also thinking more broadly about crime and criminal justice. There is something about the phenomenon of white-collar crime that always seems to invite a comparison with other types of crime, especially conventional property and violent crimes. When top executives are convicted of fraud in the savings and loan industry, we wonder what would happen to bank robbers who steal from the same institutions. On the rare occasions when corporate criminals go to prison, we wonder for how long and in which institutions they will do their time—in comparison with conventional criminals. There is always a lingering suspicion that the white-collar criminal is getting off leniently in our justice system. This ongoing comparison means that when we learn something about white-collar crime, we are simultaneously learning something about other kinds of crime and criminal justice. In this respect, an awareness of white-collar crime and how we officially handle it encourages us to think critically about the nature of crime, law, and criminal justice.

In an early analysis of white-collar crime, criminologist Donald Newman (1958: 56) recognized some of these same theoretical implications of the concept of white-collar crime. He observed that whether criminologists like it or not, they must come to terms with issues of power and privilege when they study white-collar crime. This includes examining the role of power and wealth in shaping the law: Why are some behaviors criminalized and others not? And, conversely, why and how is it that some highly questionable organizational practices are legalized? It also challenges us to think about inequalities in the administration of justice: Why do we maintain the apparent double standard in how we respond to conventional crime versus white-collar crime? Why do we allocate more resources to pursuing some crimes than others? These and other questions are basic to understanding all crime, but they are made more explicit when we take note of white-collar crime, particularly the crimes of the wealthy and powerful in society.

Steven Box (1983: 12–15) understood this when he wrote of the "mystification" of our perceptions of crime, where he argued that we are basically socialized to see crime through the eyes of the state. In this legal definition of the crime problem, the crimes of the poor are highlighted and made the focus of the investigative efforts of the criminal justice system.[2] Through this same legal lens of the state, the crimes of the powerful are concealed or obscured from view. Thinking about white-collar crime in these terms means that we must demystify our perceptions of this official view of crime.

This, indeed, is the principal task of the first two chapters: to demystify the crimes of the powerful and to make explicit our conventional wisdom about white-collar crime. In this first chapter, we shall be concerned with revealing certain myths about crime and criminals that support this traditional view of the crime problem, where criminal harms are dichotomized between those that originate with the poor and those that derive from the wealthy or powerful. It will also be necessary to demonstrate not only that the harms that flow from the privileged exist, but also that they are at least comparable to those of the economic underclass of society.

THE DUALISTIC FALLACY: THE TWO MYTHS[3]

Two widely shared myths provide ideological support to conventional thinking about the crime problem. One of these myths, the myth of the criminal type, sensitizes us to the kinds of persons who are criminals as well as to their social location in society. The other myth, the myth of the law-abiding citizen, reassures the rest of us that we are substantially different from those persons who fit that criminal type. These two myths have implications for understanding white-collar crime because, by and large, white-collar criminals are drawn from that segment of the population we designate as law-abiding. The first step to unraveling our thinking about white-collar crime necessarily involves a critical examination of these two myths.

The Myth of the Criminal Type

The belief that the world is sharply divided between criminals and noncriminals or delinquents and nondelinquents has a long history. It is a belief that not only is deeply embedded in popular thinking about crime and criminals, but also permeates much criminological thought. This false dichotomy often takes expression in the characterization of criminals as belonging to some criminal type. Where early theories of crime attempted to link the criminal to certain physical characteristics (a physical type) or mental deficiencies (a psychological type), the modern myth of the criminal type portrays the criminal as a particular social type: poor, young, male, lower class, minority (Poveda, 1970). A recent version of this myth portrays crime as highly concentrated in a small, hard-core group of offenders, variously known as "chronic offenders" or "career criminals" (Gottfredson and Hirschi, 1986; Walker, 1989: 55ff.). In this view these "career criminals" account for the vast majority of serious crime.

Many major theories of crime and delinquency, wittingly or unwittingly, reinforce the criminal-type myth by incorporating the prevailing cultural stereotypes of criminals into their search for explanations of crime. For example, the overwhelming emphasis of traditional delinquency theory was on explaining urban, male, lower-class delinquency; this reflected a widespread concern over gang delinquency in the inner cities. While this is understandable, nevertheless this collective focus neglected or completely ignored other dimensions of the problem: middle-class delinquency, nongang delinquency, and so on (Poveda, 1970). Similarly, James Q. Wilson's (1983: 5–6) justification for focusing on "predatory street crime," and for excluding white-collar crime, in a book about crime and crime policy underscores this point. It is not that theorists and policymakers must always deal with all types of crime simultaneously, but what is misleading is the appearance that they are dealing with *the* crime problem when in fact they are dealing with only one aspect of it.

Sociologist Edwin M. Schur (1969: 9–12; 1973: 10–11) designated this tendency to think about crime in a dualistic way as "compartmentalized thinking." It is manifested in many of the metaphors and stereotypes that we use to portray crime and criminals. The use of the term "war," for example, to refer to our crime policies is a common expression of this tendency. Criminals then become "enemies" of society, and any methods, accordingly, can be employed in their capture and punishment. The battle lines between the "good guys" and the "bad guys" are sharply drawn. In this manner, crime is transformed into an alien phenomenon that exists outside the mainstream of society. Its roots, as in the "war on drugs," may even lie in the crime cartels of foreign countries or in the evil tendencies of certain kinds of persons/groups within our own borders. By compartmentalizing crime in this fashion, we obscure the numerous ways in which crime and criminals are linked to mainstream values and institutions, and indeed are a product of the wider culture and social structure. In this respect the dualistic fallacy constitutes an oversimplified way of thinking about crime.

Where do our criminal-type myths come from? Clearly every historical period produces its own unique crime concerns that come to be reflected in the metaphors and stereotypes we use to characterize the crime problem, whether it be the "war on drugs" of the 1980s, the "law and order" crisis of the 1960s, or the Depression-era "gangsters" and "public enemies." There are, however, some common denominators in the production of criminal-type myths. Theodore R. Sarbin's (1967: 286; 1969: 16–17) analysis of the concept of danger is useful in this regard. He points to the origins of the word "danger" in the Latin term *dominium*, which denotes a "relative position in a social structure." Behavior that threatens the *dominium* is perceived as danger by those in power. Hence dangerous persons or groups are those who threaten the existing power structure, the status quo. Criminal-type myths are produced in the social and the political processes by which certain persons or groups are labelled as dangerous in society.

The development of our modern criminal-type myths is rooted in the "dangerous classes" of the nineteenth century, as the masses of the poor and immigrants at the bottom of the social structure were designated (Brace, 1967). In his late-nineteenth-century account of the dangerous classes of New York, Charles Loring Brace observed that the crime and pauperism of New York were not as enmeshed in the masses as in London and other European cities. However, the New York poor, who at that time were mainly children of Irish and German immigrants, were even more dangerous than their European counterparts. The dangers were expressed in terms of social unrest, such as riots and communist revolt, as well as criminal violence and the threat posed to the propertied classes (Brace, 1967: 25–31).

The invention of a variety of social institutions in the nineteenth century was in large part a response to these dangerous classes. The formation of the modern police in the mid-1800s, as a paid, paramilitary occupational group, was directly related to the urban mob violence of the lower classes, in both Europe and the United States (Reith, 1952; Parks, 1970). The creation of other modern institutions during this century—the penitentiaries for the criminals, asylums for the mentally ill, poor houses for the poor, and reformatories for delinquents—is also tied to the perceived danger of unrest and disorder from these segments of the population (Rothman, 1971).

Since the nineteenth century, criminal-type myths have consistently been linked to members of the economic underclass, but there have been times, although brief, when dangers to social order have been perceived outside of this traditional social location. During the Populist-Progressive era, from 1890 until around World War I, there were two sources of danger to social stability: (1) From the top of the social order came the "robber barons" who threatened democratic government with their huge trusts and accumulation of wealth, and (2) from the bottom came the threat of unrest from the lower classes (Poveda, 1970: 68–72). Historian Richard Hofstadter (1955: 238), in his Pulitzer Prize–winning work on this era, noted the two fronts that Progressives encountered: "On the one side they feared the power of the plutocracy, on the other the poverty and restlessness of the masses." This latter front came to be called "the social question." Hofstadter's first front was written about by muckraking journalists, among others, who exposed the abuses of the big trusts, such as Standard Oil and the meatpacking industry.

In the more recent period of the Watergate scandal[4] of the early 1970s, there was also widespread concern about crime and corruption at the top. This concern was reflected in a dramatic decline in the public's trust and confidence in major social institutions in the late 1960s and the 1970s, including not only government, but also big business, the military, the press, religion, labor unions, and so on (Simon and Eitzen, 1993: 1–12; Lipset and Schneider, 1978). White-collar crime itself even became a top investigative priority of the U.S. Justice Department during this post-Watergate era.

While criminal-type myths are on occasion linked to threats from other than the so-called dangerous classes, these threats are typically very short-lived. In his discussion of the diminished concern with trusts and political machines and the passing of Progressivism, Hofstadter (1955: 310) remarked: "And what of the old Progressive issues? They were bypassed, sidestepped, outgrown—anything but solved." As the Watergate scandal began to fade by the early 1980s, Ronald Reagan's administration similarly redirected public attention away from crime and corruption at the top by emphasizing violent crime, terrorism, and drug use as its top crime priorities. The enduring criminal-type myths remain those that are rooted in the economic underclass.

The Myth of the Law-Abiding Citizen

The other side of the dualism of the criminal-type myth is the notion that the vast majority of citizens are law-abiding. Unless they fit into the prevailing cultural stereotype of the criminal, they will not be regarded as "real" criminals. This widespread belief was captured by John Braithwaite and Gilbert Geis (1982: 292–293) when they noted President Reagan's[5] reaction to the illegal activities of the Watergate conspirators, which was recorded in the *Los Angeles Times* of May 2, 1973. Reagan contended that the Watergate offenders were "not criminals at heart," and while the Watergate break-in was illegal, "criminal" was too harsh a term to apply. "I doubt if any of them would even intentionally double park," Reagan said. Clearly the Watergate offenders, who included top officials in Richard Nixon's administration, belonged to the law-abiding majority of citizens. It was this same law-abiding majority that both Nixon and Reagan frequently enlisted on the side of "law and order" in order to "war" on the criminal elements of society. As we can see, crimes committed by this "law-abiding" group present serious conceptual and ideological problems for those seeking to maintain the dualism between criminals and noncriminals.

The existence of crime in law-abiding circles is well documented in various studies going back several decades. In one of the first attempts to show this apparent contradiction, James Wallerstein and C. J. Wyle (1947) administered a questionnaire to a convenience sample of approximately 1,700 adults, mainly in the New York City area, asking them to indicate whether they had committed any of the 49 felonies on the questionnaire during their adult life (i.e., when they were over 16 years old). Ninety-nine percent of those questioned answered affirmatively to one or more of the offenses; the mean number of self-reported offenses for men was 18, ranging from 8.2 for ministers to 20.2 for laborers.

While these findings are suggestive, it took the development of self-report measures[6] of delinquency in the mid-1950s to further substantiate the existence of delinquency among "law-abiding" juveniles. These early self-report studies found, surprisingly, that there were no social class differences in reported delinquencies (Short and Nye, 1957; Nye, Short, and Virgil, 1958). This is in contrast to traditional studies of delinquency that located most delinquency in the urban lower class. However, these traditional studies had relied upon official delinquency statistics, police arrests of juveniles and delinquency court cases, which reflected the greater involvement of lower-class juveniles with the justice system. The self-report studies tapped into the domain of unofficial or hidden delinquency, which was most characteristic of middle-class delinquency.

This apparent discrepancy in the findings from official and self-report measures was not resolved for many years. Michael J. Hindelang and his associates (1979) pointed out that these early self-reports asked respondents about relatively minor forms of delinquency. When self-report questionnaires were redesigned to include items about more serious delinquency, class and racial differences in delinquency again appear, consistent with official statistics. Delbert S. Elliot and Suzanne Ageton (1980) further pointed out that when the frequency of the offense is taken into account, class and racial differences appear at the high end of the continuum. So it appears that when only minor kinds of violations are involved, the differences in such wrongdoing among juveniles are slight. It is when we consider more serious delinquencies, committed more often, that important differences (class and race) appear among juveniles. These are also the kinds of delinquencies that are more likely to receive official attention.

The relevance of this discussion to our two myths is that these data shed light on the distribution of delinquency (official and unofficial) in the population. The two myths we have been considering (criminal type and law-abiding citizen) assume a particular distribution of offenders in the population, with a small, hardcore group accounting for the vast majority of offenses. They also assume a dichotomous, all-or-nothing phenomenon, where criminality is either present or absent. As Elliott Currie (1985: 83) has observed, there are two extreme models that can be employed to describe the reality of crime distribution. One model (the "chronic offender" model)[7] takes the position that crime is highly concentrated, and that a tiny fraction of the population accounts for most of the crime. The other extreme model asserts that crime (or delinquency) is more-or-less equally distributed in the population. Currie then proceeds to challenge both models in order to demonstrate that the truth lies in some intermediate model. Although he concedes "that a disproportionate amount of crime is committed by a *relatively* small fraction of the population" (Currie, 1985: 84), this is still not the tiny group conventionally portrayed in criminal-type myths or in this chronic offender model. Currie (1985: 85–86) goes on to estimate, based on the Philadelphia birth-cohort study of Marvin Wolfgang and his associates (1972), that some 160,000 "chronic offenders" are born in the United States each year, 1 million every six years. And while this group certainly commits more than its fair share of crime, it does not take into account the crimes committed by the less frequent offenders, which are probably understated in the official statistics.

Elliot and Ageton's (1980: 104) data on the frequency distribution of self-reported delinquency also provide some support for such an intermediate model.

Their data show a small percentage of offenders at the high end of the frequency continuum (1 to 10%, depending on the type of delinquency), with the vast majority of offenders at the low-frequency end of the continuum (70 to 80%). Clearly the frequency distribution is skewed, with most offenders at the low end of the distribution. In this regard the frequency distribution is consistent with the chronic offender model and the two myths that we have discussed, which also support that model. These data differ in one important respect from this model, however, and that is that they show law-abidingness as a continuous rather than a discrete variable. Those offenders at the low end of the continuum still commit some crimes, sometimes even serious ones, but at a less frequent rate than those at the high-frequency end. It is not clear from their data, however, how many juveniles report no delinquencies in the past year (the truly law-abiding).

It is also worth emphasizing that the only significant differences in the social characteristics of offenders (class and race) are at the extreme high end of the frequency continuum, which in terms of predatory crimes against the person accounted for approximately 2 percent of their respondents. In other words, the vast majority of offenders are not socially differentiated by their location on this frequency continuum (except those at the high end). It is also likely that our formation of criminal-type myths derives from this relatively small group where differentiation occurs, and consequently these myths do not capture the many other offenders who are committing crimes at a rate below the threshold of visibility.[8]

Although we have been examining data pertaining to adolescents and their delinquencies, it is assumed that the distribution of offenses for adults follows a similar pattern: that law-abidingness is distributed in a continuous fashion with most people at the low-frequency, less serious end of the continuum. This is a more complicated portrait of crime than is suggested by the dualism in the criminal-type and law-abiding citizen myths. It is necessary now to extend our analysis of these myths to harms outside the realm of conventional crime and also outside our cultural stereotype of the criminal. This, of course, is the realm of white-collar crime where the offenders are drawn from the "law-abiding" segment of the population.

THE CRIMES OF THE POWERFUL

When Edwin H. Sutherland first introduced the concept of white-collar crime in 1939, he was quite explicit about wanting to call attention to crimes that occurred outside the lower (or dangerous) classes, and that could not be explained by poverty. For this reason he focused on the crimes of the "respectable," mainly business and professional people, and corporate crime (Sutherland, 1940).[9] His task then was, as ours now is, to show that white-collar offenses are "real" crimes and are harmful, just like conventional crimes. In his classic study of corporate crime, Sutherland (1983) studied the law violations[10] of the 70 largest U.S.

corporations during the period from 1900 to 1944. Each corporation had at least one adverse decision against it, with 14 the average per corporation.

Although Sutherland was successful in showing illegal activity outside the traditional realm of sociological inquiry, he did not convince many of his contemporaries that white-collar crime was "real" crime. The historic Sutherland-Tappan debate in the mid-1940s, which we will consider in more detail later, centered on this very question (Sutherland, 1945; Tappan, 1947). Crime, according to Paul W. Tappan, involved violations of the criminal law that were handled by criminal courts and received criminal penalties. The vast majority of Sutherland's corporate offenses did not meet Tappan's criteria. Moreover, the kind of law violations that Sutherland studied, such as false advertising and restraint of trade, did not strengthen his argument because they involved nonviolent offenses that are typically handled by regulatory agencies (Coleman, 1989: 2).

In the mid-1970s, Marshall B. Clinard and Peter C. Yeager (1980) replicated Sutherland's research on corporate crime. Like Sutherland, they studied the law violations of the largest U.S. industrial corporations (the Fortune 500), but they only looked at a two-year period, 1975 and 1976. Clinard and Yeager found that most of these corporations (62.9%) had regulatory actions initiated against them during this period.

The important research of both Sutherland and Clinard/Yeager certainly documents lawlessness among the law-abiding, but falls short of showing that these corporate crimes are in any way comparable to the harm produced by conventional crime. Jeffrey H. Reiman (1979: 62ff.) devised one of the most effective ways of comparing the relative harm of conventional crime with that of white-collar crime. He developed a standard of harm based on the Federal Bureau of Investigation (FBI) Index Crimes (conventional crimes). Because the Index Crimes consist of property crimes and crimes against the person, the economic loss and personal injury produced by these crimes can serve as our standard of harm. We can then compare that standard to the property loss and personal injury generated by selected types of white-collar crime. First, however, we need to update Reiman's statistics on the harm produced by the Index Crimes.

Property Loss: Conventional and White-Collar Crime Compared

In its annual report on criminal victimization in the United States, the Bureau of Justice Statistics includes data on the economic loss that results from personal and household crimes. The total property loss from conventional crime, as estimated from these data, was approximately $5 billion in 1990.[11] This figure can now serve as a benchmark from which to compare the property loss generated by other crimes.

It is tempting, of course, to compare this property loss standard to various highly publicized cases involving white-collar crime, where the public was defrauded of billions of dollars. We will use two illustrations to make this point: the savings and loan scandal of the late 1980s and the "daisy chain" scandal of the late 1970s.

The cost to the U.S. taxpayer of the savings and loan scandal has been variously estimated at between $200 billion and $500 billion (Calavita and Pontell, 1990: 309). Clearly the cost of the bailout of hundreds of savings and loan financial institutions is not all due to crime.[12] Again, there are various estimates. In its study of the 26 most costly savings and loan failures, the General Accounting Office found illegal activity to be important in all of them (U.S. House, 1990: 10). The two government agencies with responsibility for managing the assets of failed financial institutions (Federal Deposit Insurance Corporation and Resolution Trust Corporation) estimated wrongdoing in more than 75 percent of the failed banks and thrifts (U.S. Senate, 1992: 29). The most conservative estimate, by a savings and loan consultant, was that 3 percent of the total cost is attributable to fraud (Calavita and Pontell, 1991: 98). Using the conservative estimates (3% of $200 billion), we still arrive at the substantial sum of $6 billion. Enforcement efforts also demonstrate the enormous scope of the problem. As of August 1990, the FBI was investigating 234 savings and loans for criminal violations, and another 300 financial institutions were the objects of preliminary inquiries (Knight, 1990: 34). The economic loss resulting from bank robberies pales in comparison to the cost of the criminal fraud in the savings and loan industry. In 1989, bank robberies in the U.S. totaled $24.6 million in losses, with the average "take" being $3,591 (U.S. Department of Justice, 1990a: 160).

A decade earlier there was a crime of comparable magnitude, involving the petroleum industry. In what was known as the "daisy chain" scandal, the domestic petroleum industry found illegal ways to circumvent the federal price regulations that had gone into effect after the Arab oil embargo of 1973—until 1981. In order to partially protect the U.S. consumer from the price explosion (1973–1974) on the international oil market, Congress established a two-tiered pricing system, distinguishing between "old" oil and "new" oil. Old oil was from domestic wells previously discovered and in operation before the Arab embargo; its price was set at $5.25 a barrel. New oil was from wells that were discovered or went into operation after the embargo and was priced at the market level established by the Organization of Petroleum Exporting Countries (OPEC), then $12 a barrel.

The daisy chains were a variety of mechanisms the oil industry devised to fraudulently "change" old oil into new oil and at the same time mark up the price until it approached the new oil price (U.S. House, 1980a; Clinard, 1990: 41ff.). The daisy chains involved the largest oil companies, such as Exxon and Texaco, as well as many smaller ones. The result of the oil industry's violation of these price regulations was in effect to illegally overcharge consumers several billion dollars for oil and gas during this seven-year period. The Department of Energy audits of the industry placed the total overcharge resulting from price control violations at $13 billion (U.S. House, 1981: 157). At the Dingell subcommittee hearings in 1979, one congressman observed that "this is perhaps the largest criminal conspiracy in the history of the United States in terms of the amount of money that has been stolen from the American people" (U.S. House, 1980a: 17).

Another way of comparing the relative property losses from conventional and white-collar crime is by looking at the average "take" in the two types of crime. As we noted above, the average loss incurred from bank robberies in 1989 was $3,591. The average property losses in 1989 from the other conventional property crimes are as follows: robbery, $701; burglary, $1,060; theft, $462; and motor vehicle theft, $5,222 (U.S. Department of Justice, 1990a: 160). In their comparison of conventional and white-collar criminals, Stanton Wheeler and his associates (Wheeler, Weisburd et al., 1988: 337–338) observed the much greater yield that results from white-collar crime. Their study of federal offenses revealed that only 2 percent of their conventional crimes involved more than $100,000, while nearly 30 percent of the white-collar crimes did so.

As a final example in our comparison, we shall consider a much less celebrated case, but nevertheless one that costs consumers millions of dollars a year. In 1981, in a book entitled *Pills That Don't Work*, Sidney M. Wolfe and Christopher M. Coley listed 607 prescription drugs that lacked evidence of effectiveness according to the Food and Drug Administration (FDA) or one of its advisory committees (as of August 1980). In 1962, Congress amended the Food, Drug, and Cosmetic Act of 1938 to require the pre-market testing of all new prescription drugs to show their effectiveness. It also required evidence of effectiveness for those approved between 1938 and 1962 (Wolfe and Coley, 1981: 193). In 1966, the FDA began the process of reviewing all the prescription drugs approved between 1938 and 1962 to see if they complied with the 1962 amendments; this involved the review of some 4,000 drugs over a two-year period.

The FDA's slowness to remove the ineffective drugs resulted in a 1970 lawsuit filed by the American Public Health Association and the National Council of Senior Citizens, which charged that the FDA was in violation of the 1962 law. Two years later a federal district court ordered the FDA to move as quickly as possible to complete its evaluation. In 1980, 607 of these drugs were still on the market and still lacking evidence of effectiveness (Wolfe and Coley, 1981: 194–196). Wolfe and Coley estimated that one out of every eight prescriptions filled in 1979 (169 million prescriptions) was for one of these ineffective drugs, costing consumers approximately $1.1 billion. While this is not what we commonly regard as theft, it is an unnecessary economic loss to consumers who believe they are purchasing an effective product.

We could extend our list of examples to demonstrate the property loss resulting from other kinds of white-collar crime, but the overall point should be clear: The economic loss from white-collar crime is certainly comparable to that of conventional crime and probably greatly exceeds it. We turn now to the other area of harm that we do not normally associate with white-collar crime—violent personal injury.

Personal Injury: Conventional and White-Collar Crime Compared

As we did with property loss, we must develop a measure of personal injury based on conventional crime. The FBI's *Uniform Crime Reports* is the source for annual statistics on murders, 23,438 in 1990 (U.S. Department of Justice, 1991: 9). The annual National Crime Victimization Survey (NCVS) is the source for nonfatal violent victimizations (rape, robbery, and assault), 2.4 million in 1990 (U.S. Department of Justice, 1992a: 16). The NCVS also reports on workdays lost due to personal and household crimes, an estimated 5.9 million in 1990 (U.S. Department of Justice, 1992a: 98).[13] These fatal and nonfatal violent criminal victimizations will serve as our benchmark of personal injury for conventional crime to which we will compare the harm of white-collar crime. For our comparison, we will focus on three areas: occupational health and safety, health care (hospitalization), and cigarette smoking and the tobacco industry.

In 1970, Congress established the Occupational Safety and Health Administration (OSHA), making health and safety in the workplace a matter of federal regulation. Two years later a *President's Report on Occupational Safety and Health* estimated that 100,000 Americans die annually from occupationally related diseases and another 390,000 suffer from job-related illnesses (Reiman, 1979: 65). A more recent study by the National Safe Workplace Institute estimated that approximately 70,000 U.S. workers die annually from occupational disease (Winslow, 1990).[14] The Bureau of Labor Statistics, which compiles an annual survey of occupational injuries and illnesses, avoids making updated estimates on long-term illnesses brought about by exposure to carcinogens in the workplace and admits that its current figures understate these types of occupational diseases. Its 1990 data show 2,900 work-related fatalities in the private sector and nearly 6.8 million occupational injuries and illnesses. Occupational injuries resulted in the loss of approximately 60.4 million workdays in 1990 (U.S. Bureau of Labor Statistics, 1992: 24–25). Regardless of the exactness of the estimates, the data reveal substantial workplace hazards resulting in both injury and illness that are comparable to the injury and death from conventional crime. In fact, the overall rate of injury at work is considerably higher than that for violent crime victimization, 58 per 1,000 adults compared to 31 per 1,000 (U.S. Department of Justice, 1988: 24).

What is not clear from the data, however, is the extent to which occupational injury and illness are avoidable and the result of law violations. Could employers have taken reasonable safety measures that would have prevented some of this harm? One study of industrial accidents indicated that 45 percent resulted from violations of state safety codes (Coleman, 1989: 7). Several scholars have argued quite convincingly that much of this is preventable (Swartz, 1975; Reiman, 1979; Box, 1983). In some notable cases companies have deliberately exposed workers to workplace hazards without informing them of the danger. The major asbestos producers concealed knowledge of the dangers of asbestos exposure from workers for many years. It is estimated that 170,000 workers exposed to asbestos in this manner will eventually die (Swartz, 1975; Coleman, 1989: 1, 35). In a 1985 case three officials of the Film Recovery Systems Corporation in Illinois were convicted of murder for the death of one of their workers (Green, 1990: 4). The causes of workplace injury and illness range from accidents to negligence and even to murder. Even if only a small percentage (10 percent) can be attributed to corporate negligence, this would still amount to a sizeable toll (10,000 deaths from occupational diseases and 680,000 workplace injuries and illnesses). It should be kept in mind, too, that occupational injuries are drawn from a much smaller population base (the labor force) than conventional crime (the total population), so any differences are actually understated.

In our second area of comparison, health care, we shall consider what a Harvard medical research team referred to as "adverse events." These adverse events were injuries to hospital patients that resulted from their hospital treatment; the injuries were caused by medical management during hospitalization. In most instances the adverse events were due to management error (by commission or omission), but in a substantial subgroup of cases, the injuries were judged to be negligent, which was defined as substandard health care.[15] In their study the Harvard research team examined 30,121 randomly selected records from 51 randomly selected hospitals in New York State in 1984. Adverse events occurred in 3.7 percent of hospitalizations, and 27.6 percent of these were judged to be negligent (Brennan et al., 1991: 370). Although most of these adverse events did not result in serious disability,[16] 13.6 percent resulted in death. The Harvard research team found that about half of these deaths were due to medical negligence. Extrapolating from their sample to the more than 2 million hospital patients discharged in New York in 1984, they estimated that 6,895 hospital patients died negligently that year in the state. By comparison, there were 1,786 murders in New York in 1984 (U.S. Department of Justice, 1985). This is not to equate murders and medically negligent deaths, but it is to establish a substantial area of harm—the adverse events—that exists outside the scope of conventional crime, that is preventable, and that rivals conventional crime in its seriousness.

Let us consider one other area of avoidable injury as it compares to conventional crime—that of cigarette smoking. It is true that it is not a crime to smoke cigarettes or to manufacture them, but nevertheless smoking is a source of personal injury in our society that is much greater than that produced by conventional crime, and it involves the deliberate actions of both manufacturer and consumer. In a recent report, the U.S. Surgeon General (1989: 11–12) found that approximately 390,000 deaths a year are attributable to cigarette smoking, and that "smoking remains the single most important preventable cause of death in our society." Even though tobacco smoke contains 43 chemicals that are carcinogenic, and even though nicotine is addictive, not unlike heroin and cocaine (U.S. Surgeon General, 1988; 1989), we have legitimated the practice of smoking and even subsidized the tobacco industry. The Commissioner of the

Food and Drug Administration (FDA), David Kessler, has recently indicated that cigarettes could be regulated by the FDA as a drug, but that he would not do so without congressional authorization (Shah, 1994: B5).[17] Paradoxically, tobacco presents a far greater danger to health and safety than the violence of conventional crime, at least in terms of avoidable deaths.

This brings us back to the original task of this chapter, which is to demystify the crimes of the powerful. It should be clear by now that there is a substantial arena of harm that exists outside the scope of our criminal-type myths. Some of these noncriminal harms are controlled as regulatory offenses, as in the pharmaceutical and savings and loan industries; others are even legitimated, as in the tobacco industry. The traditional dualism of criminals and law-abiding citizens has functioned to alert us to the dangers posed by conventional crime and the economic underclass. At the same time, however, it has concealed the dangers, even the avoidable injuries and deaths, that flow from the "law-abiding" segment of society, especially the crimes of the wealthy and powerful and those of large organizations. Demystifying the crimes of the powerful sensitizes us to this collective blindspot that is fostered by our traditional myths about crime.

NOTES

1. The various issues involved in the definition of white-collar crime will be taken up in Chapter 3. For purposes of discussion at this stage, white-collar crime is being defined broadly to include occupational and organizational (corporate and governmental) crimes. These include the law violations of individuals in the context of their occupations, whether the gain is personal or organizational in nature. Emphasis will, however, be given to those white-collar crimes that are organizational, and that involve elite offenders.

2. These are essentially what we shall designate in this volume as conventional crimes. They are the Federal Bureau of Investigation's Index Crimes, which are used as a measure of major crime in the United States in its annual *Uniform Crime Reports*. They are murder and nonnegligent manslaughter, forcible rape, robbery, aggravated assault, burglary, larceny-theft, motor vehicle theft, and arson.

3. Sue Titus Reid (1976: 97) first used "dualistic fallacy" in this particular context to describe the assumed dichotomy that exists between criminals and noncriminals.

4. The Watergate scandal involved a variety of illegal activities carried out by officials of President Richard Nixon's administration, beginning with the break-in at the Democratic National Committee headquarters at the Watergate office building in Washington, D.C., in June 1972. The scandal eventually encompassed a cover-up by top Nixon White House officials when the Watergate burglars were later linked to the Committee to Re-elect the President. In addition to the conviction of the five Watergate burglars, several top Nixon aides were convicted of crimes stemming from the break-in and its cover-up. President Nixon himself resigned in August 1974 when it became clear that the House Judiciary Committee intended to impeach him (Congressional Quarterly, 1975).

5. Ronald Reagan was governor of California at the time of the Watergate scandal in 1973–1974.

6. Self-report measures refer to questionnaires that ask a given sample of people to report on their own crimes or delinquencies over a certain period of time from a checklist of items on the questionnaire. These items may include serious as well as minor infractions of the law. Self-report measures are in contrast to official crime statistics, which include data collected by the official agencies of the criminal justice system, such as crimes reported to the police, arrests, prosecutions, and so on. Self-report measures are also distinct from victim surveys, which ask subjects about their victimization experiences rather than their offenses.

7. The term "chronic offender" was used by Marvin Wolfgang and his associates (1972) to refer to the delinquents in their Philadelphia birth cohort who were arrested five or more times by the age of 18. This 6 percent of the 10,000 boys accounted for 52 percent of all the arrests and 83 percent of the arrests for Index Crimes.

8. In the frequency distribution of predatory crimes against persons (their most serious delinquency category), Delbert S. Elliot and Suzanne Ageton's (1980: 104) data show about 2 percent of their respondents reporting 55 or more offenses and another 2 percent committing between 30 and 54 offenses. Approximately 16 percent committed between 5 and 29 offenses, and 80 percent committed 0 to 4 offenses. They do not report how many of their respondents had a frequency rate of zero for their various types of delinquent acts. Their data are from a national probability sample (National Youth Survey) of 1,726 adolescents aged 11 to 17 who reported on their delinquencies in the past year (in 1976).

9. Sutherland was president of the American Sociology Society at the time. It was in his presidential address that he added the term "white-collar crime" to our vocabulary (Sutherland, 1983: xii–xiii).

10. Sutherland examined four types of law violations: restraint of trade (antitrust); false advertising; infringement of patents, trademarks, and copyrights; and unfair labor practices.

11. In the National Crime Victimization Survey (NCVS), personal crimes are robbery, rape, assault, and theft; household crimes include burglary, household larceny, and auto theft. These are victimizations reported in interviews from a nationwide sample of approximately 50,000 households. Because the property loss for each type of crime is reported in five mutually exclusive categories (less than $50, $50 to $99, etc.), it was necessary to estimate the total loss for each crime by multiplying the midpoint of each category by the number of crimes in each category. Table 91 in *Criminal Victimization in the United States, 1990* provides the relevant data (U.S. Department of Justice, 1992a: 94).

12. The bankruptcy of several hundred savings and loan institutions in the 1980s has been variously attributed to their deregulation by the Reagan administration, increased federal protection of their deposits, the failure of regulators, and collective embezzlement (Calavita and Pontell, 1990; 1991).

13. An estimation procedure similar to that described in note 11 for property loss was employed to estimate workdays lost.

14. The National Safe Workplace Institute is an advocacy group headquartered in Chicago. Its estimates were based on 1987 data from the National Center for Health Statistics, using established methods for calculating the percentage of deaths from major diseases that could be attributed to the workplace. The Institute's estimate of occupational-disease deaths was actually a range, from 47,377 to 95,479 (Winslow, 1990: B8).

15. In distinguishing between management error and negligence, the Harvard research team relied on tort law: "medical negligence is defined as failure to meet the standard of practice of an average qualified physician practicing in the specialty in question. Negli-

gence occurs not merely when there is error, but when the degree of error exceeds an accepted norm. The presence of error is a necessary but not sufficient condition for the determination of negligence" (Leape et al., 1991: 381).

16. In approximately 70 percent of the adverse events, patients completely recovered in less than six months (Leape et al., 1991: 378).

17. Although denied by the Tobacco Institute, the FDA has found increasing evidence that the tobacco companies have deliberately manipulated the level of nicotine in cigarettes in order to ensure that smokers become addicted. If this is confirmed, it could provide a legal basis for the FDA regulation of cigarettes as a drug (Shah, 1994: B4).

■ CHAPTER TWO ■

Accidents, Isolated Episodes, and Rotten Apples: The Conventional Wisdom About White-Collar Crime

Perhaps the foremost obstacle to understanding white-collar crime is an ideological one: our inability to think about white-collar offenses as crime. As we saw in the last chapter, our culture and legal system skew our perceptions in such a manner that we are much more likely to recognize and criminalize the harmful acts of the poor, powerless, and marginal groups of society. The predatory acts of these dangerous actors are conventionally viewed as *the* crime problem. By making white-collar crime largely invisible, and by targeting law enforcement resources on conventional crime, we in effect limit our view of crime, criminals, and criminal justice.

In this chapter we shall explore some of the means we commonly employ to render invisible many of the avoidable injuries in our society. While our criminal-type myths focus our attention on the dangerous classes, this is just part of the story. There are additional elements to our conventional wisdom about white-collar crime that also serve to reduce its visibility. If there is a common theme to our conventional wisdom about white-collar crime, it is that we do our best *not* to see it when it occurs, and on those occasions when we must acknowledge the existence of white-collar crime, we are likely to view it as a fleeting phenomenon or as something that we can attribute to a handful of individuals. And, as a fallback position, we can even argue that, after all, white-collar crime is not "real" crime. By examining three cases—the space shuttle *Challenger* disaster, the General Motors transportation conspiracy, and police corruption in New York City, we shall see how different aspects of this wisdom manifest themselves in events that are sometimes characterized as "accidents," "isolated episodes," or events that are attributed to "rotten apples." The net effect of these cultural characterizations is to conceal or obscure the criminality of some of the actions that may be involved in these events.

THE SPACE SHUTTLE *CHALLENGER* DISASTER

On January 28, 1986, as thousands watched from Kennedy Space Center, and as millions watched live on national television, the space shuttle *Challenger* exploded some 73 seconds into flight. This 25th flight of the Space Shuttle Program, which resulted in the death of the *Challenger's* seven crew members, appeared to be normal up to the time of the explosion. National Aeronautics and Space Administration (NASA) officials could offer no immediate explanation as to the cause of the explosion and refused to speculate (Rensberger, 1986: A6). Both the *Washington Post* and the *New York Times* noted that it was the worst accident in the history of the U.S. space program. News accounts variously characterized the explosion as an "accident," a "disaster," and a "tragedy." The Rogers Commission,[1] which was the presidential commission set up to investigate the *Challenger* explosion, also characterized it as an accident in its final report (Presidential Commission, 1986a).

Clearly the demise of the *Challenger* and its crew was not only a disaster, but also a national tragedy of the first order. Whether it was an accident is open to question, given the dictionary definition of that term as an unanticipated, unintentional event. Certainly no one intended the *Challenger* explosion, but, as the Rogers Commission revealed in its investigation, it was not the unanticipated event that the public and the media were initially led to believe. It was quite the contrary. The mechanical problem that ultimately resulted in the failure of the *Challenger* mission (51–L), the O-ring problem,[2] was well known to engineers who worked on the Space Shuttle Program long before the 1986 explosion.

The erosion of O-rings in the joint seal of the solid rocket booster, especially at low temperatures, was noted by Morton Thiokol and NASA engineers in the early stages of development of the shuttle's rocket motor in the late 1970s. During this period one of NASA's engineers at the Marshall Space Flight Center in Alabama wrote a report indicating that Thiokol's joint seal design was "unacceptable." Despite these early concerns regarding the O-rings, the joint seal design was not changed (Presidential Commission, 1986a: 123–124).

During the 1980s, when the space shuttle became operational, inspection of the O-rings after shuttle flights caused further alarm among engineers. On July 31, 1985, Thiokol engineer Roger Boisjoly wrote an internal memorandum marked "company private" to his vice-president of engineering, expressing serious concern about the O-ring erosion in shuttle flight 51–B: "This letter is written to insure that management is fully aware of the seriousness of the current O-ring erosion problem in the SRM joints from an engineering standpoint." He further warned of "a catastrophe of the highest order—loss of human life" (Presidential Commission, 1986b: 691). A Thiokol O-ring task force was set up to assess the problem, and a "launch constraint" was placed on the shuttle system by the project manager of the rocket booster at Marshall Space Flight Center (Presidential Commission, 1986a: 136–140). However, in December 1985, the O-ring problem was erroneously "closed out" even though no corrective action had been taken to change the joint seal design (Presidential Commission, 1986a: 142–144).

Finally, on the evening before the *Challenger* launch, when Thiokol engineers became aware of the cold temperatures forecast for the following morning, a teleconference was arranged to discuss the impact of the cold temperatures on the O-rings and the joint seal, and to assess the feasibility of launch under those conditions. The teleconference included Thiokol managers and engineers (in Utah) and project managers at the Marshall Space Flight Center and the Kennedy Space Center. Thiokol Vice-President of Engineering Robert Lund presented the position and concerns of the Thiokol engineers, which constituted essentially a recommendation not to launch. Their conclusion was that they "should not fly outside of our data base, which was 53 degrees" (Presidential Commission, 1986a: 90). One of the Marshall officials indicated that he was "appalled" at this conclusion, but that he would not go against the contractor's recommendation.

At that point one of the Thiokol managers asked for a five-minute off-net caucus of the Thiokol personnel. During the caucus the Thiokol engineers continued to express objections to the launch, but the burden of proof seemed to have shifted to the opponents of the launch to prove that it would fail. Unable to do so, Thiokol's senior vice-president asked the managers present to put on their management hats in order to make a management decision. The teleconference resumed with Thiokol management stating that they had reassessed the problem; they were still concerned about the low temperatures, but their data were inconclusive, and they were therefore recommending that NASA should proceed with the launch, a reversal of the earlier position (Presidential Commission, 1986a: 92–96). NASA officials at Marshall (level III) accepted this recommendation without passing on the temperature and O-ring concerns to the top levels of NASA management (levels I and II).[3]

The Rogers Commission (Presidential Commission, 1986a: 104) concluded that NASA's decision-making process was flawed: "Thiokol Management reversed its position and recommended the launch of 51–L, at the urging of Marshall and contrary to the views of its engineers in order to accommodate a major customer." The Commission was further troubled by the failure of the Marshall officials to communicate the issues raised in the teleconference to levels I and II of NASA management, who made the final decision to launch. Top-level NASA officials testified at the 1986 hearings that if they had been aware of the engineering concerns expressed at the teleconference, they would not have launched that morning (Presidential Commission, 1986a: 103).

We return now to the cultural characterization of the *Challenger* explosion as a "disaster" and an "accident." It is important that we recognize these designations as two of several categorizations that could have been applied to the events of that day. Just as events and actions that we label "crime," "negligence," or "justifiable" involve a judgment about what occurred, so do the labels "accident" and "disaster." By placing the *Challenger* explosion in those categories, we are grouping it with other unintentional, unexpected misfortunes such as hunting accidents, floods, earthquakes, and famines. The implication of categorizing what happened to the *Challenger* in this manner is that it skews our perceptions in a certain direction: We see it not only as an unintended and unanticipated event, but also as an unavoidable event—something that could not reasonably have been prevented. It also implies that what happened was an act of fate—the result of impersonal forces—and to the extent that human actions were involved, they would not be regarded as "causing" the unexpected event. The net effect of this cultural classification of the *Challenger* explosion is to obscure the role of human actions in the production of this disaster and to minimize the criminality, if any, that might have contributed to it as well. It should be noted that no criminal charges have ever been brought against NASA, its officials, or its contractors, although a case of organizational misconduct could be made based on the exposing of its workers (the shuttle crew) to unsafe work conditions (Green, 1990: 144; Bancroft, 1989: 32).

The visibility of much white-collar crime in our society is reduced accordingly by our cultural misclassification of many organizational actions and events that place them in a category of unavoidable injuries and deprivations. Many everyday events are conventionally viewed in this manner: illnesses acquired in the workplace (Swartz, 1975), injuries and deaths from automobile accidents (Nader, 1966), accidental injuries around the home while using unsafe consumer products (Box, 1983: 29), and even deaths resulting from health care delivery (Horowitz, 1988; Brennan et al., 1991; Leape et al., 1991). Rethinking white-collar crime entails reassessing the fatalism we normally attribute to these kinds of events.

THE CAMPAIGN TO MOTORIZE AMERICA

The cover story of the March 30, 1981, issue of *Time* magazine, "Rumbling Toward Ruin," deplored the terrible condition of the nation's urban mass transit systems. This decline of mass transit was set against a background of a precarious international oil market and a society highly dependent on oil for energy and on the internal combustion engine for transportation. The *Time* article documented the dramatic nationwide decline in transit passengers from 1950 (17.2 billion) to 1980 (8.2 billion). In addressing the causes of this decline, three groups were singled out: politicians, inept managers, and inflexible labor unions. Also cited were a number of long-term trends, including the popularity of the automobile in the 1950s: "Americans fell in love with the automobile, honeymooned on new highways and married into the suburbs. Subways and buses were not part of the post–World War II American dream." During the energy crisis of the 1970s, "mass transit was going to be the methadone that would help America withdraw from its addiction to foreign oil" (McGrath, 1981: 13).

What is most striking in this mainstream media account of what happened to our mass transit systems is what has been omitted from its popular portrayal of "America's romance with the automobile." A significant omission in this account is any reference to a 1949 federal antitrust case in Chicago. In that case General Motors, Standard Oil of California, Phillips Petroleum, Firestone Tire and Rubber, and Mack Manufacturing were convicted (upheld on appeal) of criminal violations of the Sherman Antitrust Act (Kwitny, 1981). For approximately 14 years, beginning in the mid-1930s, these corporations conspired to acquire the electric transit systems of cities across the country and to replace them with General Motors (GM) buses.[4]

Their strategy was to establish a holding company, National City Lines, which the several conspirators then used as a front organization to finance their acquisition of local transit systems. After acquiring each local system, they proceeded to replace it as quickly as possible with GM buses. Once conversion was complete, they resold the bus operations, in this way ensuring that their capital would continuously be reinvested in additional transit systems. To prevent the return of the old transit systems, they often pulled out the old tracks or paved them over, and contracts with the new transit companies prohibited the purchase of equipment that used any fuel except gas (Snell, 1985: 324–325). In this manner the conspirators sought to secure expanded markets for their products, especially automobiles.

At the time of their conviction in federal court, General Motors and its fellow conspirators had acquired and replaced more than 100 electric transit systems in 45 cities, including New York, Los Angeles, Philadelphia, St. Louis, Salt Lake City, and Oakland (Snell, 1985: 326). General Motors was apparently not deterred by its criminal conviction, as it continued its campaign to motorize America through September of 1955, when approximately 88 percent of the nation's electric transit systems had been purchased and destroyed. This is perhaps not surprising given the $5,000 fines each of the guilty corporations had to pay, the maximum fine at the time under the Sherman Antitrust Act, and the $1 fines paid by the guilty executives (Snell, 1985: 326).

How do we explain the rather curious omission of this case that clearly had a bearing on the condition of urban mass transit in the 1980s? Unlike the *Challenger* explosion where wrongdoing was masked by the cultural characterizations of "accident" and "disaster," in this instance the wrongdoing was labeled a "crime"—an antitrust matter. So why this historical amnesia regarding this 1949 criminal conspiracy case? I would argue that it is a little-remembered case because it does not fit into the dominant ideology of how corporations are supposed to conduct themselves. That ideology asserts that there is an identity of interest between corporations and the public welfare. This ideology is reflected in Calvin Coolidge's famous quote earlier in this century: "The business of the country is business." Similarly, Charles E. Wilson, president of General Motors (a major defense contractor) in the early 1950s, defended himself against conflict of interest allegations after his nomination as secretary of defense during the Eisenhower administration by telling senators, "What is good for General Motors is good for the country and what is good for the country is good for General Motors" (Stone, 1963: 7). Ironically, Wilson's own corporation, as we saw, was at this very time engaged in an ongoing criminal conspiracy that would adversely affect transportation and energy policy in the United States for decades to come.

Because the corporate conduct of these several companies appears to contradict our traditional ideology, there is a tendency to see their behavior as an exception to the rule or as an isolated episode. It is this process of selective perception that allows us to quickly forget episodes of corporate or government conduct that depart from the dominant ideology. In this manner the disclosure of corporations manufacturing unsafe products or the revelation of scandal in government tends to be perceived as an "isolated episode" where individuals or organizations have momentarily departed from conduct that is consistent with the public or national interest. These events not only fail to register in the societal memory (unless they are of such an enormous magnitude), but also are not likely to be viewed as part of an ongoing pattern of questionable or illegal practices, which they sometimes are.

THE POLICE AND ROTTEN APPLES

In its investigation of police corruption in New York City in the early 1970s, the Knapp Commission[5] encountered departmental resistance to recognizing the widespread nature of corruption throughout the department, although it was especially flagrant in the gambling and narcotics units. This resistance was expressed in a departmental attitude that the Commission designated as the "rotten apple" theory of corruption (Knapp Commission, 1972: 6). This theory amounted to an unofficial department doctrine as to how corruption, when exposed, is to be handled. The theory asserts that corruption is a problem of individual misconduct and not something that should reflect on the department as a whole. A police officer involved in corruption is "a rotten apple in an otherwise clean barrel" (Knapp Commission, 1972: 6). The Commission (Knapp Commission, 1972: 6–7) further argued that the rotten apple theory served two purposes: (1) Department morale required that there be no official recognition of corruption, and (2) the department's image and effectiveness required this official denial.

In 1993, the Mollen Commission, which again uncovered corruption in the New York City Police Department 20 years after the Knapp inquiry, encountered this same reluctance by police officials to view corruption in a systemic way. Instead, when corruption surfaced in spite of the "blue wall of silence," it was largely viewed in terms of "rogue officers" and "pockets" of corruption, rather than as behavior that might be more deeply embedded in police culture. This was clearly the interpretation of events that Police Commissioner Raymond Kelly favored (James, 1993: B1, B3).

In his report to the National Commission on the Causes and Prevention of Violence, Jerome H. Skolnick (1969: 259ff.) also observed that the police view of crime and disorder in general can be characterized by this "rotten apple" theory of human nature. In this view crime is a function of evil individuals making bad choices; such choices are apparently made in relative isolation from external factors such as past experience, culture, and society. Crime, like police corruption, is personified, and the solution becomes linked to identifying the individual troublemakers—the "rotten apples." Skolnick (1969: 260) further noted that this rotten apple view is not unique to the police world view; quite the contrary, it is widely shared in our society.

When Rodney King was severely beaten by members of the Los Angeles Police Department in 1991 after he led them on an extended car chase,[6] the question again arose: Was this brutality due to the aggressive tendencies of a handful of officers, or was it more deeply ingrained in the Los Angeles Police Department? Los Angeles Police Chief Daryl Gates apparently subscribed to the "rotten apple" view, attributing the problems to just a few officers, 300 at most, in a force that had over 8,000 members (Reinhold, 1991: A14). An independent commission that inquired into the King incident, as well as brutality and racism in the department, reported four months later that there were a "significant number" of officers who repeatedly used excessive force.[7] However, rather than singling out officers or even the chief for blame, the commission viewed the problem as a "management and leadership failure." It concluded that there was "an organizational culture that emphasizes crime control over crime prevention and that isolates the police from the communities and the people they serve" (Reinhold, 1991: A1). There was also evidence that members of this "problem group" of officers were seldom punished for using excessive force and, in fact, often received glowing evaluations for their performance.

Although the Los Angeles commission, like the Knapp Commission before it, provided evidence for a more systemic view of the problem, it is the rotten apple view that typically prevails. While polls showed that most of the U.S. public (whites and blacks) believed the four Los Angeles police officers were guilty (Pope and Ross, 1992), it is not likely that they would have also viewed the King beating as a wider institutional problem of the police. At best, the misconduct of the officers might be attributed to the leadership of the police chief. In fact, Chief Gates was replaced the following year.

John A. Gardiner (1977: 68) observed a similar phenomenon in his study of gambling and corruption in Wincanton, where corruption seemed to be an ongoing problem. Periodic efforts to solve the problem, however, always seemed to follow a similar policy of "throwing the rascals out." This, of course, is another version of the rotten apple theory in which criminality is viewed as an individual trait, rather than as something that is rooted in wider social forces.

The rotten apple theory is another way in which our conventional wisdom conceals or minimizes the harm of white-collar crime Even though criminality is acknowledged, whether it be corruption, police brutality, or some other wrongdoing, the solution is deceptively simple: Get rid of the "rotten apples" or the "rascals." By emphasizing the *individual* misconduct in white-collar crime, this view obscures the links such behavior may have to its organizational and social context, wider cultural patterns, and ongoing institutionalized practices.

ETHNOCENTRISM AND THE CONVENTIONAL WISDOM

In this chapter we have explored three aspects of our conventional wisdom about white-collar crime. We have considered how this wisdom is expressed in events that we culturally characterize as "accidents," "isolated episodes," and "rotten apples." We have also observed how one of the net effects of this labeling is to mask or obscure the criminality that may be involved in these events.

Perhaps the more fundamental question is, Why do we attempt to make white-collar crime invisible as a social phenomenon and avoid seeing the full extent of the harm that it produces? Why do we have this collective blindspot? I suggest that the answer relates to one of the basic concepts in sociology and anthropology: the idea of ethnocentrism. This is the tendency in human societies to think of one's own culture and institutions as superior to those of other cultures. In the context of this discussion ethnocentrism translates into a powerful desire to have trust and confidence in one's own leaders and major social institutions. The accumulated disclosure of crime in high places, whether it be scandals in government or corporate misconduct, erodes this sense of public confidence we like to have in our own institutions. If this erosion is severe enough, what begins as a political crisis of the moment might evolve into a wider crisis of legitimacy, where the authority that supports those institutions may be fundamentally questioned. The dramatic decline in public trust in government and big business in the United States in the late 1960s and early 1970s, for example, has been linked to the numerous revelations of wrongdoing surrounding the Vietnam War and the Watergate scandal (Lipset and Schneider, 1978; Katz, 1980; Cullen, Maakestad, and Cavender, 1987; Simon and Eitzen, 1993: 1–12). Thus, to the extent that white-collar crimes are linked to our mainstream institutions, their disclosure is antithetical to this ethnocentric tendency.

Our collective blindspot regarding white-collar crime supports this tendency that seeks to view one's own culture and institutions in the most favorable light. It is much more reassuring, as Jeffrey H. Reiman (1979) has noted, to feel that our criminal justice system is protecting us from the most harmful acts in society, those that stem from dangerous individuals and groups on the lower rungs of our social ladder.

The contemporary cultural stereotyping of conventional criminals as young, black, and male similarly supports this ethnocentric process. Focusing on the danger in a narrow segment of the population allows us to retain an overall sense of legitimacy about our major social institutions. To widen the scope of danger to include white-collar crime would not only be very alarming, but also call into question the integrity of our economic and political institutions. The conventional wisdom that we have elaborated in this chapter clearly reinforces this ethnocentism, which circumscribes our view of danger in society.

CRIME MYTHS AND WHITE-COLLAR CRIME

A final consideration is the marked contrast between our conception and definitions of the white-collar crime problem and our comparable conceptions and definitions of conventional crime. Victor E. Kappeler and his associates (1993) refer to these collective views of the crime problem as crime myths. Crime myths provide a way to organize how we think about crime, criminals, and the criminal justice system. Kappeler and his associates (1993: 10ff.) observed that the construction of crime myths follows a certain pattern. These myths typically target a particular unpopular group, such as immigrants or minorities. There are innocent victims who are affected by the criminal conduct of this group. Furthermore, the behavior in question has reached epidemic proportions, so that it threatens traditional values in some way. This, of course, is the pattern that we noted in our discussion of the formation of criminal-type myths. Such myths are generated to create alarm or panic about a particular aspect of the crime problem, such as drugs, organized crime, or serial murder, with the intention that a societal response will be forthcoming. Crime myths necessarily shape the social and political agenda concerning crime, in terms of which crimes are targeted for public attention and how we should respond to them.

The myths that we have generated about white-collar crime—our conventional wisdom—are, however, fundamentally different from those of conventional crime in two important respects. They do not involve unpopular or marginal groups in society, and they do not create panic or hysteria about a problem. Quite the contrary, as Kappeler and his colleagues (1993: 102) argued, the mythology of white-collar crime justifies policies of less enforcement and weaker punishments. Corollary to this, the mythology also serves to protect white-collar criminals, especially those who are wealthy and politically powerful, from the criminal justice system. The reasons for this differential treatment of conventional and white-collar crime are numerous and complex, and will be considered in a later chapter on the double standard of justice. Meanwhile, we need to be cognizant of our conventional wisdom (crime myths), the role it plays in shaping our thinking about white-collar crime, and how it affects our response to the problem. Next, however, we will trace the evolution of white-collar crime as a concept within criminology and examine the two schools of thought that have emerged in the controversy over defining white-collar crime.

NOTES

1. William P. Rogers was chair of the Presidential Commission on the Space Shuttle Challenger Accident, which President Ronald Reagan established on February 3, 1986, to investigate the cause(s) of the accident. It issued its five-volume report on June 6, 1986, after holding public hearings. The Commission inquired into the causes of the mechanical failure of the *Challenger* as well as the flaws in the decision-making process that led up to the launch.

2. The O-rings were designed "to prevent hot gases from leaking through the joint during the propellant burn of the rocket motor" (Presidential Commission, 1986a: 40). Low temperatures made the rubber O-rings hard and less resilient, and therefore more susceptible to leakage. The air temperature at the time of the *Challenger* launch was 36 degrees F., well below any previous launch. Once this leakage begins, it leads to a progressive erosion of the O-rings and ultimately to a failure of the joint seal. The escape of hot gases resulted in combustion in the right solid rocket motor that eventually penetrated the *Challenger's* external tank which is when the main explosion occurred (Presidential Commission, 1986a: 70–71).

The Morton Thiokol Corporation was the contractor that developed the solid rocket boosters for NASA's Space Shuttle Program. Each shuttle has two rocket boosters that provide 80 percent of the total thrust at liftoff. After launch they are separated in flight from the shuttle and may be reused in future missions.

3. The Space Shuttle Program management structure was organized into four levels. Level IV consists of the contractors for the shuttle components such as Morton Thiokol, the designer and producer of the solid rocket booster. Level III includes the NASA project managers (at Marshall, Johnson, and Kennedy Space Centers) for the various shuttle components, such as the rocket booster, the external tank, and the orbiter itself. Level II centers on the shuttle program manager, who oversees the review for the flight readiness process that culminates in Level I, the NASA associate administrator (Presidential Commission, 1986a: 83, 102).

4. These local electric rail and streetcar systems had been the main form of urban public transportation since early in this century. The Los Angeles area, for example, had the world's largest interurban electric rail system, established in 1911, which linked 56 cities within a radius of 75 miles and transported 80 million people annually (Snell, 1985: 325). Ironically, in July 1990, several decades after the destruction of its old rail system, Los Angeles opened a new commuter electric-rail service, the Blue Line, covering 22 miles and carrying approximately 20,000 passengers daily. The Blue Line covers only a small fraction of the territory of the old system, but Los Angeles plans to expand this service to 150 miles of rail line, costing approximately $5 billion ("Los Angeles Tries Out New Rail Train," 1990).

5. Following the disclosures of Frank Serpico, a former New York City police officer, and a series of *New York Times* articles alleging corruption in the New York City Police Department, the Knapp Commission was appointed by Mayor John Lindsay to investigate the charges. The Commission, chaired by Whitman Knapp, conducted a two-and-one-half-year investigation, held public hearings, and issued its recommendations and findings on August 3, 1972.

6. Rodney King's beating on March 3, 1991, happened to be videotaped by a citizen bystander who later released the video to the media. The scene of one black male motorist being struck repeatedly by numerous white police officers made the national news programs and was shown often in the following weeks. Four officers from the Los Angeles Police Department were tried on various charges of using excessive force. When the acquittal verdict was announced, one year later in May of 1992, the city of Los Angeles erupted into several days of rioting. Relative calm returned to the city only after National Guard troops were called to restore order. In a subsequent federal case, two of the Los Angeles police officers were convicted of violating King's civil rights.

7. The independent commission, chaired by Warren Christopher, reported that 243 officers had four or more allegations of improper conduct, and that 10 percent of the officers accounted for 33 percent of all the incidents of excessive force (Reinhold, 1991: A14).

■ CHAPTER THREE ■

From Sutherland to the Justice Department: The Evolution of a Concept

Now that we have explored some of the ideological obstacles that confront us in thinking about white-collar crime, we must consider in more detail how these issues have affected the concept of white-collar crime itself. In this chapter we trace the idea of white-collar crime from its introduction in criminology in the 1930s to its eventual assimilation in the 1970s. The problem of incorporating white-collar crime into the mainstream of criminology is central to understanding its evolution as a concept. It will be clear that the idea of white-collar crime was surrounded by controversy from the beginning, and to this day there continues to be disagreement over its definition. There are two broad contemporary schools of thought on these issues. As we shall see, what is at stake in this controversy is not only what we mean by white-collar crime, but also the validity of some core concepts in the field of criminology.

SUTHERLAND'S "DISCOVERY"

It has been more than 50 years since Edwin H. Sutherland introduced the concept of white-collar crime in his 1939 American Sociological Society presidential address. Sutherland's (1940: 38) stated purpose was to reform criminological theory; he was not interested in "muckraking or . . . reforming anything except criminology." Sutherland (1940; 1945; 1983) wished to demonstrate the existence of a type of crime that had been traditionally ignored by criminologists—crime committed by "respectable" and "high social status" persons—and, at the same time, to convince his colleagues that white-collar crime was "really" crime. It is this latter purpose that gets to the significance of Sutherland's contribution.

Sutherland "discovered" white-collar crime in the sense that he was pointing to a phenomenon that existed outside the scope of traditional criminology. Moreover, this discovery may also be considered an "anomaly," to use Thomas S. Kuhn's (1962) term, if it does not fit into the conventional framework of criminology inquiry—what Kuhn referred to as "normal science" and "paradigms."[1] If the idea of white-collar crime was an anomaly in the Kuhnian sense, it meant that criminology could not readily assimilate this concept without fundamentally altering its core concepts. One way of interpreting the historical (and contemporary) debate over white-collar crime relates to the implications of the concept of white-collar crime for redefining the subject matter of criminology. Was the notion of white-collar crime an idea that could readily be absorbed by the field of criminology? Was white-collar crime just another type of crime that could be added to the existing taxonomy of crimes that criminologists study, or did it represent something more—a conceptual challenge to the way in which criminologists think about all crimes? A paradigm challenge?

Sutherland seems to have understood the implications of his own discovery in reformist rather than radical terms. He argued that his demonstration of the existence of a pattern of crime among the upper classes invalidated the traditional explanations of lower-class crime. Sutherland saw these explanations as flawed primarily by sampling bias. Because traditional theories relied exclusively on lower-class samples, they could not possibly explain all crime (Sutherland, 1983: 5). Sutherland (1983: 240) maintained that a general theory of crime should also explain white-collar crime. His resolution of this problem was simply to employ his own general theory of crime, differential association theory. White-collar crime, in Sutherland's view, could apparently be assimilated within the "normal science" (Kuhn, 1962: 24) framework of traditional criminology—by testing rival hypotheses and by improving sampling methods. This seems to be what Sutherland had in mind when he called for the reformulation of criminological theory. In his view it evidently was not necessary to invent new concepts and to rethink paradigmatic assumptions in order to incorporate his discovery.

There is certainly an awareness on the part of both Sutherland's critics and his defenders that he had discovered something of importance. Donald J. Newman (1958: 50) recognized the concept of white-collar crime as one of the most significant developments in criminology since World War II. Hermann Mannheim (1965: 470) proposed awarding Sutherland a Nobel Prize in criminology for his work on white-collar crime, if such an award had existed. Although Sutherland's critics took issue with his formulation of white-collar crime, they, too, recognized the serious challenge that it posed to the existing legal paradigm in the field. Robert G. Caldwell's (1959: 282) commentary on the significance of white-collar crime is revealing:

In this, white-collar crime becomes a propagandistic weapon, which under the meretricious guise of science, is to be used for the establishment of a new social order. Apparently sociologists are to be mechanics of collectivism. Some sociologists may want to play this role, but let them not delude themselves into believing that they are being scientific.

Newman (1958: 56), furthermore, recognized some of the theoretical implications underlying the controversy: "Whether he likes it or not, the criminologist finds himself involved in an analysis of prestige, power, and differential privilege when he studies upperworld crime."

THE HISTORIC DEBATE REVISITED

From the outset, Sutherland's critics seemed well aware of the significance and conceptual challenge posed by the introduction of white-collar crime to the discipline of criminology. Herbert Bloch and Gilbert Geis (1962: 399) noted that the severest critics of the concept seemed to be those with legal training, most notably Paul W. Tappan and Robert G. Caldwell, who were both legally trained sociologists. The main thrust of their criticism of white-collar crime was that it was outside the traditional scope of the criminal law. Tappan's (1947: 276–277) classic article entitled "Who Is the Criminal?" referred pejoratively to "white-collar criminologists" who employ terms that do not clearly differentiate criminal and noncriminal behavior, and who encourage "individual systems of private values to run riot in an area (economic ethics) where gross variation exists among criminologists as well as others." His solution to this definitional dilemma was for criminologists to rely upon the more precise and explicit standards of the criminal law, which presumably is free of the above pitfalls.

Caldwell (1958: 33) echoed Tappan's arguments in a subsequent reexamination of the white-collar crime concept. He, too, was concerned with the potential for "corruption of the terms 'crime' and 'criminal,' the integrity of which the law has sought so vigilantly to preserve . . ." Both Tappan and Caldwell attempted to make the case for maintaining the sanctity of the criminal law and the concepts that support it as well as the traditional view of crime. While their concerns are often couched in terms of the greater precision and objectivity of the criminal law, there does seem to be a genuine inability on their part to "see" the criminality of white-collar offenses. For Tappan (1947: 276), "all are within the framework of the norms of ordinary business practice." Caldwell (1958: 34) similarly has difficulty understanding the term "crime" except in terms of its strict legal meaning. These criticisms represent some of the ideological obstacles that white-collar crime had to overcome in order to be assimilated into the field of criminology. The dominance of the legal definition of crime was a critical obstacle to its inclusion.

Sutherland (1945) was equally insistent on the criminality of the offenses he had documented in his research on corporate crime. He accounted for the apparent lack of stigma associated with these offenses by the different administrative procedures that are used to handle white-collar offenses. Moreover, Sutherland's later writings also reveal his own ideological orientation that seemed to underly his concern with the crimes of big businessmen. In his classic work *White-Collar Crime*, which was originally published in 1949, Sutherland expressed outrage at the undermining of the nineteenth-century economic order by white-collar offenders. Big businessmen are likened to socialists in their disrespect for antitrust laws (Sutherland, 1983: 55). White-collar offenders are also characterized as subversives insofar as their illegal behavior has "fundamentally changed the economic and political institutions of the United States" (Sutherland, 1983: 90). At another point in the text, the utility companies are compared to Nazis in their "organized propaganda designed to develop favorable sentiments" (Sutherland, 1983: 221). Even Geis and Colin Goff (Sutherland, 1983: xiv), in their introduction to *White-Collar Crime: The Uncut Version*, observed that there is little in Sutherland's background or earlier work that would have anticipated this kind of expression of indignation, particularly in regard to white-collar crime.

In hindsight, the historic debate over the definition of white-collar crime may be reinterpreted as involving more than simply a controversy over rival theories. It also entailed an ideological and paradigmatic conflict over the anomaly that Sutherland had discovered. The emotional tone of the debate over the inclusion of white-collar crime in the discipline of criminology suggested the seriousness of the conceptual challenge that it posed. Although the historic debate is usually regarded in terms of the Sutherland-Tappan exchange in the 1940s, it was also an ongoing problem of inclusion that persisted into the 1950s and 1960s, and it remains part of the definitional controversy today.

THE PROBLEM OF INCLUSION: THE SCIENTIFIC ISSUES

The critics of white-collar crime had clearly put the "white-collar criminologists" (Tappan, 1947: 281) on the defensive early in the debate. Both Tappan (1947) and Caldwell (1958) questioned the scientific utility of the concept. For Tappan, white-collar crime was much too nebulous and variable a term to be of scientific value. "Vague, omnibus concepts defining crime are a blight upon either a legal system or a system of sociology that strives to be objective" (Tappan, 1947: 277). Caldwell (1958: 33–34) similarly emphasized the imprecise and ambiguous meaning of the term "white-collar crime," and thought that the whole controversy reflected "the immaturity of the social sciences" (Caldwell, 1958: 36).

Clearly there was some merit to this criticism, as acknowledged by Geis (1962), Bloch and Geis (1962), Richard Quinney (1964), and Mannheim (1965). Various defenders of the white-collar crime concept responded to the Tappan and Caldwell objections by offering clarification of Sutherland's definition and theoretical concepts.

Geis (1962: 160–161), for instance, recognized that the imprecision of Sutherland's definition limited its utility. Clarification was necessary not only to pacify the critics, but also to establish white-collar crime as a respectable subject of inquiry. As Geis (1962: 165) expressed it at the time, "such attacks have understandably tended to distract from the essential elements of Sutherland's position and to hinder its reexamination and the absorption of its more viable portions into the main body of criminological theory." The problem, as Geis saw it, was to further specify the kind of illegal activities to be included under the term "white-collar crime." Moreover, Geis contended that explanations of crime should then be sought for specific types of crime that are relatively homogeneous. In this respect Sutherland's attempt to apply differential association theory to all crime, including white-collar crime, was misguided in Geis's view.

Finally, Geis advocated that white-collar crime be tied to the legal codes in order to restrict the definition in some objective way. In these various ways Geis hoped to head off the criticisms of the detractors of Sutherland's concept so that it could more readily be absorbed into mainstream criminology (Geis, 1962: 165, 171).

In a similar manner, Mannheim (1965: 469–498) systematically considered the definitional and theoretical weaknesses of Sutherland's work. As with Geis, the general thrust of Mannheim's remarks was to acknowledge and correct the weaknesses of Sutherland's position, but at the same time to establish white-collar crime as a respectable subject in mainstream criminology.

Writing about the same time, Quinney, too, sought to correct some of the inadequacies of Sutherland's formulation of white-collar crime with an objective similar to that of Geis and Mannheim. Quinney (1964: 285) argued, "It is apparent, then, that such efforts to distinguish categories of white-collar crime, or to restrict the definition of white-collar crime itself, must be undertaken in order to give the concept any scientific utility." Quinney's contribution to increasing the scientific utility of white-collar crime was to expand the concept to include legal violations committed in the course of all occupational activity, not just those involving "respectable" or "high social status" offenders. Accordingly, he advocated changing "white-collar crime" to "occupational crime."

While the defenders of white-collar crime all made contributions in their own right, at this stage of the controversy their clarifications and refinements of Sutherland's work served to legitimate white-collar crime as a scientific concept and to facilitate its assimilation into the discipline of criminology. However, as we shall see, some of these efforts at operationalizing white-collar crime as a scientific concept also served to transform Sutherland's meaning of the term. By delineating white-collar crime as just another type of crime, by expanding its meaning to include all occupational crime, or by excluding organizational crime from the province of criminological inquiry, all contributed to subtle shifts in the meaning of white-collar crime. The unintended consequence of these changes may have been to blunt the more serious conceptual challenge posed by Sutherland's idea of white-collar crime.

THE PROBLEM OF INCLUSION: THE LEGAL ISSUES

In addition to the scientific issues that had to be considered in white-collar crime's assimilation, there were some legal issues that had to be resolved. While the scientific utility of white-collar crime could be demonstrated through the clarification and refinement of ambiguous concepts, the legal questions raised by Sutherland's "white-collar crime" were much more intractable. They strike at the very core of the meaning of crime, including the political and ideological bases for its definition.

Tappan and Caldwell both insisted on the hegemony of the law in defining crime. Tappan (1947: 279) did not regard white-collar criminals as criminals unless they were convicted of a violation of the criminal law, which was a rare occurrence. He considered the concept of white-collar crime as an imposition of the private values and meanings of "white-collar criminologists." Caldwell (1958: 34) shared this view and pointed to how "the legal profession is already entrusted by society with the responsibility of interpreting and administering the criminal law." He further pointed out that "the legal profession has always insisted upon a strict interpretation of the meaning of the term 'crime' " and that we should resist attempts to change its meaning "through academic decree or fiat."

The Tappan/Caldwell position on the legal definition of crime, which is widely shared and represents the traditional criminological view, was a formidable obstacle to the assimilation of white-collar crime. This legal definition has rarely been challenged in the criminology literature. In his plea for greater autonomy among social scientists in defining their own terms and subject matter, Thorsten Sellin (1938: 9) argued "that the study of conduct norms would afford a sounder basis for the development of scientific categories than a study of crimes as defined in the criminal law." More than 30 years later, Herman Schwendinger and Julia Schwendinger (1970) argued for an alternative to the legal definition based on notions of human rights and egalitarianism. Harold E. Pepinsky (1974) similarly sought to reformulate white-collar crime in terms of the broader category of exploitation. For the most part, these critics of the legal definition have not provided a viable alternative.

Sutherland, however, accepted the legal or state definition of crime, as noted by the Schwendingers in their analysis of the controversy, but he did advocate its reform. Sutherland sought the inclusion of white-collar offenses into criminological inquiry by extending such inquiry beyond the criminal law to violations of the civil and administrative laws. This constituted an expansion of the legal and traditional meaning of the term "crime," but it was not the more radical redefinition argued for by Sellin and subsequently by the Schwendingers and by Pepinsky.

Why this traditional adherence to the legal definition of crime? What was the nature of the threat posed by Sutherland's proposed reform of this legalistic view? In order to understand the resistance to the notion of white-collar crime as crime, we must also understand the ideological underpinnings of the legal definition, which was defended so well by Tappan and Caldwell.

The Schwendingers (1970) astutely pointed to some of the mainstream sociological concepts that unwittingly serve to maintain the legalistic view. They argued that pluralism[2] and structural functionalism,[3] for example, advance a particular view of the state and a theory of social control. The state is viewed as a neutral arbiter of competing interests, and the problem of order is one of maintaining harmony and consensus among these diverse interest groups. Individuals or groups whose behavior violates this stability through dissent, conflict, or deviance are likely to be viewed as criminal, subversive, or dangerous because their actions are dysfunctional to the prevailing social order. An integral part of this perspective was the assumption that the poor and the lower class constituted the criminal and dangerous elements of the population. The neutrality of the law in this process of criminalizing behavior, like the accompanying notion of a value-free sociology, tended to obscure its ideological character. The discovery of white-collar crime threatened to expose this myth of neutrality by pointing to the role of power and privilege in the shaping of the law as well as to the existence of a double standard of justice in the application of the law to upper-class and lower-class offenders.

Adherence to the legal definition carried additional ideological implications. These are embedded in our historical notions of criminal responsibility and the scope of the criminal law. Among these is the individualistic bias of the criminal law. Although the legal construct of "juristic person" was invented around the twelfth century to recognize the existence of organizational entities, the application of criminal liability to organizations was several centuries in its evolution (Coleman, 1974; Bernard, 1984). The emergence during the Middle Ages of *mens rea*, or criminal intent, as a necessary element of criminality securely linked criminal responsibility to the guilt of individuals for the purposes of conviction and punishment (Cullen, Maakestad, and Cavender, 1987: 114–115). Corporations were largely immune from criminal liability until the twentieth century when it was established "that criminal intention could be attributed to a corporation through the intent of its agents" (Bernard, 1984: 10). Eventually even the barriers to prosecuting corporations for homicide were brought down, with the 1980 criminal trial of Ford Motor Co. for reckless homicide in the Pinto case as the outstanding example (Cullen, Maakestad, and Cavender, 1987).

Given the entrenchment of the legal definition of crime, not only in the legal profession, but also in the discipline of criminology, the prospect of assimilating Sutherland's "white-collar crime" was not very favorable. In spite of the historic debate over white-collar crime and its defense by a variety of prominent sociologists and criminologists over two decades, Sutherland's concept remained largely out of the mainstream of criminology until the 1970s. Geis (1988: 26) recently noted that work on white-collar crime was at a "virtual standstill" in the decade after 1964, a development that he found to be somewhat puzzling. In Kuhn's (1962) terms, white-collar crime remained an anomalous phenomenon, unincorporated in the paradigms of the discipline.

FROM ANOMALY TO ASSIMILATION

A number of students of white-collar crime have observed the strong initial influence of Sutherland in producing research on white-collar crime, followed by a period of relative inactivity and then by a sudden turnabout of interest in the topic in the 1970s. Geis and Robert F. Meier (1977: 1), for example, referred to the early research on white-collar crime, following Sutherland's discovery, as the "classic core" of white-collar crime investigation. They also noted in the preface to this same volume that "the challenge offered by white-collar crime . . . has continued to be unanswered. We still know relatively little about the social, economic, and legal dynamics that contribute to its appearance and form." Francis T. Cullen and his associates (1987: 49–50) similarly noted the "long hiatus" in the study of corporate crime after Sutherland's initial influence.

Writing a few years later, Geis (1982: 177–179; 1988: 27) observed the turnabout in interest in white-collar crime, both in the political arena and in criminology. He called attention to some of the developments that signaled this new concern with white-collar crime: the sudden proliferation of colloquia specifically focusing on this subject, sessions on white-collar crime that are now routinely part of the meetings of the professional associations of criminologists and sociologists, congressional hearings on white-collar crime, and the reordering of priorities and resources by the U.S. Justice Department.

Besides these impressionistic accounts of the evolution of white-collar crime, there are also some objective indicators that support these developments. A survey of the criminology literature from 1945 to 1980 for changes in the use of the concept of white-collar crime reveals the same trends as noted above. If we use the production of journal articles and books on white-collar crime as a measure of the utilization of the concept in criminology, we can get a relative sense of how marginal or central to the discipline the subject of white-collar crime is over time. Using Wolfgang's bibliography (1974) and index (Wolfgang, Figlio, and Thornberry, 1975) of all significant articles and books in criminology in the years 1945 to 1972, it was determined that 31 journal articles and 13 books on white-collar crime were written during that period.[4] Over this 28-year time span, no year had more than six publications (1969), with an average of 1.6 per year.

Although there are no works comparable to the Wolfgang bibliography and index for the period after 1972, other bibliographies can be used to provide suggestive results. One such bibliography on white-collar crime publications, primarily from 1977 to 1980, was compiled by Herbert Edelhertz and Thomas Overcast (1982: 205–224). A search of this bibliography reveals that there were 37 journal articles and 35 books published with white-collar-crime-related titles between 1977 and 1980.[5] This total (72) exceeds the total published works on white-collar crime for the entire 28-year period from 1945 to 1972.

These data appear to support impressionistic accounts that white-collar crime was not a major area of inquiry before 1970, remaining out of the core of the discipline of criminology. They also confirm the sudden transformation that was taking place, with the explosion of publications on white-collar crime topics in the 1970s. This renewal of interest in white-collar crime has been likened by some to a social movement that includes not only criminologists but also prosecutors, the media, and consumer crusaders (Katz, 1980; Cullen, Maakestad, and Cavender, 1987; Kramer, 1989). Its roots have been traced to the political crisis generated by the Watergate scandal of Richard Nixon's administration and, even more broadly, to a legitimation crisis of the U.S. political economy. This social movement against white-collar crime will be examined in a later chapter when we consider the Justice Department's sudden concern with white-collar crime during this same period.

Clearly it is widely recognized that there was a major revival of interest in white-collar crime in the 1970s. A recent study (Wright and Friedrichs, 1991) showed that criminology textbooks dramatically increased their coverage of white-collar crime in the 1980s. However, this same study found that this was not true of criminal justice textbooks and the criminal justice curriculum as a whole. Richard A. Wright and David O. Friedrichs (1991) concluded that white-collar crime topics still do not receive adequate attention in criminal justice education. Although the idea of white-collar crime has moved away from the margins of the discipline (from anomaly) to the mainstream, it appears that the process of assimilation is far from complete.

TWO SCHOOLS OF THOUGHT

Although the concept of white-collar crime had its origin in Sutherland's challenge to the legal/theoretical paradigm of traditional criminology, the eventual assimilation of the white-collar crime idea was achieved only after its more radical implications were blunted. In this process of selectively incorporating aspects of Sutherland's idea, two schools of thought can be delineated, both of which can be traced to the Sutherland-Tappan debate in the 1940s. One school of thought continues the Sutherland tradition of focusing on the offender as the defining characteristic of white-collar crime. The other school departs from the Sutherland definition by emphasizing the offense as the central criterion of white-collar crime. As white-collar crime has become a mainstream concept, this latter school has become the more dominant of the two.

The Sutherland Tradition

It should be recalled that Sutherland was concerned with the crimes of the upper class—big business, the wealthy, and the powerful. In his often-criticized definition, he stated that white-collar crime is "a crime committed by a person of respectability and high social status in the course of his occupation" (Sutherland, 1983: 7). The primary focus of his definition is on *who* was committing these illegal acts rather than on the kind of offenses they were committing. This, of course, is a major ambiguity in his definition: What offenses are to be included as white-collar crimes? It is also the point of departure for the competing school of thought, which has operationalized white-collar crime in terms of a legal typology of offenses. Nevertheless, those students of white-collar crime who maintain the Sutherland tradition have sought to preserve the historic meaning of the term by focusing on the characteristics of the offender. In this manner the crimes of the economic and political elites are highlighted rather than those of the dangerous classes.

There is a long line of research that fits into this tradition, going back to what Geis and Meier (1977: 1) called the "classic core" of white-collar crime research. This includes the work of Marshall Clinard (1946) on the violation of wartime price regulations, Frank E. Hartung's (1950) study of offenses in the Detroit wholesale meat industry, and Robert E. Lane's (1953) inquiry into why businessmen violate the law. Geis's (1967) own study and analysis of the heavy electrical equipment antitrust cases of 1961 are also firmly in this tradition. The more recent works of Clinard and Peter C. Yeager (1980) on corporate crime, John Braithwaite (1984) on crime in the pharmaceutical industry, M. David Ermann and Richard J. Lundman (1992) on corporate and governmental deviance, David R. Simon and D. Stanley Eitzen (1993) on elite deviance, and James W. Coleman (1989) on the criminal elite all continue in the Sutherland tradition. Although these volumes encompass an enormous variety of offenses, their common denominator is a concern with the illegal or deviant acts of the upper class or large organizations in society.

The Legal Tradition

This second school of thought can be traced to Tappan's viewpoint in his debate with Sutherland. In that historic exchange Tappan argued for the primacy of the law in defining crime. The law, of course, specifies which acts are to be criminalized regardless of who commits them. In this view the defining characteristic of white-collar crime is the offense rather than the offender. The problem of defining white-collar crime from this perspective becomes one of deciding which subset of crimes is "white collar." By separating white-collar crime from the characteristics of the offender, white-collar crime in the legal tradition ceases to be linked to any particular social class.

Edelhertz (1970: 3) was one of the first to develop a definition and typology of white-collar crime based on the nature of the offense. His definition emphasized illegal acts committed by "nonphysical means and by concealment" in order "to obtain money or property, . . . or to obtain business or personal advantage." As a former head of the Fraud Section of the U.S. Justice Department, his definition was influential in shaping the official Justice Department definition of white-collar crime in the 1970s. Former Federal Bureau of Investigation (FBI) Director William H. Webster (1980: 276), in fact, noted the FBI's indebtedness to Edelhertz for his definition. Simon Dinitz (1982: 140ff.) later referred to Edelhertz's departure from the Sutherland definition as the "Edelhertz modification."[6]

Susan P. Shapiro (1980; 1990) also argued persuasively for an offense-based definition of white-collar crime. She contended that Sutherland's definition is an "imprisoning framework for contemporary scholarship," and that the concept of white-collar crime should be "liberated" by "disentangling the identification of the perpetrator with their misdeeds" (Shapiro, 1990: 346). In a review of four books on corporate crime, which were mainly in the Sutherland tradition, Shapiro (1983) took many of the authors to task for imposing their own moral agendas on white-collar crime, rather than limiting themselves to acts that are law violations. She reminded some of these authors, whom she called the "new moral entrepreneurs" and "corporate crime crusaders," that "crimes" are only those acts that violate the criminal law. Shapiro's criticism of the modern proponents of the Sutherland tradition is strongly reminiscent of Tappan's criticism of Sutherland himself.

This legal school of thought has become the dominant view among practitioners in the justice system and among a growing number of criminologists. It is of interest that in its effort to standardize the use of terms, including "white-collar crime," in the justice field, the Bureau of Justice Statistics (BJS)—in the Justice Department—has developed *The Dictionary of Criminal Justice Data Terminology*. In its definition of white-collar crime, it largely accepts the Edelhertz modification, although it does retain an element of the Sutherland definition by restricting the white-collar offender to someone who is "entrepreneurial, professional or semi-professional." In an annotation to its definition, the BJS dictionary refers to the original meaning of white-collar crime, that is to say, Sutherland's definition, and describes how current criminal justice usage departs from it: "the focus of the meaning has shifted to the nature of the crime instead of the persons or occupations" (U.S. Department of Justice, 1981: 215).

The ascendance of an "official" definition of white-collar crime has implications for the two rival schools of thought in academic criminology. It tends to give more legitimacy to the legal tradition over the Sutherland one. For example, as an important source of criminal justice research funding, the National Institute of Justice (NIJ)—part of the Justice Department—can favor certain kinds of research over others. In fact, proposals submitted for the white-collar crime research program should be consistent with this official definition (U.S. Justice Department, 1990b: 42). Moreover, those doing research and preparing special reports that emanate from the BJS often use the BJS dictionary as their reference when defining white-collar crime (Manson, 1986: 2; U.S. Department of Justice, 1987: 1–2). Furthermore, as the justice system begins to collect its own white-collar crime statistics, which are based on the statutes designated by the Justice Department as being "white collar," researchers relying upon these official statistics will unwittingly be accepting this official definition of white-collar crime.

In this and in other ways the domain of white-collar crime can be subtly skewed toward supporting the official view of white-collar crime—the legal tradition.

The Abandonment of White-Collar Crime?

In their pursuit of a general theory of crime, Travis Hirschi and Michael Gottfredson (1987; 1989) recently advocated abandoning the typological approach inherent in the concept of white-collar crime and questioned the theoretical value of the idea itself. In comparing white-collar criminals with conventional criminals, they found the age, gender, and race distributions in both white-collar and conventional crime to be remarkably similar. Hirschi and Gottfredson (1987: 970–971) observed that the distinction between white-collar crime and conventional crime is an offense rather than an offender distinction. According to their analysis, white-collar and conventional offenders share similar characteristics. It should be pointed out that they arrived at this rather surprising conclusion by employing the "official" definition of white-collar crime as well as *Uniform Crime Reports* statistics as the basis for their analysis.[7] Hirschi and Gottfredson's reliance on official statistics and on certain designated white-collar offenses, such as fraud, forgery, and embezzlement, probably accounts for their unexpected results. Darrell Steffensmeier (1989: 347) questioned the use of such data as a measure of white-collar crime, arguing that these offense categories are broad and heterogeneous, are not occupationally related, and include a variety of types of offenders. Kathleen Daly (1989: 790), too, cautioned against the use of federal data on embezzlement, fraud, and forgery as a measure of white-collar crime. Because most of the offenders in these data are non-elite offenders ("little fish" in terms of their socioeconomic profile), especially the female white-collar offenders, she questioned the appropriateness of "white-collar" as a description of them or their crimes.

Stanton Wheeler and his associates at Yale,[8] using federal court statistics on eight "white-collar crime" statutes, arrived at a different conclusion than Hirschi and Gottfredson. They maintained not only that white-collar crime is systematically different from conventional crime, but also that conventional and white-collar offenders are drawn from very different sectors of the population (Wheeler, Weisburd et al., 1988; 337ff.; Weisburd et al., 1991: 171). While conventional criminals are disproportionately poor and marginal, the white-collar offenders in the Yale studies more closely resemble the profile of ordinary, middle-class people and, in the vast majority of cases, are not the powerful and affluent offenders typically portrayed as white-collar criminals.

In their discovery of this large "middle class" of white-collar offenders, the Yale group is in effect amending Sutherland's definition to include this non-elite group that he neglected. They suggested another way of thinking about white-collar crime. If crime is thought of as a continuum from the "pure" white-collar type (the elite offender) at one end to the "pure" conventional type (the underclass offender) at the other, then there is also a vast middle group, which has grown in size since the time of Sutherland. The question then becomes where to draw the line on this continuum between elite and middle-class offenders as well as which statutes to designate as "white collar" (Weisburd et al., 1991: 178ff.).

There is no definitive answer to this question except to say that where one draws the line depends on one's theoretical purposes. If we as researchers are interested in calling attention to the crimes and differential treatment of elite offenders, as Sutherland was, then the traditional definition is appropriate. If, on the other hand, we wish to focus on still another neglected group of offenders, the non-elite white-collar offenders, then the Yale group's definition better serves that purpose.

In the end we must also be mindful of how such definitions may actually work against our understanding of white-collar crime. By sensitizing us to certain aspects of the phenomenon, they are also neglecting others. Shapiro (1990: 362) made this point in her critique of the restrictive Sutherland definition. She argued that the focus on the characteristics of the offender has hindered our understanding of the nature of white-collar violations as well as of the role of organizational and macro processes in producing them. It can similarly be argued that by focusing on the act itself regardless of who commits it, we are moving away from an understanding of the social and cultural forces that not only produce elite crime, but also define it in a different manner than underclass crime. As we saw in Chapter 1, *who* the offender is, is central to our labeling of certain acts as dangerous in society.

The evolution of the concept of white-collar crime has brought us full circle. With its assimilation into the mainstream of criminology, and with the ascendance of the legal school of thought, there has been a blurring of the distinction between conventional and white-collar criminals. It is ironic that this challenge to the typological approach has resulted in the renewed questioning of the value of the idea of white-collar crime itself. The persistence of the Sutherland tradition, however, reminds us that white-collar crime is more than just an additive phenomenon (another type of crime). The historic meaning of Sutherland's idea is linked to a more critical understanding of the nature of law and to a greater sensitivity to inequalities in the justice system, particularly as they relate to upper-class and lower-class offenders. Regardless of definition or school of thought, this core meaning should not be lost.

NOTES

1. Kuhn's (1962) work on how science evolves offered a challenge to the traditional view that science develops by the accumulation of individual discoveries and inventions. In that view each new discovery simply builds upon the knowledge of the past. In contrast, Kuhn argued that science develops by the selective incorporation of discoveries that are consistent with the dominant "paradigm" of the prevailing scientific community. Discoveries that fall outside the realm of that paradigm and contradict its basic tenets are con-

sidered "anomalies" and tend to be disregarded. It is only when there is an accumulation of anomalies that gain acceptance among some segment of the scientific community that competing paradigms develop, which ultimately might lead to a "scientific revolution."

2. Pluralism refers to the view of political power that maintains that power is widely distributed in society among diverse interest groups. No group is so dominant that its interests would prevail across the spectrum of issues. Pluralism is usually contrasted with the elite view of political power, which sees power as highly concentrated in the hands of a dominant elite.

3. Functionalism pertains to the sociological perspective that views the institutions of society as being closely integrated and related to each other in terms of reciprocal functions. It also emphasizes those aspects of social systems that contribute to order, harmony, and stability.

4. The subject index in *The Criminology Index* (Wolfgang, Figlio, and Thornberry, 1975) was employed to search for key terms related to white-collar crime that might appear in the titles of books and journal articles. The following key terms were used in the search: white-collar crime/criminal, economic crime, occupational crime, corporate crime, organizational crime, elite crime/deviance, embezzlement, fraud, corruption, and business crime.

5. The same key terms used to search the titles of articles and books in the Wolfgang index were used to search the Edelhertz bibliography.

6. Edelhertz himself was aware that he was departing from Sutherland's definition. He noted that his definition "differs markedly from that advanced by Edwin H. Sutherland" (Edelhertz, 1970: 3). Although critical of Sutherland's definition, Edelhertz went on to point out Sutherland's contributions to the study of white-collar crime.

7. Hirschi and Gottfredson (1989: 363) denied that they were taking sides in the definitional controversy. They contended that they did not depend on the traditional (Sutherland) definition, but, apparently without being aware of it, they are depending on an offense-based definition, consistent with Edelhertz's and the Justice Department's definition.

8. Wheeler and a number of colleagues at Yale University have produced a four-volume series entitled the Yale Studies on White-Collar Crime. Much of this research was funded by the National Institute of Justice and focuses on the social control of white-collar crime. These volumes are Shapiro's (1984) *Wayward Capitalists*; Kenneth Mann's (1985) *Defending White-Collar Crime*; Wheeler, Kenneth Mann, and Austin Sarat's (1988) *Sitting in Judgment*; and Weisburd, Wheeler, Elin Waring, and Nancy Bode's (1991) *Crimes of the Middle Classes*. Their work is in the legal tradition because they adopt an offense-based definition of white-collar crime.

CHAPTER FOUR

White-Collar Crime and the Double Standard

THE DOUBLE-STANDARD ISSUE

One of the core ideas of the Sutherland tradition in white-collar crime is that there is a double standard of justice in our differential handling of conventional and white-collar crime. Besides insisting on the criminality of white-collar offenses, Sutherland (1940; 1945: 266ff.) also maintained that the differential application of the law to conventional and white-collar crimes "blurred and concealed" the criminality of the white-collar offenses. By inventing special administrative agencies and commissions to handle white-collar crimes, rather than using the criminal courts, the stigma of crime is minimized. One of the factors to which Sutherland attributed this differential treatment was the status of businessmen in society, which, he argued, made legislators and officials in the criminal justice system reluctant to antagonize them. In effect Sutherland contended that there is a double standard of justice with respect to how society responds to the crimes of the underclass and those of the upper class, with white-collar offenders clearly receiving the more lenient treatment of the two classes of offenders. This would appear to be particularly true if those white-collar offenders happen to be white, male, wealthy, and politically powerful.

Christopher Stone (1975: 64) cited two Georgia cases as a glaring example of the double standard. Those cases involved sentencing in the same court on the same day in 1973: one case for bank embezzlement, the other for bank robbery. In the former case the president of the First National Bank of Cartersville was sentenced to 10 years for embezzling $4.6 million; this amounts to approximately $400 for every resident of Cartersville. In the bank robbery case three men who stole $13,834 from a bank in Balton, less than 1 percent of the embezzlement take, were sentenced to 16 years each.

To further explore the complexity of the problem involved in whether we judge the crimes of the wealthy and powerful by a different, and more lenient, standard than those of the poor, let us consider another case. This is one of the classic cases in the white-collar crime literature, occurring a decade after the publication of Sutherland's book. In 1961, 29 corporations and 45 executives in the electric industry were convicted in federal court of violating the antitrust laws. They had been charged with price-fixing conspiracies in contract bidding on heavy electrical equipment, going back to the mid-1940s and involving $7 billion in sales (Smith, 1961; Geis, 1967; Green, Moore, and Wasserstein, 1972: 154ff.). As a white-collar crime case, it was exceptional because it was dealt with as a criminal matter, and because it marked the first time in the history of the Sherman Antitrust Act of 1890 that business executives were incarcerated (Green, Moore, and Wasserstein, 1972: 156). At first glance it appears the industry was handled rather harshly. Not only did seven executives receive 30-day jail sentences, but also criminal fines totalling nearly $2 million were assessed on both the corporations and the individual defendants. Additionally, because the Sherman Antitrust Act provides for treble damages in civil claims, the corporations paid out approximately $500 million in civil settlements (Green, Moore, and Wasserstein, 1972: 174). At the sentencing the judge in the case also registered his surprise and dismay at the defendants' behavior:

This is a shocking indictment of a vast section of our economy, for what is really at stake here is the survival of the kind of economy under which America has grown to greatness, the free enterprise system. The conduct of the corporate and individual defendants alike . . . flagrantly rocked the image of [this] economic system . . . and destroyed the model which we offer today as a free world alternative to state control and eventual dictatorship. (Quoted in Green, Moore, and Wasserstein, 1972: 156)

In spite of the apparent harshness of the judge's words and the criminal sentences, closer examination reveals a lenient side to the case. Although the total of the criminal fines ($2 million) is a considerable sum, this amount was spread over a whole industry, with General Electric (GE) paying the largest fine of $437,500. While this, too, may appear to be a sizeable amount, Gilbert Geis (1967: 120) observed that, considering GE's profits in that year, this would be no more than a $3 parking fine for an individual earning an annual income of $175,000. Clearly the more serious financial costs to the industry were the civil fines, but the threat of these civil settlements to corporate profits was blunted by an Internal Revenue Service ruling that these payments were deductible from corporate income taxes as "ordinary and necessary" business expenses (Mintz and Cohen, 1971: 104). Moreover, in spite of the substantial civil and criminal fines, the industry's criminal conspiracy had still turned a profit of approximately $300 million—after the fines (Green, Moore, and Wasserstein, 1972: 174). Finally, even though the case was unique for the seven executives who were sent to jail, the top executives (presidents and CEOs) still escaped punishment. The president and board chairman of GE was in fact selected as man of the year for 1960 (the year before the convictions) by the National Association of Manufacturers (Green, Moore, and Wasserstein, 1972: 157).

An integral part of the notion of the double standard is a comparison of white-collar and conventional crime, with the implication that those convicted of conventional crimes receive much harsher treatment for comparable, or even lesser, offenses. If we compare the penalties in the electric industry price-fixing case (relatively harsh for a corporate crime) with those for the typical larceny-theft, the results seem to confirm the double standard. Larceny-theft is roughly comparable to corporate theft insofar as both involve the taking or stealing of property without the use of force or violence; larcenies of $50 or more were regarded as serious enough to be part of the Federal Bureau of Investigation (FBI) Index of major crime in the United States in 1961. The FBI estimated that the average value of property stolen in larcenies in that year (the same year as the convictions in the electric conspiracy case) was $74, with the total value of all larcenies estimated at $70 million (U.S. Department of Justice, 1962: 89). In 1960, 9,303 convicted larceny offenders were received in state institutions, serving an average of 20 months each (Cahalan and Parsons, 1986: 43, 52).[1] This is substantially more than the 25 days served by the seven industry executives for a crime resulting in total property loss that exceeded the combined value of all the larcenies in a single year.

The disparity in punishment for corporate price-fixing and larceny seems quite apparent, especially if we take into account the value of the property loss in both kinds of cases relative to the penal sanction. Is this disparity the result of criminal justice officials blatantly favoring elite defendants over poor defendants? Or is it due to more subtle processes relating to how we perceive and define crime? In other words, is there still a sense in which we feel that white-collar offenses, such as price-fixing, are not "real" crimes and therefore should not be punished as such?

This brings us back to the question raised in the historic Sutherland-Tappan debate: Is white-collar crime "really" crime? This is more fundamentally a question about the nature of crime, not just white-collar crime. Why are some behaviors labeled "crime" and others not? Are some acts, such as murder and robbery, intrinsically criminal? Who has the authority to make these judgments? Why do we respond to conventional crimes through a different set of administrative agencies and procedures than white-collar crimes? The traditional answer to this series of questions is to rely upon the legal definition, which is the state's definition of crime. What is crime in this view is simply what violates the criminal law and is punishable as such through the criminal courts. Furthermore, as we discussed in Chapter 3, what makes some of these crimes "white-collar" depends upon the school of thought to which one subscribes, the legal or the Sutherland tradition.

The issue of the double standard remains a source of controversy among students of white-collar crime. It should be pointed out that the fact of differential treatment does not in itself constitute evidence of a kind of class or race discrimination in the justice system. There may be sound legal and policy reasons for this differential handling, rather than it reflecting a discriminatory attitude that systematically favors one class of offenders over another. This historic claim by Sutherland of a double standard of justice will be further explored in this chapter. We shall begin by examining the different kinds of public law that have been traditionally applied to conventional and white-collar crime. Moreover, we shall explore the "war on drugs" as an example of how society responds to certain aspects of a social problem as a "criminal" matter and to other aspects as a "regulatory" problem. Finally, we shall consider some recent empirical evidence on the double-standard issue.

THE ADMINISTRATIVE LAW VERSUS THE CRIMINAL LAW

Since the late nineteenth century an administrative and regulatory apparatus has developed to deal with offenses that involve the activities of business and professional groups. This administrative law[2] serves as the legal basis for most white-collar crimes (Newman, 1958: 53). There are, of course, certain white-collar crimes that are violations of the criminal law and are typically processed through the criminal justice system: Examples are embezzlement, forgery, criminal fraud, and bribery. There are also offenses that fall under the jurisdiction of these regulatory agencies and, if regarded as serious enough, may be referred to the Justice Department for criminal prosecution. In the domain of white-collar crime these strictly criminal violations are in the minority.[3] In assessing the differential treatment of conventional and white-collar crime, it is important to understand the different underlying assumptions of the administrative and the criminal laws, and the official rationale for handling offenses under one or the other of these public laws.

Donald J. Newman (1958: 53) provided one of the best analyses of how the administrative and the criminal laws differ. He identified five major differences: "1) in origin, 2) in determination of responsibility, or intent, 3) in philosophy, 4) in enforcement and trial procedure, and 5) in sanctions used to punish violators."

Let us consider each of these differences in more detail. The first difference rests on the common law distinction between crimes that are *mala prohibita* and those that are *mala en se*. Behaviors that are proscribed by the criminal law are regarded as *mala en se* (bad in themselves). This implies that such acts are inherently wrong ("natural" crimes), and the criminal law simply reflects the widespread moral outrage over crimes such as robbery, rape, and murder. Offenses that are *mala prohibita* are not so self-evidently wrong. They are unlawful because certain rules are necessary for the maintenance of social order. Traffic laws are a good example. It is not inherently right or wrong to drive on a certain side of the road, but in order to maintain some semblance of orderly traffic flow, some convention must be established. In this sense it is arbitrary which convention is adopted (driving on the right or on the left side). These kinds of regulatory matters are the subject of the administrative law, whether it regards the emission of toxic gases into the atmosphere, the labeling of food and drug products, or the advertising of various commodities.

The second difference pertains to the intentionality of the law violation. The criminal law is based on the principle that all crimes should consist of an act (*actus reus*) and a given state of mind or criminal intent (*mens rea*) that accompanies that act. Both of these elements must be present in order for a crime to be committed, and in order to hold a particular individual responsible. The punishment of criminal behavior requires this concurrence of act and intent. In contrast, the administrative law is simply concerned with whether a particular law or regulation was violated and not the state of mind of the offenders. If an automobile manufacturer does not meet the Environmental Protection Agency (EPA) pollution standards on auto emissions, it does not matter to the EPA whether this was a deliberate violation, what the state of mind of top executives was, or even whether responsibility can be individually pinpointed. In enforcing the administrative law the main concern is with the overt act—the violation of pollution standards in this case. If, however, there was also some intentionality (*mens rea*) on the part of top officials to violate pollution laws, then this might also be a criminal matter.

A third area of difference relates to the underlying philosophy and objectives of these two kinds of public law. The main aim of sanctions in the criminal law is to punish offenders. Although there are various reasons for using criminal sanctions, retribution, deterrence, and incapacitation have always been central; reforming the offender has been much more secondary. Clearly we wish to catch bank robbers and rapists in order to punish them for their criminal behavior. If they are rehabilitated in the process, this is an added bonus. On the other hand, the main purpose of the administrative law is much more remedial and corrective in nature. The range of sanctions available to regulatory agencies includes warnings, recalls, cease and desist orders, consent decrees, injunctions, fines, and referrals to the courts for civil or criminal action. In Marshall B. Clinard and Peter C. Yeager's (1980: 122) study of corporate crime, 44.2 percent of all the sanctions imposed by 25 federal agencies in a two-year period consisted of warnings or recalls. The main purpose of such administrative actions is to stop some ongoing illegal practice—the marketing of an unsafe drug, false advertising, and so on— and not to "get even" with the offending firm. It is difficult to find a comparable sanction for violators of the criminal law, where they would be enjoined from committing future crimes, but not punished for past misdeeds.

In the fourth difference between the criminal and the administrative laws, different organizational mechanisms operate to handle violators. The criminal law has the personnel and resources of the criminal justice system—the police, the criminal courts, and the jails and prisons at various levels of government— at its disposal. The administrative law, as we noted above, has regulatory agencies at the state and federal levels to enforce its provisions. Unlike the agencies of the criminal justice system, regulatory agencies, such as the EPA, the Occupational Safety and Health Administration (OSHA), and the Food and Drug Administration (FDA), not only have responsibilities for enforcing the law, but also have the power to make rules that have the effect of law. Administrative law judges may also be called upon to settle matters that fall under the jurisdiction of each of these agencies.

The final difference pertains to the kinds of sanctions available to each type of public law. This difference is really a corollary of the third. Because the criminal law is more punitive in its philosophy, its sanctions emphasize various forms of punishment of the offender—probation, imprisonment, and even the death penalty. The administrative law, in contrast, focuses on remedial actions to prevent future violations—injunctions, cease and desist orders, and product recalls. Criminal sanctions would be measures of last resort for the administrative law and are not within the enforcement powers of regulatory agencies. Such sanctions must be carried out through the courts.

Even if it is conceded that there are different public laws and organizational structures for handling conventional and white-collar crime, as we pointed out, this in itself does not establish that our justice system is discriminatory toward these two classes of offenses/offenders. Again, as we observed, there may be some very sound legal and policy reasons for this differential treatment. Let us consider what these are.

Sue Titus Reid (1976: 225ff.) offered one of the more cogent rationales for the official handling of white-collar crime under the administrative law. She pointed out that there are various advantages to using the administrative law. These include the speed with which matters can be handled. In using the example of a restaurant that is serving spoiled food and operates a kitchen that does not meet cleanliness standards, Reid pointed out that a health inspector may act quickly to close such an establishment. Under the criminal law the resolution of this problem might take months, and the outcome would be uncertain. In this case, she argued, public safety is much more effectively ensured through the mechanisms of the administrative law.

Another advantage of using regulatory agencies to handle white-collar violations is the expertise possessed by the staff of such agencies in the particular area they are charged with regulating. The FDA, for example, has the knowledge and skills to determine the effectiveness and safety of prescription and over-the-counter drugs that a criminal court would not have. In addition, the informality and flexibility of the regulatory process might develop a spirit of voluntary compliance and cooperation, rather than the adversary system fostered in the criminal courts.

Reid also cautioned against the tendency to overcriminalize behavior in our society, and against the wisdom of labeling individuals criminal when their conduct can be controlled by less severe and more effective methods. She pointed out that ultimately if there is not a political will to pursue white-collar crime through the administrative law, it will still not be pursued simply because criminal sanctions are made available.

Each of the advantages that Reid mentioned has its disadvantages as well. The informality of the regulatory process also offers opportunities for bribery and corruption. The expertise possessed by given regulatory agencies may also be based on conflict of interest insofar as much of this expertise stems from staff or officials who are drawn from (or destined to be part of) the very industry being regulated. Similarly, the observation about the lack of political will to pursue white-collar crime, whether it be in terms of the administrative or the criminal law, could also be taken as a reflection of the double standard that Sutherland talked about. Before picking up on this debate in more detail, we shall explore the differential handling of the drug problem in our society, with careful attention to understanding why some aspects are defined as a "criminal" problem and others as a "regulatory" matter. This should give us additional insight into the social, political, and cultural dynamics of this process.

THE "WAR ON DRUGS"

The "war on drugs" of the 1980s and early 1990s is largely equated with the measures taken by the administrations of Ronald Reagan and George Bush to control, if not eliminate, drug use in the United States. What is not so widely recognized is that there is another "war" relating to drugs that has paralleled the more publicized attack on the use and distribution of illegal drugs. This less visible war entails, ironically, a massive promotion of drug use—albeit legal drugs, both prescription and over-the-counter ones. The war is the intense competition among pharmaceutical and generic companies for market share and profits. At the same time the Bush administration was spending over $9 billion a year to combat various aspects of the illegal drug problem (Maguire and Flanagan, 1991: 17), the pharmaceutical industry was spending about $5 billion a year promoting its products (U.S. Senate, 1991a: 1).

It might be objected that this is an unfair comparison, and that we should not place legal and illegal drugs in the same category; we are essentially comparing "apples" and "oranges." But are we? This is another version of the debate that we have been considering that involves not only the double standard, but also the whole question of what crime is and what "white-collar" crime in particular is. This objection assumes that there is an underlying rationality in the distinction we make between legal and illegal drugs that justifies our differential labeling and handling of legal and illegal drugs. It is difficult to identify any criterion that consistently differentiates the legal from the illegal drugs. Perhaps the most frequently cited is that illegal drugs are the most dangerous and harmful, and have no medicinal value, while legal drugs in various degrees have some health benefit.

Arnold S. Trebach (1987), a critic of the Reagan and Bush administrations' drug war, emphasized the basic "irrationality" of the drug laws as well as the myths that support them. He pointed to the harm produced by legal drugs, such as alcohol and tobacco, and compared it to the deaths from the most popular illegal drugs in 1985—heroin, cocaine, PCP, marijuana. The deaths from diseases derived from alcohol and tobacco overshadow the deaths from the above illegal drugs by 500,000 to 2,177 (Trebach, 1987: 3). Trebach also pointed out that some illegal drugs, especially heroin and marijuana, have medicinal value, and that the use of such drugs, even for medical purposes, remains criminalized in the United States.

The 1992 crackdown by the FDA on practitioners of alternative medicine further clouds the presumed rationality in the distinction we make between legal and illegal drugs. In May of 1992, state health inspectors in Texas raided health food stores across the state, seizing hundreds of products, including vitamin C and herbal teas. About the same time, FDA agents, who were armed and wearing bulletproof vests, raided the Tahoma Clinic in Kent, Washington, where practitioners of alternative medicine allegedly injected themselves with megadoses of vitamins and minerals in order to treat a variety of ailments. The FDA said the raids were part of a crackdown on manufacturers of nutritional supplements who make unproven claims for their products. In addition, the Tahoma Clinic, according to the FDA, was making illegal drugs, including "vitamin-mineral concoctions" (Williams, 1992: 1, 34). If we substitute cocaine and marijuana for vitamin and mineral concoctions, these raids are reminiscent of the "war on drugs." So how are we going to make sense of this process by which some drugs (and their use) are criminalized and others are legitimated? The history of drug legislation may give us a clue.

Stigma and Drugs

A common element in the passage of drug legislation has been the stigma associated with the user of a particular drug. Rather than criminalization being related to the pharmacological properties of a drug, which is the conventional wisdom, a much stronger case can be made for a relationship between the characteristics of the user and criminalization.

A cursory examination of the history of drug legislation indicates that drugs are most likely to be criminalized when their use is strongly associated with the poor, minority, or marginal segments of society. Perhaps the first to recognize this connection was Alfred R. Lindesmith in his study of opiate addiction. He observed that, during the nineteenth century, addiction, except for opium smoking, was not linked to crime. The rapid spread of opium smoking in the criminal underworld of the late nineteenth century established this link between addiction and crime, and it was gradually extended to include all types of addicts (Lindesmith, 1947: 188). Roger Smith (1966) and Theodore J. Raynor (1968) placed more emphasis on race than on the criminal underworld in their interpretations of this process of stigmatizing the opiate addict. Because Chinese immigrants introduced opium smoking on the West Coast in the latter part of the nineteenth century, this practice was strongly identified with the Chinese and taken as a symbol of their depravity, keeping in mind that prejudice and discrimination against the Chinese were mounting at this time in U.S. history, especially on the West Coast.

Similarly, federal marijuana legislation was passed in the United States when its use was largely confined to Mexican laborers in the Southwest, black jazz musicians, and some elements of the black, urban lower class (Becker, 1963: 135; Polsky, 1967: 168). The criminalization of marijuana was certainly facilitated by its link to minority and marginal groups in society. It was also greatly facilitated by a highly stigmatized image of the marijuana user, an image that was actively fostered by the Federal Bureau of Narcotics in its efforts to gain passage of the Marijuana Tax Act of 1937 (Becker, 1963; Lindesmith, 1965; Oteri and Silvergate, 1967).

Even the passage of the Volstead Act of 1920, which ushered in the Prohibition era, involved a symbolic attack on the drinking practices of immigrants and minorities. As historian Richard Hofstadter (1955: 289ff.) noted, Prohibition symbolized not only a distaste for the evils of alcohol, but also the rural Protestant aversion to the urban, immigrant, Catholic drinking masses. One interpretation of the failure of Prohibition was that it could not maintain support when drinking cut across social-class lines, and when there was no highly stigmatized image of the average alcohol drinker.[4]

In the mid-1980s, it was the emergence of "crack" cocaine that fueled the Reagan war on drugs and added to the public panic over the drug problem. Cocaine had existed in the illegal marketplace for many years, and in the 1970s it had a reputation as an expensive glamour drug that was popular with some celebrities and some upper- and upper-middle-class drug users. The "scared summer of 1986," as Trebach expressed it, when the "crack" epidemic was officially announced and promoted, actually preceded any hard data from official sources that such an epidemic existed, in terms of either increasing use or increasing deaths from overdose (Trebach, 1987: 1–21).

The advent of "crack," which was considerably less expensive than cocaine in its traditional form, meant that it was much more available to the non-elite (Kappeler, Blumberg, and Potter, 1993: 153). Indeed, it was the smoking of "crack" cocaine in the inner cities that became one of the chief targets of law enforcement in the drug war of the 1980s. The data on the arrest rates for drug offenses show a tripling in the arrest rate of nonwhites (mainly blacks) during the 1980s as compared to a steady rate for whites. This disparity is even more pronounced in the arrest of nonwhite and white juveniles for drugs after 1985. Between 1965 and 1980, white and nonwhite juveniles had about the same arrest rate for drugs, with whites slightly higher in the 1970s. In the late 1980s, the arrest rate for nonwhites increased dramatically while that for whites declined (Blumstein, 1993: 3–5). Like the drug panics of previous eras, this one focused on the drug use of the poor and the minorities. It also served some of the same purposes: to divert attention away from other public issues, and to present drug use as a cause rather than a symptom of social problems (Johns, 1991).

Clearly key contributing elements in determining which drugs become criminalized in society are the existence of a stigmatized image of the user and a strong identification of the drug with the poor, minority, or marginal groups in society. This is another expression of the myth of the criminal type discussed in Chapter 1, where certain persons or groups who are designated as dangerous or threatening in society become the cultural material for our criminal-type myths. It can conversely be argued that when the diffusion of drug use spreads to more mainstream groups, there will be social and political efforts to alter the legal status of that particular drug. The spread of marijuana use to white, middle-class high school and college students in the 1960s in this respect set the stage for subsequent decriminalization efforts.

The Pharmaceutical Industry and Drugs

The other side of the criminalization coin is the mobilization of resources to legitimate drugs and their uses. Clearly the pharmaceutical industry is at the forefront of efforts to legitimate certain drugs and their uses, including the legitimation of some questionable practices in the promotion of these drugs. The pharmaceutical industry is historically one of the most profitable manufacturing industries.[5] The Clinard and Yeager (1980) study of corporate crime in the mid-1970s found that it is also one of the most lawless industries.[6] The lawlessness has included bribery, negligence in the safety testing of drugs, unsafe manufacturing practices, and illegal promotion practices (Mintz and Cohen, 1971; Braithwaite, 1984). To illustrate the process by which some drugs are criminalized and others are legitimated we will consider what happened to amphetamines when Congress passed the Comprehensive Drug Abuse Prevention and Control Act of 1970.

James M. Graham's (1972) analysis of the politics surrounding passage of this Act showed the dynamics of this process. Congress held hearings on this legislation, which was essentially the program of Richard Nixon's administration to combat drug abuse. Much of the debate concerned which schedule (II or III)[7] in the bill the various controlled substances, particularly the 6,000 drugs in the "amphetamine family," should be placed. Amphetamines, whether used legally or illegally, almost all originate from the same source—the pharmaceutical industry. The initial bill proposed by the Nixon administration had placed the amphetamines in schedule III, which would exempt them from any quotas on production and would lessen controls and penalties. Some senators and representatives had attempted to amend the bill by moving the amphetamines to schedule II, which would have made them subject to government quotas and stricter controls. This effort to bring the amphetamines under tighter regulation was, however, unsuccessful in spite of testimony that more than half of the legally manufactured amphetamines were being diverted to the black market; medical experts also testified on the limited medicinal value of amphetamines. In the final compromise only liquid injectable methamphetamine ("speed") was transferred to schedule II. This category of amphetamines (only 5 of the 6,000 amphetamines) was abused primarily by mainlining "speed freaks," and no evidence had been presented at the hearings that there was a problem with the illicit diversion of this particular amphetamine group. President Nixon signed the bill in November of 1970. It was not much different than the original version that had been submitted to Congress, which the pharmaceutical industry had helped to draft. As Graham (1972: 14–15) noted, "the end result is a national policy which declares an all-out war on drugs which are *not* a source of corporate income. Meanwhile, under the protection of law, billions of amphetamines are overproduced without medical justification." In the final analysis, although this 1970 law was publicized as part of the Nixon administration's effort to combat drug abuse, it essentially criminalized amphetamine use at the street level after it had been diverted to the black market, but it did little to control the initial source of supply, which was the domestic pharmaceutical companies. The legislation in effect legitimated the traditional manufacturing practice of the drug firms, which was to overproduce amphetamines given the limited medical needs they served.[8]

The Double Standard and the Two Wars

We return now to the two wars on drugs that began this discussion. There is the familiar "war on drugs" that criminalizes certain harmful drugs and their use, mainly involving the poor and the minorities. There is also the "war" involving the promotion of other drugs that are generally viewed as being safe and effective for given medical purposes. The social control of this latter war is traditionally handled as a regulatory matter through the FDA. The social control of the former war is delegated to the Justice Department and local police forces. Does this differential handling reflect a double standard of justice? It does not if we accept the rationality of the conventional distinction between legal and illegal drugs. It is problematic, however, if we reject the criteria on which that distinction is based. To the extent that we view the traditional distinction between legal and illegal drugs as irrational, as Trebach (1987) maintained, then the differential handling of these two problems may also be called into question. Furthermore, Christina Johns (1991: 147) argued that not only do we treat legal and illegal drugs differently, but also the overwhelming focus on the dangers of illegal drugs serves to divert attention from the dangers of legal drugs, which are a more integral part of our culture and economy.

Two decades ago Henry L. Lennard and his associates (1971) noted this same disparity in our response to illegal and legal drugs. At that time they were concerned with the lack of attention given to the increasing use of prescription and over-the-counter drugs for everyday problems. They saw the pharmaceutical industry expanding its market through a process they referred to as "mystification." This entailed the creation of demand for industry products (drugs) by redefining certain human problems as medical ones, thus requiring medication/drugs as a solution. In their view the pharmaceutical industry's promotion of its products in this manner was communicating a basic model for solving personal problems: drug use (Lennard et al., 1971: 18–23). The promotion of pharmaceutical products in this fashion has made chemical solutions to everyday problems a growing aspect of our consumer culture, whether those chemicals happen to be legal or not.

In 1990, the promotion practices of the pharmaceutical industry came under the scrutiny of the Senate Committee on Labor and Human Resources. The Committee, chaired by Senator Edward Kennedy, found that industry spending on certain questionable promotion practices—the use of gifts, reminders, and symposia to influence physicians' prescribing practices—had increased fourfold between 1974 and 1988, from $40.4 million to $165.8 million, in 1988 dollars (U.S. Senate, 1991a: 5, 10). This increase was attributed to a number of factors. David C. Jones,[9] a former top executive with several pharmaceutical firms, testified that until 1970 the industry had accepted the principle that demand for prescription drugs was inelastic, that is to say, limited by the dictates of good medical practice. Jones observed that when Tagamet was introduced in the early 1970s, the industry learned an important lesson. This was that publicity and education could make both doctors and consumers interested in a drug, even before it became available, and that demand could be expanded beyond the medical need of the drug. Moreover, Jones argued, the industry discovered that prescription drugs could be marketed like cosmetics or candy (U.S. Senate, 1991a: 19).

Gerald Mossinghoff, president of the Pharmaceutical Manufacturers Association (PMA), testified at the Senate hearings as to the crucial role of generics in the mid-1980s in producing an enormous surge in competition once the patent on a brand-name drug expires (U.S. Senate, 1991a: 164).[10] This has meant an even greater emphasis on marketing and promotion by the brand-name firms in order to ensure the profitability of their drugs, both before and after patent expiration ("Doctors' Dilemma," 1990).

The issue of when legitimate advertising of pharmaceutical products spills over into illegal, and even criminal, promotional practices came into focus with the testimony of Dr. Sidney Wolfe, director of the Public Citizen Health Research Group. Dr. Wolfe quite blatantly referred to the widespread "doctor bribing" that was being carried out by the pharmaceutical companies. His organization has set up a national hotline for doctors to report questionable industry promotional practices aimed at influencing physicians' prescribing behavior. One such effort was the Wyeth-Ayerst "frequent prescriber, free-flying doctor" program. This was a program aimed at maintaining the profitability of Inderal when its patent expired in 1986 and generics became available. For each prescription of Inderal LA, a doctor would receive 1,000 points toward a free trip on American Airlines anywhere in the continental United States. It would take 50 such prescriptions to win the trip. Ayerst defended the program as "research" for which the doctors were being appropriately compensated (U.S. Senate, 1991a: 55–57). Dr. Wolfe made clear that this was not an isolated episode and proceeded to provide the Committee with additional examples of promotional programs from other firms.

When Wolfe was questioned by the Committee, Senator Orrin Hatch objected to Wolfe's use of the term "bribery" in reference to these promotional campaigns. In Hatch's view, "I think it is stretching it to say that that is a bribery campaign" (U.S. Senate, 1991a: 83). Wolfe defended his use of "bribery" by pointing out that some of these programs involved violations of FDA regulations on promoting unapproved uses of drugs.[11] Additionally, he noted that 36 states and the federal government have anti-kickback laws that are not being enforced (U.S. Senate, 1991a: 79, 82). Apparently not persuaded, Hatch again questioned Wolfe on the use of "bribe" to describe payments to doctors for attending a meeting or a dinner. Hatch regarded this as fair compensation for a doctor's time. Hatch also objected to using the term "white-collar crime" to describe these practices: "Now, that is a very strong statement" was his view of the matter (U.S. Senate, 1991a: 84–88). This exchange between Dr. Wolfe and Senator Hatch nicely epitomizes the double-standard issue as well as the definitional controversy over what crime is. It reveals the traditional reluctance to see illegal corporate practices as criminal matters.[12] It is also reminiscent of the Sutherland-Tappan debate on whether white-collar offenses are crime.

If we can generalize from this example of the two drug wars, it would appear that what distinguishes those commodities and behaviors (drugs and their use) that are criminalized from those that are legal or subject to regulation is the social, economic, and political power of the groups whose behavior is in question. Powerless and marginal groups are more likely to have their behavior (drug use) labeled as dangerous and criminalized. More powerful groups, such as pharmaceutical companies, have the resources to mobilize public opinion so that their commodities and behaviors (drugs and certain uses) are favorably perceived and culturally categorized; they are also better able to influence the legal status of their practices.

Because most white-collar crime, such as the illegal promotional practices of the pharmaceutical industry, is handled by regulatory agencies and the administrative law (Coleman, 1989: 167), is this what we mean by the double standard? It is if the decision on how to handle different types of crime, through the administrative law or the criminal law, is determined by the backgrounds of offenders who typically commit those crimes, with more powerful offenders (economically and politically) more likely to be handled by the mechanisms of the administrative law. In this manner elite groups may systematically receive more favorable treatment than others, not because their crimes are less serious, but because they have the power to influence public perception and legislation. This, of course, was the argument that Sutherland made: that we have institutionalized a kind of cultural bias in how we handle the crimes of the business and professional classes and those of the poor (Sutherland, 1945: 266ff.). Although our drug example supports the Sutherland position, the empirical evidence on this issue is mixed. Let us consider some of the more recent research.

SOME RECENT EVIDENCE

Basically, what we wish to know is whether elite offenders systematically receive more lenient treatment than non-elite offenders? One approach is to examine the penalties that elite and non-elite offenders receive when they commit the *same* crime. Another approach is to consider the penalties given to different types of crimes, distinguishing between those crimes that are more likely to involve elite and non-elite offenders, respectively—that is to say, white-collar and conventional crimes.

The research of Stanton Wheeler and his associates (1982) took the former approach. They found a significant positive relationship between one's socioeconomic status and the probability of imprisonment. In other words, the higher the social-class background of the offender, the *more* likely the offender would be sentenced to prison. This was a consistent finding in their research; it held for all eight types of white-collar crime as well as each of the seven federal districts in their study. The probability of imprisonment for truck drivers was 28 percent; bank tellers, 42 percent; managers, 47 percent; accountants, 53 percent; and lawyers, 60 percent (Wheeler, Weisburd, and Bode, 1982: 650–651). This finding is surprising, as they also observed, because it is contrary to the double-standard hypothesis. They interpreted this finding as an indication that judges hold those in higher positions to be more blameworthy. They also pointed out that harsher sentences might be due to the post-Watergate climate, when there was a heightened awareness of the harm of white-collar crime. It is also possible, as they noted, that the apparent harsher sentencing of high-status offenders may have occurred because only the relatively "little fish" make it to the sentencing stage. In this interpretation high-status offenders are much more likely to have their cases disposed of prior to sentencing; this prior leniency is thus not reflected in their data. Moreover, a limitation of the Wheeler research is that it was based on white-collar offenses that were handled as criminal matters. Because the vast majority of white-collar offenses are dealt with as regulatory violations, the generalizability of these findings is in question. Furthermore, their research did not examine whether the unexpected relationship they found also held for conventional crime—that is, that high-status offenders were more harshly penalized for robbery, rape, murder, and so on.

Susan P. Shapiro's (1984; 1990) study of the Securities and Exchange Commission (SEC) looked at the double-standard issue in a regulatory context. In her analysis of the enforcement actions of the SEC, Shapiro (1990) pointed out that, regardless of the seriousness of the offense, the availability of civil and administrative options increases the likelihood of legal action and at the same time decreases the risk of criminal prosecution. This affects lower- and upper-status offenders differently. Because there tend to be fewer civil or administrative legal options for lower-status offenders, they are more likely to be criminally prosecuted, especially for serious offenses, and they are also more likely to be convicted and sent to prison. Shapiro (1990: 360–361) also maintained that the prosecution of upper-status offenders, even for serious offenses, tends to be diverted away from criminal processing. However, upper-status offenders are much more likely to receive civil or administrative sanctions for their less serious violations than their lower-status peers.

Shapiro's interpretation of this differential response to lower-status and upper-status offenders, even for the same crime, was that the bias is due to the distribution of legal options and not the social standing of the offender (Shapiro, 1990: 362). But why are different legal options (administrative versus criminal) available to lower- and upper-status offenders? Shapiro's response was that violations of trust are not a function of social class, but a function of how positions of trust are distributed in society. Therefore, the availability of legal options is related to the appropriate mechanism for handling violations of trust for a given position rather than to who happens to occupy that position.

It should be emphasized that the Wheeler and Shapiro research focused on what happens to different kinds of offenders when sentenced for committing the same crime. Do lower-class offenders receive harsher penalties than upper-class offenders? This still does not address variation in sentencing between different kinds of crime, which is also a critical element of the double-standard notion. In general, are white-collar offenses handled more leniently than conventional crimes?

This second approach to the double-standard hypothesis was taken in a Bureau of Justice Statistics study, which was based on felony cases in eight states in 1983. It found that white-collar offenders,[13] when compared to property and violent criminals (1) were slightly more likely to be prosecuted; (2) had a slightly lower rate of conviction than property offenders, but a higher rate than violent offenders; (3) were somewhat less likely to be sentenced to prison than either property or violent offenders; and (4) were much less likely to be sentenced for a term of over one year (Manson, 1986). As Coleman (1989: 173) observed, this study probably understates the differences in the sentencing of white-collar offenders and other types of offenders as a result of the white-collar crimes selected for comparison. Coleman questioned whether offenders convicted of forgery, counterfeiting, fraud, and embezzlement are all really white-collar criminals.

Another study by David Weisburd and his colleagues (1991) used federal crimes in their comparison of the treatment of white-collar and conventional criminals.[14] Overall, they found that those convicted of white-collar crimes were about as likely to go to prison (46.4%) as those who committed common crimes (49.7%), although for slightly less time (21.3 months versus 25.1 months). They did, however, find considerable variation in sentencing between different types of white-collar crimes, with antitrust violators the least likely to go to prison— 19.2 percent for a 1.8-month average sentence (Weisburd et al., 1991: 131).

In their assessment of the evidence regarding the double-standard issue, Weisburd and his colleagues (1991: 144) concluded that their data did not fit the discrimination model (the double-standard hypothesis). In their view judges largely draw upon common legal principles, such as seriousness of the crime, blameworthiness of an individual, and so on, rather than the race or class background of a defendant, in their decisions. The researchers did note, however, that judges do seem to weigh the criteria differently when deciding common crime and white-collar crime cases. In common crimes the backgrounds and attributes of defendants, especially prior criminal records, are much more damaging to them (Weisburd et al., 1991: 162–163). This observation again seems to open the door of the double-standard issue. Moreover, as with the Manson study above, the selection of common and white-collar crimes in the comparison can understate or overstate any differences in the two groups.

In a study of Medicaid fraud, Robert Tillman and Henry N. Pontell (1992) examined what they called the leniency (double-standard) hypothesis by comparing the penalties received by health care providers convicted of defrauding California's Medicaid system (known as Medi-Cal) with the sanctions received by a group convicted of grand theft (more than $400). The Medi-Cal fraud sample consisted largely of professionals, including physicians, psychiatrists, and dentists, while the grand theft sample was characterized by persons in clerical and retail jobs (and no professionals). Both samples, however, were made up of first-time offenders. Tillman and Pontell (1992) found that the Medi-Cal fraud offenders were much less likely to be incarcerated than the grand theft offenders. Overall they concluded that their white-collar sample received more lenient treatment even when the civil and administrative sanctions received by this group were taken into account.

While the elite/non-elite status of the offender may be important in sentencing, perhaps even more important is the type of offense, particularly the "collar" that is typically attributed to that offense. This is not surprising because variation in sentencing is a function of the perceived seriousness of the offense. What is not clear, however, is the extent to which seriousness becomes confounded with the "collar" of the offense. The research of Francis T. Cullen and his colleagues showed that although the perceived seriousness of white-collar crime has increased more than any other crime category, white-collar crime is still regarded as less serious than most other types of crime. They also pointed to the considerable variation in how the public regards different types of white-collar crime, with corporate violence the most serious (Cullen, Link, and Polanzi, 1982). Tillman and Pontell (1992: 564–565) also observed changing attitudes on the part of judges and prosecutors regarding white-collar crime. They argued that until recently prosecutors have not typically sought incarceration for Medi-Cal offenders. The older attitude, which has not disappeared, is that the professionals who commit Medicaid fraud should not be subject to the same indignities as common criminals. Although crime seriousness appears to be an objective, legal criterion for determining sentences, it really cannot be separated from attitudes regarding the differential treatment that should be accorded offenders with different class backgrounds.

As we can see, Sutherland's historic claim of a double standard of justice in our treatment of elite and lower-class offenders turns out to be much more complex than we might have imagined. It is essentially an allegation of class discrimination in the justice system and involves many of the same difficulties of proof as the discrimination issue itself (Wilbanks, 1987). It is also an issue that we will pursue in the chapters in Part Three, which relates to the social control of white-collar crime.

In closing, let us consider the relevance of the distinction between individual and institutional discrimination for this issue. We need to distinguish between blatant acts of discrimination by individual officials in the justice system and more systemic forms of favoring or disadvantaging certain kinds of defendants. Studies that focus on the decision-making of justice officials (judges' sentencing decisions, etc.) are looking for the former kind of discrimination. The more subtle form of discrimination is the institutional variety, which is much more ingrained in the justice system's day-to-day operations. It is reflected in our attitudes regarding the seriousness of different crime categories. It is also apparent in our discussion of the drug problem, where some drugs are routinely handled as criminal matters and others as regulatory problems. Shapiro's work also alluded to this in terms of the differential availability of civil and administrative actions to different kinds of offenders. These differential organizational procedures we have devised clearly represent institutionalized mechanisms by which we routinely respond to different kinds of problems. It is this systemic, taken-for-granted quality of our official handling of white-collar crime that makes the double-standard issue so difficult to come to terms with and that causes it to remain a point of controversy.

NOTES

1. Given the rarity of incarceration for price-fixing, it is also instructive to compare the probability of incarceration for larceny. Although data are not available for the 1960s, data based on 37 urban jurisdictions in 1981 indicate that 44 percent of felony larceny convictions resulted in some incarceration, 13 percent for more than one year (U.S. Department of Justice, 1986: 30). In 1960, 14.3 percent of all state prisoners under felony commitment were there for larceny (Cahalan and Parsons, 1986: 48).

It is also instructive to compare the severity of the penalties in the heavy electrical equipment conspiracy (again, relatively harsh for a corporate crime) with those for embezzlement and fraud, which are also white-collar crimes, but which typically involve non-elite offenders in an occupational crime. In 1960, the average time served before first release in state and federal institutions for embezzlement and fraud was 17 months (Cahalan and Parsons, 1986: 52).

2. The administrative law is one type of public law. It is created when state legislatures or the Congress establish administrative agencies or commissions with authority to regulate certain spheres of economic or professional activity. These agencies also typically have rule-making authority and some enforcement powers in the area that they regulate. The Federal Trade Commission (FTC), the Occupational Safety and Health Administration (OSHA), parole boards, and human rights commissions are examples of such agencies (Reid, 1976: 12).

3. In Sutherland's (1945: 260–265) classic study of corporate crime, only 9 percent of the adverse decisions against corporations were made by criminal courts. Sutherland conceded that although all of these decisions involved unlawful behavior, they were not necessarily criminal. He argued, however, that 473 of the 547 adverse decisions involved crimes.

4. While the reasons for ending Prohibition in 1933 are complex, the absence of a stigmatized image of the average drinker is certainly a contributing element. Another key ingredient was the Great Depression. The drys had argued for years that Prohibition was responsible for the prosperity of the 1920s. The Depression exploded that myth. The wets then argued that repeal would create thousands of jobs in alcohol-related enterprises (Folliard, 1970).

5. In the 1980s, the profitability (% of profits/sales) of pharmaceutical companies ranged from 12 to 20 percent; all manufacturing enterprises during the same period fluctuated from 6 to 8 percent (U.S. Senate, 1991a: 4).

6. In Clinard and Yeager's study of the enforcement actions of some 24 federal agencies during 1975 and 1976, the pharmaceutical industry accounted for 10 percent of the total violations and 20 percent of the manufacturing violations. All 17 drug firms had at least one enforcement action against them, with two drug firms having 21 or more violations (Clinard and Yeager, 1980: 120). The other two most lawless industries in their study were the automobile and the oil refining industries. These three industries accounted for nearly half the total violations in the Clinard and Yeager study.

7. Federal law classifies controlled substances into five categories, with schedule I the most strictly controlled (includes heroin, marijuana, and LSD) and schedule V the least controlled (includes codeine-based cough syrup). Cocaine and morphine are in schedule II, the amphetamines and barbiturates are mostly in schedule III, and valium and librium are in schedule IV (Inciardi, 1992: 292–293).

8. As James A. Inciardi (1992: 39) pointed out, the 1970 legislation did represent a tightening of controls on the prescribing and distribution of amphetamines, but this is relative to the unregulated state of affairs at that time regarding amphetamines. Inciardi also claimed that legitimate amphetamine production was ultimately cut by 90 percent. This can only be a rough estimate because until 1970 the manufacturers of amphetamines were not legally required to keep an exact accounting of their production. At the time of the 1970 legislation, amphetamine production was estimated at 8 to 10 billion pills annually (Graham, 1972: 14).

9. David C. Jones was a former vice-president for Abbott Laboratories, a former executive director of government and public affairs at CIBA–GEIGY, and, in the early 1970s, a spokesperson for the industry with the Pharmaceutical Manufacturers Association (PMA). Jones resigned from Abbott and left the industry because, as he put it, "I got to a point where I began to learn what the truth was, and I could no longer tolerate the truth" (U.S. Senate, 1991a: 36). Senator Edward Kennedy later explained at the hearing that Jones left Abbott "after confronting unconscionable corporate policy which exploited patients with Lou Gehrig's Disease by promoting an ineffective drug in order to bridge a revenue gap at the company." Also, as Jones was about to leave Abbott, the company was planning "to promote a very expensive drug, Lupron, for a variety of unapproved uses" (U.S. Senate, 1991a: 153).

10. Because of the enormous expense in the development and pre-market testing of new drugs, the pharmaceutical firm that develops a particular drug is entitled by law to a monopoly on the manufacture and distribution of that drug until the patent expires. At

that point generic drugs may be introduced into the market, providing they meet the bioequivalence test. The Drug Price Competition and Patent Restoration Act of 1984 is the governing legislation in this process ("Big Lie," 1987). According to the PMA, it takes more than 12 years and $230 million to bring a new prescription drug to market (U.S. Senate, 1991a: 163).

11. When the FDA approves a prescription drug for marketing, it approves it for specific uses or indications. It is still illegal to promote that same drug for an unapproved use.

12. In a 1991 note in the *New England Journal of Medicine*, Dr. David Kessler, Food and Drug Administration (FDA) commissioner, warned the medical profession that "the FDA will no longer exercise regulatory restraint" regarding the role of medical experts in illegal promotional efforts. Under provisions of the Food, Drug, and Cosmetic Act, the FDA has responsibility for ensuring that there is no promotion of unapproved drugs or of unapproved uses of approved drugs (Kessler, 1991: 201–202). Although the FDA is still not dealing with illegal promotion of drugs as a criminal matter, it is clearly showing a much greater willingness to exercise its regulatory authority in these matters.

13. The study used forgery, counterfeiting, fraud, and embezzlement as its white-collar crimes. It traced the actions taken against those arrested for these crimes (as well as property, violent, and public order crimes) from arrest to sentencing, using the Offender-Based-Transactions Statistics program (Manson, 1986).

14. The eight white-collar crimes were violations of securities laws, violations of antitrust laws, bribery, bank embezzlement, mail and wire fraud, tax fraud, false claims and statements, and credit fraud. The comparison group of nonviolent, financially oriented common criminals consisted of those who had committed postal theft and postal forgery (Weisburd et al., 1991: 9–10, 17).

Part Two

THE PROBLEM OF
EXPLANATION

CHAPTER FIVE

What Are the "Facts" of White-Collar Crime?

Let us begin exploring the problem of explanation by making an unwarranted assumption: that white-collar crime is randomly distributed in society. By this we mean that there are no differences between groups in their incidence and prevalence of white-collar crime.[1] Men commit white-collar crimes at the same rate as women. There are no racial or social-class differences. White-collar crime does not depend upon age, occupation, education, income, or any of the standard variables sociologists typically employ. White-collar crime is not only widespread, but also equally distributed across groups in society. If this were true, then what would an explanation of white-collar crime entail? The answer is basically nothing, except perhaps to attribute the constancy and uniformity of white-collar crime to human nature. Clearly this is not the case. Not too many social phenomena, if any, are distributed in this way. What we need to know about white-collar crime is just how it is distributed in society. How does it vary in relation to all of the standard sociological variables? What are the patterns and trends of white-collar crime? These relationships between white-collar crime and various theoretically relevant variables are what might be called the "facts" of white-collar crime.[2] It is precisely these facts that need to be explained in any theory of white-collar crime.

In 1980, at a colloquium on a research agenda for white-collar crime, Herbert Edelhertz noted that one of the problems in the field was the lack of such facts about white-collar crime (Edelhertz and Overcast, 1982: 18). Although there have been advances in our knowledge since then, it is still not comparable to what we know about conventional crime or delinquency. Unlike for conventional crime, there is no centralized government recording system for white-collar crime that monitors its distribution and trends.

There are two main sources of national crime statistics for conventional crime:

Uniform Crime Reports (UCR) and the National Crime Victimization Survey (NCVS). The U.S. Justice Department is responsible for collecting the statistics for both—the UCR by the FBI and the NCVS by the Bureau of Justice Statistics (BJS). The UCR is based on crimes reported to the police, and the NCVS is a victimization survey conducted on a national sample of households. Both, however, measure essentially the same types of offenses, major property and violent crimes (U.S. Department of Justice, 1988: 11). When we hear media reports about crime in the United States, invariably they are based on one or both of these two national sources. As we noted, there is no comparable national source of statistics on white-collar crime.[3]

The development of explanations of white-collar crime requires the very knowledge about variation and patterns that we are so lacking. This chapter nevertheless will set forth the facts of white-collar crime as we know them through various scholarly studies and official data. First, however, we must deal with the question of typology: What are the types of white-collar crime that we are trying to explain?

TYPOLOGIES OF WHITE-COLLAR CRIME

The question of types of white-collar crime is, of course, clouded by the definitional dispute. If there is disagreement about what we mean by white-collar crime (the Sutherland tradition versus the legal tradition), then certainly there will be differences in the typologies generated from those disparate definitions. As Marshall B. Clinard and Richard Quinney (1973: 1–14) observed, there are many possible typologies of the same phenomenon, depending upon the theoretical assumptions, interests, and purposes of the researcher. Whatever those might be, theory construction is advanced by the development of typologies. Accordingly, we are trying to explain not only a general phenomenon, such as white-collar crime, but also more specific subtypes of that phenomenon, such as antitrust violations and embezzlement. The specific types of white-collar crime will produce variation and patterns somewhat different from the more general phenomenon. It is important to know the diversity that exists in the various types, and yet we also need to know how these specific types fit into a more comprehensive theory of white-collar crime.

As noted above, various typologies of white-collar crime are possible. A legalistic typology is one possibility. It delineates types of crime according to the criminal act as defined in statutes—bribery, forgery, price-fixing, mail-order fraud, and so on. This is useful for investigative purposes, but it probably does not advance our understanding of the illegal conduct. In contrast, individualistic typologies base their classifications on the personal characteristics of those who commit the crime. This may be useful from the standpoint of treatment and corrections, but it is of limited value for sociological explanation. The typologies most beneficial in the development of theory are those that take into account the motivation of the offender and the social context of the offense. Several typologies of white-collar crime are based on these dimensions, but they vary according to the theoretical interests of the proponent.

Edelhertz (1970) classified white-collar crime into four categories: personal crimes, abuses of trust, business crimes, and con games. The motivation of the offender and the context of the offense are the two principles of classification for his typology. Abuses of trust and business crimes both occur in the context of a legitimate occupation. In the case of the former (e.g., embezzlement), the gain is typically a personal one, with the employer the victim. In business crimes, while there might be personal gain, the business as an entity is the beneficiary of the crime (e.g., antitrust violation), and the perpetrator is likely to be a middle- or upper-level official. Personal crimes involve frauds by individuals for personal gain in a nonoccupational context (credit card fraud, welfare fraud, individual income tax violations). Finally, con games involve businesses that are set up with the intention of defrauding the public (phony contests or land frauds). This category is distinguished from business crimes in that the illegal activity is central to the business's operation; it is only incidental in a business crime. Edelhertz saw the main benefits of his typology in terms of the prevention and deterrence of white-collar crime. As we saw in Chapter 3, Edelhertz's definition and typology of white-collar crime were an important influence on the U.S. Justice Department's conception of white-collar crime.

One of the earliest, and also influential, typologies was that of Marshall B. Clinard and Richard Quinney (1973: 188). They simply divided white-collar crime into two categories: occupational crime and corporate crime. Occupational crime is similar to Edelhertz's category of abuses of trust, and corporate crime is equivalent to his business crime category. Personal crimes and con games were not part of Clinard and Quinney's typology because they were conforming with Edwin H. Sutherland's definition, which required that white-collar crime take place in the context of occupational activity. They did, however, depart from that definition by including occupations that were not "white collar."

In a more recent typology Gary S. Green (1990: 10–18), in the interest of conceptual preciseness, revised the concept of white-collar crime to include only occupational crime. By occupational crime he meant acts that are punishable by law, and that are committed through opportunities made available in a legal occupation. He then proceeds to construct four categories of occupational crime: organizational, state-authority, professional, and individual occupational crime. Organizational occupational crime is comparable to Clinard and Quinney's corporate crime (and Edelhertz's business crime), where the employer is the principal beneficiary of the illegal conduct. The second of Green's categories of occupational crime involves persons who commit crimes in the exercise of their governmental authority and powers. This would include police who engage in brutality and corruption, politicians who receive bribes and kickbacks, and public officials who make or enforce policies of torture and genocide. The third category, professional occupational crime, is specific to those in certain recognized professions, such as lawyers and doctors, who commit illegal acts because of their occupational opportunities—performing unnecessary surgery, perpetrating health insurance fraud, overbilling clients, falsifying documents, and the like. Green's fourth category, individual occupational crime, consists of all the remaining occupational crimes not encompassed by the other three categories where the individual is the primary beneficiary of the illegal conduct. Employee theft, individual income tax evasion, and insider trading are examples of crimes in this category.

Still another typology is offered by James W. Coleman (1989: 9–10), who argued that an offender-based typology is most effective for a sociology of white-collar crime. His typology dichotomizes white-collar crime into organizational and occupational crime. Organizational crime involves illegal conduct committed on behalf of a formal organization (corporation or government agency) to benefit that organization and to advance its goals. Occupational crime consists of illegal conduct by employees for personal gain, whether it be in the business world, in government, or in the professions. In Coleman's typology, all white-collar crimes are occupational, but the critical differentiation is between organizational and individual offenders.

From the standpoint of a Marxist criminology, Quinney (1977: 50–52) developed a typology based on types of domination in a capitalist society. He distinguished four types of crimes of domination: crimes of control, crimes of government, crimes of economic domination, and social injuries. The first type involves violations of individual liberties by the agents of social control, especially law enforcement. The second type involves offenses committed by elected or appointed government officials in order to maintain their position in government or to suppress domestic or foreign groups that may appear to threaten the national security. The crimes of the Watergate scandal during Richard Nixon's administration and the Iran-Contra affair during Ronald Reagan's administration illustrate this category. Crimes of economic domination are offenses committed by corporations or individual businesspersons in order to ensure capital accumulation and the survival of the capitalist system. Price-fixing and environmental pollution are among these economic crimes. The fourth category, social injuries, consists of acts by the capitalist class and the state that are not necessarily illegal, but that involve the denial of human rights. Racial or gender discrimination and the economic exploitation of workers are part of this type of domination. In Quinney's view, all four types of domination are an illegal part of the capitalist political economy. These crimes further consolidate the position of the capitalist class.

Clearly the formulation of a typology depends upon the theoretical biases and purposes of the researcher. Although we need not adopt a particular typology for the purposes of this book, we do need to be mindful of the importance of considering the diversity of white-collar crime in its explanation. Each of the various types of white-collar crime may have its own distinctive distribution in society. This variation, assuming that it exists, is another of the facts of white-collar crime that needs to be explained.

THE EXTENT AND NATURE OF CORPORATE CRIME

In our examination of the facts of white-collar crime, we shall first consider what we know about the distribution of one of the major types of white-collar crime: corporate crime. The lack of national governmental statistics on the incidence and prevalence of white-collar crime has on occasion generated independent attempts at producing this kind of systematic data. Sutherland's (1949; 1983) landmark study of corporate crime was the first major effort in this regard. Clinard and Peter C. Yeager's (1980) replication of Sutherland's work 30 years later was the second such effort. Although we have noted the significance of these two studies previously, we need to examine more closely the variation and patterns that they discovered with respect to corporate crime.

Sutherland's Lawless Corporations

In his study of the 70 largest U.S. corporations, Sutherland (1949; 1983) documented their offenses between 1900 and 1944 with respect to four types of law violations: restraint of trade (antitrust); false advertising; infringement of patents, trademarks, and copyrights; and unfair labor practices. In Chapter 2, "The Statistical Record," Sutherland (1949: 17–28) presented his findings in table form. There is no sophisticated analysis of the data, just a simple cross-tabulation of the results. Table III, for example, lists each of the 70 corporations and the court decisions against each of them by type of law violation.[4] The unit of analysis in the study is a decision against a corporation; this included the formal decisions and orders of courts, decisions by administrative commissions, and settlements ordered or approved by courts. There were 980 such adverse decisions made against the corporations by various courts and administrative commissions; only 16 percent of these decisions were made by criminal courts. Each corporation had at least 1 adverse decision against it, with 14 the average per corporation; the range was 1 to 50. Even if the data were limited to the decisions of the criminal courts, 60 percent of the corporations had at least one criminal conviction, with an average of four convictions each. Sutherland suggested that those corporations with four or more convictions might be designated "habitual criminals." In the uncut version of Sutherland's *White-Collar Crime* (1983: 15), the firms at the top of the list of law violators were Armour and Company (50 adverse decisions), Swift and Company (50), General Motors (40), Sears Roebuck (39), and Montgomery Ward (39).

Table V in *White-Collar Crime* presents the data on decisions against corporations over time. Most of the adverse decisions were made in the most recent time period of his study (60 percent between 1935 and 1944, and 40 percent between 1900 and 1934). Sutherland offered several possible explanations for this. One possibility, of course, is that there was an actual increase in corporate crime during this period. Because there are other factors that influence the number of adverse decisions, these have to be considered as well. One such factor is that there were more corporations in existence in 1944 than in 1900. This, however, did not seem to be much of a factor because the vast majority of the corporations in his study were in existence for the entire 45 years. Second, some of the laws that Sutherland included in his research had only been enacted in the mid-1930s; therefore, this skewed the results toward the most recent time period. Sutherland conceded that this had some effect, but noted that the concentration of adverse decisions in the 1935–1944 period also held for laws that had been passed much earlier. An additional factor is the possibility that corporations were more aggressively prosecuted from 1935 to 1944. It is this last explanation that Sutherland thought most plausible along with an actual increase in certain types of corporate crime.

When Sutherland examined the evidence pertaining to the early illegal activities of the 70 corporations, he found that nearly half (30) were either illegal in their origin or began illegal activities shortly thereafter. Most commonly these early illegal activities involved antitrust violations.

Finally, in explaining the differences in illegal activity among corporations, Sutherland (1983: 258–263) attributed this variation to four factors: the age of the corporation, the size of the corporation, the individual traits of business executives, and the position of the corporation in the economic structure. It was this last factor that Sutherland believed to be most important. He also noted a tendency for firms in the same industry to have similar numbers of offenses. For example, the two firms with the highest frequency of offenses were both meat-packers, Armour and Swift. Similarly, two of the major retailing companies, Sears and Montgomery Ward, had the same number of violations. He accounted for this correspondence in terms of the diffusion of illegal practices within the same industry and the need for each company to remain competitive if other firms in the industry were engaging in illegal practices; in some instances the illegal activity may have been in concert with the other corporations in the industry.

Clinard and Yeager's Fortune 500

In their update of Sutherland's research Clinard and Yeager (1980) studied the 477 corporations of *Fortune* magazine's list of largest U.S. manufacturing corporations in both 1975 and 1976 (the Fortune 500 list). Except for the shorter two-year period, in most respects the Clinard and Yeager study was broader in scope than Sutherland's research. Not only did they include a larger number of corporations, but also they examined a wider assortment of offenses. All of the law violations within the jurisdiction of some 24 federal agencies were within the study's scope; they were grouped into six categories: administrative violations (e.g., noncompliance with an agency or court order), environmental violations (e.g., air or water pollution), financial crimes (e.g., bribery), labor law violations (e.g., discrimination, occupational health and safety deficiencies), manufacturing violations (e.g., defective consumer products), and unfair trade practices (e.g., antitrust violations). Two indicators, agency actions initiated against corporations and actions completed, were employed to measure corporate crime. The first indicator is the equivalent of arrest or prosecution in the processing of conventional crimes; the second indicator is comparable to conviction in the criminal justice system. Clearly there were many more violations than are reflected in these two indicators because most corporate offenses go undetected; their study, like Sutherland's, is a conservative estimate of corporate crime.

Clinard and Yeager (1980: 113, 116) nevertheless found that 62.9 percent of these Fortune 500 corporations had regulatory actions initiated against them in 1975 and 1976 for a total of 1,724 actions. Law violations were not evenly distributed among these corporations. Thirty-eight corporations, 8 percent of the total, accounted for 52 percent of all the violations (an average of 23.5 violations per corporation), with the largest corporations the most frequent violators.

When Clinard and Yeager (1980: 119–122) examined the distribution of law violations by industry, they also found illegal activity much more concentrated in some industries. The oil, automobile, and pharmaceutical industries were the most lawless, accounting for nearly one-half of all the violations. In addition, almost all of the firms within each of these industries had at least one violation, with a few of them having substantial numbers of violations. For example, all 17 corporations in the pharmaceutical industry had at least 1 violation, and the two most lawless had 21 or more.

Although Clinard and Yeager revealed through their research the variation and patterns that we discussed above, they were less successful in identifying variables that had much explanatory value. They pointed out that the law-violating corporations, on the whole, were larger, were less financially successful, experienced less growth, and were more diversified than the conforming firms (Clinard and Yeager, 1980: 132). These relationships were only moderate in strength, however, and were insufficient to explain the corporate crime that their study had documented.

Other Surveys of Corporate Crime

Although the research studies of Sutherland and Clinard/Yeager comprise the major efforts thus far to determine the prevalence of corporate crime, additional surveys of a more modest nature have been conducted by journalists. Irwin Ross (1980) produced such a survey for *Fortune*, and Orr Kelly (1982) did the same for *U.S. News and World Report*. Both of these surveys were concerned with the relatively serious violations of the largest corporations, as measured by convictions or consent degrees.

Ross compiled the violations of 1,043 major corporations[5] during the 1970s for five federal crimes: bribery, criminal fraud, illegal political contributions, tax evasion, and criminal antitrust violations. During that decade, 117 corporations (11 percent) had at least one conviction for the above crimes. These corporations are listed on Ross's "Roster of Wrongdoing," which includes the name of the firm along with the one or more convictions against it in the 1970s. Gulf Oil, for example, was a multiple offender: In 1973, Gulf was convicted of making illegal political contributions; in 1975, there were charges of a $10 million slush fund for political contributions (settled by consent decree); in 1977, Gulf pleaded guilty to charges of giving illegal gifts to an Internal Revenue Service (IRS) agent; and in 1978, the company also pleaded guilty to fixing the price of uranium (Ross, 1980: 60). Although Ross documented the illegal activity of major corporations in the decade of the 1970s, he admitted that he was unable to determine from his data whether there was an actual increase in corporate lawlessness during this period, or just more prosecution of such crimes in the aftermath of Watergate. In his assessment of the explanatory factors, Ross found competitive pressures and industry custom and structure to be significant variables in accounting for corporate crime.

Kelly's (1982) compilation of corporate crime was based on Justice Department, Securities and Exchange Commission, and court records for serious violations involving the 500 largest U.S. corporations over the preceding decade. He found that 23 percent of these companies either had been convicted of a criminal offense or had been penalized in a civil action for a serious noncriminal offense. The 25 largest firms had an even higher rate of corporate crime, with 56 percent involved in some kind of serious law violation. Kelly listed these top 25 corporations and their violations between 1976 and 1982. Although he was not concerned with explaining corporate crime, Kelly emphasized the role of corporate leadership and the ethical tone that it sets as important in influencing corporate conduct.

A serious limitation of all of these studies is that they are based on official statistics of corporate wrongdoing, whether the statistics are convictions, consent decrees, actions initiated by regulatory agencies, or other types of court or regulatory decisions. What, of course, is not revealed in these data is the unreported or undetected corporate offenses and, even if detected, the unprosecuted cases. In the measurement of conventional crime, there are two ways of getting at this hidden or unreported crime: victim surveys and self-report studies.[6] No comparable research strategies have been developed to measure the prevalence of corporate crime.

OFFICIAL STATISTICS

Although official crime statistics have emphasized conventional property and violent crimes in their data collection, there are nevertheless a few selected white-collar crimes on which *Uniform Crime Reports (URC)* collects arrest data, namely, embezzlement, fraud, forgery, and counterfeiting. Additionally, since 1980, the Bureau of Justice Statistics (BJS) has collected information on the processing of federal criminal cases. Two of the offense categories in its annual *Compendium of Federal Justice Statistics* involve types of white-collar crime: fraudulent property offenses and public order/regulatory offenses. In reviewing these white-collar crime statistics from both the *UCR* and the BJS, we shall limit our analysis to official trends in the 1980s.

These official data are suggestive in terms of white-collar crime trends although limited insofar as they also measure the behavior of the criminal justice agencies in the processing of these cases. It is difficult to distinguish the effects of the two unless we assume a constancy in the behavior of the criminal justice system in the arrest and prosecution of white-collar crime cases. Indeed, there is evidence that criminal justice agencies tend to process cases in a similar manner over time; Samuel Walker (1989: 46) referred to this steady-state tendency as the "law of criminal justice thermodynamics." It typically requires a major reordering of priorities to bring about changes in the behavior of local courtroom work groups in the criminal justice system. The campaigns in the 1980s to crack down on drunk drivers and on drug offenders (the "war on drugs") produced such changes. Such a reordering of investigative priorities also occurred at the federal level with respect to white-collar crime, but that took place in the mid-1970s. The official white-collar crime statistics must necessarily be viewed with caution.

If we combine the UCR's three white-collar crime categories—forgery and counterfeiting, fraud, and embezzlement—in assessing trends in the 1980s, there was only a slight increase in the arrest rates for these offenses from 1981 to 1990 (11.9 percent).[7] This is basically similar to the trend in arrests for the Federal Bureau of Investigation (FBI) Index Crimes during this period, which increased by 12.4 percent. Among the three white-collar crime categories, only embezzlement showed a substantial increase in arrest rate—63.2 percent (U.S. Department of Justice, 1991; 1982).

Rita J. Simon's (1990: 3, 5) analysis of these UCR data provides some additional insights into these trends. She noted that the pattern of women's crime that formed in the late 1960s and early 1970s continued into the 1980s. The two areas where women's involvement in crime continued to increase significantly were property crimes, especially larceny, and white-collar crimes (embezzlement, fraud, forgery, and counterfeiting). In fact, the only UCR offense that has a higher rate of female participation than the three white-collar offenses is prostitution. Simon attributed this pattern of female crime to the greater labor force participation of women and to the particular occupational opportunities that have become available to women.

The BJS statistics on federal criminal cases during the 1980s also show growth in the number of white-collar-crime cases (fraudulent property offenses and regulatory offenses) processed, although the growth rate is basically similar to that in all federal criminal cases (see Table 5.1).[8] Clearly the increase in drug cases far exceeds that of any other offense category.

The federal data do not differentiate between individual and corporate defendants, but given the nature of fraudulent property offenses and regulatory offenses, it would appear that the two offense categories are roughly comparable to occupational and corporate crime. Insofar as this is the case, these official statistics offer limited insight into these two major types of white-collar crime.

These data on federal criminal cases also shed some light on the characteristics of white-collar offenders (see Table 5.2). Overall, the offenders in these two white-collar offense categories are similar in most respects, but they are also

Table 5.1
Number of Suspects in Federal Criminal Cases, 1980–1990[a]

	1980	1985	1990	Percent Change 1980–1990
Fraudulent Offenses[b]	16,594	19,554	28,768	+73.4%
Regulatory Offenses[c]	6,218	6,505	8,554	+37.6%
Other Property Offenses	4,835	3,954	3,677	−24.0%
Drug Offenses	9,546	15,669	33,265	+248.5%
Violent Offenses	3,861	3,828	5,070	+31.3%
All Offenses	63,344	78,407	109,949	+73.6%

[a]Number of suspects who were involved in investigative matters received by U.S. Attorneys in which
    a prosecution decision was reached.
[b]Property offenses involving the elements of deceit or intentional misrepresentation, including em-
    bezzlement, fraud, forgery, and counterfeiting.
[c]Violations of regulatory laws enforced in agriculture, antitrust, labor, food and drug, motor carrier,
    and other regulatory agencies.
Source: U.S. Department of Justice, 1992b: 1

different from the profile of all federal offenders. Both fraudulent property offenders and regulatory offenders are more likely than other offenders to be older,
better educated, and employed; to have no prior convictions; and to have no
known history of drug abuse. They do, however, differ in two important respects
from each other. Fraudulent property offenses have a higher percentage of female
and black offenders than the regulatory offenses, although male and white offenders predominate in both categories. This is undoubtedly a function of the
relative occupational opportunities of these groups, as Simon noted in her analysis of the UCR data.

Clearly the official data on white-collar crime are much more limited and less
enlightening than the voluminous crime statistics on conventional crime. In
recent years, however, scholars have gained access to federal files on white-collar
crime cases. That research, as cited below, provides a richer picture of both white-
collar offenses and offenders.

YALE STUDIES ON WHITE-COLLAR CRIME

During the 1980s, Stanton Wheeler at Yale University directed a series of
studies on white-collar crime, supported by grants from the National Institute of
Justice. This research has been published in four volumes, each dealing with a
different aspect of the control of white-collar crime (Shapiro, 1984; Mann, 1985;
Wheeler, Mann, and Sarat, 1988; Weisburd et al., 1991). An important part of
their work was a comparison of white-collar and conventional crimes and criminals. The research of Wheeler and his associates provides a much more detailed
portrait of the white-collar offender than one can glean from the official data. It
does, however, have its limitations. It focused on eight white-collar offenses in

Table 5.2
Characteristics of Convicted White-Collar Offenders in Federal Criminal Cases,
1989 (N = 34,146 offenders)

Offender Characteristics	Type of Crime (% offenders convicted)		
	Fraudulent Offenses	Regulatory Offenses	All Offenses
Gender			
Male	71.2%	84.1%	83.1%
Female	28.8%	15.9%	16.9%
Race			
White	68.5%	84.3%	71.3%
Black	28.7%	11.6%	25.8%
Other	2.8%	4.1%	2.8%
Age			
16–18 years	.6%	.7%	1.3%
19–20 years	2.6%	3.1%	4.0%
21–30	29.4%	27.1%	34.7%
31–40	32.5%	28.8%	31.4%
Over 40	34.9%	40.4%	28.6%
Education			
Less than H.S. grad.	33.1%	39.6%	50.3%
H.S. grad.	12.4%	11.6%	13.6%
Some college	35.3%	28.4%	24.9%
College grad.	19.2%	20.4%	11.2%
Employment Status at Arrest			
Unemployed	34.1%	26.7%	40.1%
Employed	65.9%	73.3%	59.9%
Criminal Record			
No convictions	63.1%	64.2%	49.8%
Drug Abuse			
No known abuse	87.2%	87.9%	76.4%
Drug history	12.8%	12.1%	23.6%

Source: U.S. Department of Justice, 1992c: 33

the federal system, which may or may not be representative of the total domain of white-collar crime.[9] Not included in their analysis were violations of civil or administrative regulations, organizational/corporate crimes, and a variety of other federal white-collar offenses. Finally, their analysis only considered convicted offenders, who may or may not be representative of all white-collar offenders.

In the Yale research white-collar offenders were compared to conventional criminals[10] in terms of a variety of background and demographic characteristics. They also compared these offenders to the general public. The following differences emerged in the comparison (Wheeler, Weisburd et al., 1988: 339–342; Weisburd et al., 1991: 47ff.):

1. White-collar criminals are much more likely to be employed steadily than conventional criminals and are slightly less likely to be unemployed than the general public.

2. White-collar criminals are better educated than either conventional criminals or the general public.

3. White-collar criminals are more likely to be male and white than conventional offenders.

4. White-collar offenders are generally older than either conventional criminals or the general public.

5. White-collar offenders are much better off financially than conventional criminals, but not as well off as the general public.

6. White-collar offenders are more likely to have a prior arrest than the general public, but less likely than conventional criminals.

In conclusion, Wheeler and his colleagues noted that white-collar and conventional offenders come from very different sectors of the population. They also pointed out that white-collar criminals are much closer in background to the average American than they are to the wealthy and powerful—the common stereotype of the white-collar offender.

Besides these differences between white-collar and conventional offenders, Wheeler and his colleagues considered the diversity within white-collar crime, that is to say, the differences between the eight white-collar offense categories they selected for their research. They organized these categories into three types, varying by complexity of the offense (Wheeler, Weisburd et al., 1988: 343). Those offenses that are most organized, that are ongoing, and that require several people in an organizational context are at the high end of the complexity continuum. Antitrust and securities fraud are at this end. Intermediate are mail fraud, false claims, credit fraud, and bribery. At the low end of the continuum are tax fraud and bank embezzlement.

In addition, when one looks at the kinds of offenders who commit different types of white-collar offenses, still other differences appear. The antitrust and securities fraud offenders emerge as the elite among the white-collar offenders and come closer than any other crime category to the traditional image of the white-collar offender as wealthy and powerful. They are overwhelmingly white (99%), male (98%), middle-aged, very likely to be owners or officers in their companies (about 70%), and well above average in their financial standing (Wheeler, Weisburd et al., 1988: 346; Weisburd et al., 1991: 49). At the lower end of this white-collar-crime continuum are credit fraud, false claim, and mail fraud offenders.

In her subsequent analysis of the Wheeler data, Kathleen Daly (1989) examined the gender differences in white-collar criminality. She found that while only a minority of male offenders fit the conventional stereotype of the affluent white-collar criminal, women were even less likely to approach that stereotypical image. In fact, for about 20 percent of the women convicted of postal fraud and false claims, the primary means of support was welfare and unemployments benefits— a far cry from the stereotype of the wealthy, powerful white-collar offender. Daly took issue with Simon's claim that the increase in female white-collar crime is a function of increasing economic opportunities in the 1970s and 1980s. Instead, Daly argued that her data support the thesis that female white-collar crime is more a reflection of economic marginality than opportunity.

Wheeler and his colleagues (Wheeler, Weisburd et al., 1988: 353) also pointed out that female white-collar offenders are more similar to conventional criminals than to their male counterparts. Given the socioeconomic profile that emerges of the female white-collar offender, Daly also raised questions about the appropriateness of applying the "white-collar" label to these illegalities and criticized the use of embezzlement, fraud, and forgery as measures of white-collar crime. They are not all occupationally related crimes, and they can be committed without being part of the white-collar world (Daly, 1989: 790).

Wheeler and his associates concluded that in spite of the variation in white-collar crimes, they are still more alike than different when compared to conventional crimes. But perhaps their most striking conclusion is that the vast majority of white-collar offenders are non-elite offenders who more closely resemble the average American. They argued that Sutherland's traditional definition was too restrictive in focusing on upper-class offenders and neglecting this middle group of offenders, which is far more numerous. This middle group is also clearly distinct from conventional offenders, who are drawn disproportionately from the lower classes (Weisburd et al., 1991: 171ff.).

A RESEARCH STRATEGY FOR WHITE-COLLAR CRIME

In spite of this recent work on white-collar offenses and offenders, our knowledge of white-collar crime is much more circumscribed than that of conventional crime and draws more heavily upon official crime statistics. It is perhaps time to think about alternate approaches to gaining knowledge about white-collar crime, approaches that circumvent the official statistics.

In this section we shall develop one such strategy of collecting data on white-collar crime, a strategy that is particularly suited to the crimes of large organizations. Large organizations possess the power and resources to control public information about themselves to a much greater extent than other kinds of offenders. It is accordingly necessary to develop an approach that will penetrate the secrecy that surrounds much organizational behavior, especially if that behavior entails illegal conduct. Moreover, the strategy cannot assume the research subjects will willingly disclose sensitive information about internal organizational practices. Such cooperation is assumed in much of traditional sociological research: that is, that the research subject will voluntarily respond to a questionnaire or answer questions in an interview setting. Because this problem of access is much more serious when the researcher confronts large organizations, particularly if one is an outsider to that organization, it is often necessary to depart from traditional research methods.

The alternative strategy proposed here is based on the "accident research" methodology first suggested by Harvey Molotch (1970: 125) in his analysis of the Santa Barbara oil spill of 1969. Accident research may be thought of as a strategy for revealing aspects of social structure and large organizations, including white-collar crime, that are normally hidden in the everyday functioning of society. An understanding of this strategy requires the development of a sociology of news as well as some basic concepts about large organizations.

In Molotch's study of the Santa Barbara oil spill, he showed how this "accidental" event led to a series of revelations about the relationship between the community of Santa Barbara and political power in the United States. These revelations included relationships between the oil industry and Congress, the executive branch of government (including regulatory agencies), and science and technology (including universities). In regard to each of these sectors of society the residents of Santa Barbara became progressively disillusioned with the behavior of these public officials or university experts. Disclosures in the aftermath of the oil spill showed that these officials were not acting in the public interest, but rather seemed to be "in the pockets of Big Oil." These disclosures were all made possible, according to Molotch, by the oil spill in the Santa Barbara Channel. Molotch designated events such as the oil spill as "accidents"—unplanned events that lead to revelations about society and organizational behavior (Molotch, 1970).

In a series of subsequent articles Molotch and a colleague, Marilyn Lester, further developed accident research methodology by showing how various kinds of news events can be resources for revealing information about society. "Routine" news events are the most common type of news and, at the same time, are the least informative because they are the most highly managed or staged type of news. Press conferences, speeches, news releases, and the like are routine in the sense that they are events promoted by major social and political actors in society—large corporations, labor unions, the president, cabinet members, members of Congress, and so on. These actors, according to Molotch and Lester, are trying to get their messages into the news and, in doing so, are defining issues and events for the public; they are socially constructing the news. Only "accidents" and a second type of news event, "scandals," penetrate this constructed reality of the news by catching these major actors off guard. While accidents are unplanned, scandals involve planned events, but they must typically be disclosed by an inside informer to an organization because they involve sensitive information. Both accidents and scandals have the attribute of revealing hidden aspects of social structure and organizations (Molotch and Lester, 1973; 1974; 1975).

The relevance of this to white-collar crime research is that these "accidents" and "scandals" may often include revelations of white-collar crime. The explosion of the space shuttle *Challenger*, which we discussed in Chapter 2, was an "accident" that subsequently led to disclosures of questionable judgment by the National Aeronautics and Space Administration (NASA) and Morton Thiokol Corporation, both in the decision to launch on that day in 1986 as well as in the original design of the O-ring in the solid rocket motor. Numerous "scandals" have similarly revealed crimes of large organizations. The savings and loan scandal of the late 1980s and the Iran-Contra affair of Ronald Reagan's administration, for example, represent major scandals where illegal practices in the thrift industry and in high levels of government were disclosed that otherwise would have been concealed.

"Accidents" and "scandals" may also be thought of as a process rather than as discrete events. In this process the public disclosure of illegal conduct is part of a series of events where major social and political actors are promoting their view of the "accident" or "scandal." This might be manifest in "routine" news that attempts to manage or even cover up the damage of the revelations. It might also be expressed in further revelations, resulting from additional leaks from insiders, civil suits and/or criminal cases, congressional hearings, independent commissions, and investigative reporting. The celebrated Ford Pinto case of the 1970s involved a combination of investigative reporting,[11] a series of major civil suits, and a highly publicized criminal trial in which the Ford Motor Company was prosecuted for the deaths of three Indiana girls who were killed in their Ford Pinto in 1978 (Cullen, Maakestad and Cavender, 1987).

Similarly, the illegal activities of the intelligence agencies were disclosed in the 1970s through a combination of investigative journalism, a presidential commission, and congressional inquiries.[12] Once the researcher is sensitive to the resources made possible by "accidents" and "scandals," these events can become invaluable sources of information on white-collar crime, with journalists, members of Congress, and others serving as unwitting research assistants. From the standpoint of white-collar crime research, "accidents" and "scandals" should be viewed as unique research opportunities that can be exploited for the information and insights that suddenly become public information.

IMPLICATIONS FOR THEORY

Clearly the development of a theory of white-collar crime is dependent upon an adequate database on white-collar crime and its various types. Theory construction requires knowledge of the variation and patterns of white-collar crime because it is precisely these "facts" that a theory must explain.

Some progress has been made in the development of official statistics on federal white-collar crimes and to a lesser extent on regulatory violations. There is, however, still no centralized governmental recording system for white-collar crime that monitors its distribution and trends. In addition, federal data are severely limited because they essentially involve data on the processing of offenders by the criminal justice system (from arrest to conviction and sentencing) and do not provide data on crimes reported to police (or other official agencies). These data are also lacking in their differentiation between the types of white-collar offenses, especially between individual and corporate offenders. Moreover, these official statistics are not particularly valuable in correlating data on the incidence of offenses with other theoretically relevant variables (demographic and background characteristics of offenders).

Finally, there is an absence of any measurement of unofficial white-collar crime except in particular case studies. Much needs to be done, both in the improvement of existing official statistics and in the development of measures of unofficial white-collar crime. Until such time, white-collar crime theory will remain in its infancy. In the following chapter we will examine the state of theory in white-collar crime.

NOTES

1. Prevalence is a measure of the relative involvement of groups in criminal behavior. For example, what percentages of males and females report shoplifting, burglary, embezzlement, and so on? In contrast, incidence denotes the frequency with which such acts are committed. Even if there are no gender differences in prevalence, there may be differences in incidence—the number of burglaries, assaults, and other crimes reported in the two groups.

2. La Mar T. Empey (1982) used "facts" in a similar way in his discussion of the extent and nature of delinquency.

3. *Uniform Crime Reports* (*UCR*) does collect data on a few white-collar offenses, such as embezzlement and forgery, but these are not part of what is called the Crime Index, the eight major crimes that represent serious crime in the United States. Aside from this, there has been no effort in the *UCR* to develop an index of white-collar crime.

Since 1980, the Bureau of Justice Statistics (BJS) has collected information on the processing of federal criminal cases. Two of the offense categories in its annual *Compendium of Federal Justice Statistics*—faudulent property offenses and public order/regulatory offenses—clearly involve white-collar crime (U.S. Department of Justice, 1992c). This BJS report, however, deals with prosecution, adjudication, and sentencing in criminal cases. As a result, it does not provide a good measure of the incidence or the prevalence of white-collar crime in society because these stages are far removed from the actual commission of the crime. Nevertheless, we will consider some of these data later in the chapter.

4. When *White-Collar Crime* was originally published in 1949, Sutherland's publisher, Dryden Press, and the administration at Indiana University, where Sutherland taught, pressured him to delete the actual names of the corporations from the book. Because the companies were being accused of criminal behavior, both feared libel suits. Thirty-four years later an uncut version of Sutherland's book was published that identified the corporations by name (Sutherland, 1983: x).

5. These were the corporations that appeared at some time during the 1970s on *Fortune*'s list of the 800 largest corporations.

6. Both victim surveys and self-report studies circumvent official statistics by collecting data directly from the population at large. Victim surveys question subjects to deter-

mine what persons have been victimized, what kinds of crimes they have been subjected to, whether these crimes have been reported, and so on. Self-report studies ask subjects about their own involvement in crime—as offenders.

7. Because *Uniform Crime Reports* (UCR) reports offenses known to the police for only the eight Index Crimes, it is necessary to rely on arrest rates as the measure for white-collar crimes. These are reported as the number of arrests per 100,000 population in the United States.

8. The measure of crime employed is the number of suspects in federal criminal cases.

9. The eight statutory offenses are securities violations, antitrust violations, bribery, bank embezzlement, mail fraud, tax fraud, false claims and statements, and credit fraud.

10. For this comparison Stanton Wheeler and his associates selected two nonviolent, financially oriented property crimes for their conventional offenses: postal theft and postal forgery. In this manner they were attempting to choose somewhat similar crimes for their comparison, with one type generally regarded as "white collar" and the other as "common" crime, to use their term (Wheeler, Weisburd et al., 1988: 334–335).

11. Mark Dowie's 1977 exposé, "Pinto Madness," in *Mother Jones* magazine, produced damaging revelations about the unsafe location of the Pinto's gas tank, which made it susceptible to rupture and fire, and the occupants to burn injuries and death. Perhaps most damaging was an internal memo that Dowie obtained in which Ford had conducted a cost-benefit analysis that placed a value on human life. In the analysis Ford decided against an $11 modification to the gas tank design because it was estimated to be less expensive to pay the costs of civil suits from burn injuries and deaths (Dowie, 1977: 31).

12. President Gerald Ford's Rockefeller Commission issued a report in 1975 on the CIA's illegal domestic spying. In 1975, both the U.S. House of Representatives and the U.S. Senate established select committees (the Pike and Church Committees, respectively) to hold hearings and issue final reports on the activities of all of the intelligence agencies, including the Central Intelligence Agency (CIA) and the FBI. These hearings and the final report of the Church Committee provide a rare glimpse inside these normally secret organizations (Halperin et al., 1976).

CHAPTER SIX

Toward a Theory of White-Collar Crime

THE CHALLENGE

Just as white-collar crime has been a perennial definitional problem, so it is also problematic for theory. How do we explain the criminal conduct that derives from what are normally regarded as the law-abiding segments of the population, particularly the powerful and wealthy? How do we account for the crimes of people such as Ivan Boesky and Michael Milken, who were both wealthy and highly successful in their world of high finance during the 1980s.[1] What about the crimes of large organizations in society that are otherwise reputable and legitimate enterprises: Sears Roebuck making unnecessary auto repairs (Patterson, 1992), Eastern Airlines falsifying its safety and maintenance records (Marcus and O'Brian, 1990), and companies in the generic drug industry cheating on pre-market testing ("Generic Drugs," 1990)?[2] How do we explain the crimes of government agencies, such as the Federal Bureau of Investigation (FBI) or the Central Intelligence Agency (CIA), each of which has at times exceeded its authority in the pursuit of legitimate objectives (Halperin et al., 1976; Poveda, 1990)?[3] These and numerous other crimes that fall within the scope of white-collar crime pose a challenge for traditional crime theories insofar as these theories have assumed that crime is largely a lower-class phenomenon.

This was a problem that Edwin H. Sutherland (1940) observed when he first introduced the concept of white-collar crime. At that time he noted the important role of poverty, and some associated personal and social characteristics, in explaining crime in traditional theories. He argued that traditional theories were flawed because they only took lower-class crime into account. He further maintained that because these traditional theories identified factors specific only to lower-class crime, not only were they inadequate as an explanation of all crime, but also they did not even explain lower-class crime. In Sutherland's view, what was needed was a general theory of crime that would account for crime in both the lower and the upper classes. His theory of differential association was offered to fill the void.

Of course, criminological theory has advanced since the time of Sutherland, but some of the same problems remain. How do we integrate the phenomenon of white-collar crime into traditional theories? Can we explain specific types of crime without offering a general theory of all crimes? Are completely new theories necessary in order to incorporate white-collar criminality? In this chapter we shall trace the history of efforts to come to terms with these questions.

"OLD WINE, NEW BOTTLES"

Many of the early studies in white-collar crime, which followed soon after Sutherland's work, were case studies of particular white-collar crimes that seemed more concerned with demonstrating the existence and the criminality of white-collar offenses than with developing theory. Marshall Clinard's (1946) description of the violation of price and rationing regulations during World War II, Frank E. Hartung's (1950) study of these same types of violations in the Detroit wholesale meat industry, Donald R. Cressey's (1953) research on embezzlers, and Gilbert Geis's (1967) study of the electric industry conspiracy were of this genre. To the extent that theory was considered, it was a matter of applying their case study to the benchmark theory of the day, which was Sutherland's differential association theory. Most of these case studies found some support for the principles of differential association theory, although they found limitations as well.

Differential Association Theory

The basic propositions of Sutherland's differential association theory include the ideas that crime is a learned behavior, that it is learned primarily in intimate personal groups, and that it is a function of contact with criminal and noncriminal patterns of behavior. Individuals will acquire the cultural patterns that surround them unless there are conflicting patterns. In those circumstances the individual will become criminal only if criminal associations exceed the noncriminal ones. What determines the outcome of these differential associations and their impact is basic principles of learning theory relating to the frequency, duration, priority, and intensity of the associations (Sutherland and Cressey, 1960: 77–79).

Although differential association theory was useful in explaining individual differences in the process of becoming criminal, it did not account for group, community, or national differences in crime rates. To explain this dimension, Sutherland invoked the concepts of culture conflict and social disorganization (later changed to differential social organization). Communities that exhibited more social disorganization were more likely to have higher crime rates. In Sutherland's view social disorganization could take two forms. It could be expressed as "anomie," where there is a sense of normlessness or uncertainty as to what constitutes proper conduct. It could also be expressed as "culture conflict," where there are competing norms that prescribe different behaviors in the same situation (Sutherland and Cressey, 1960: 79–84). These two levels of explanation comprise Sutherland's general theory of crime, including white-collar crime.

Gilbert Geis's (1967: 122–123) study of the electric industry price-fixing cases of 1961 provided clear support for differential association theory by his showing that the conspirators had learned their price-fixing conduct as an integral part of their jobs; it had become part of an "established way of life" in the electric industry. There were both criminal and noncriminal patterns of behavior in the industry, and the conspirators had learned both as necessary to the performance of their jobs. The electric industry case also revealed the culture conflict that existed with respect to price-fixing behavior, with the business community showing widespread acceptance of this practice in contrast to the political community's definition of it as illegal.

Cressey's (1953) study of embezzlement was, however, less supportive of Sutherland's theory. He found that embezzlers as a group were committed to conventional norms and engaged in embezzlement only when they had a "non-shareable financial problem," and only when they could rationalize it as "borrowing" and not "stealing." Embezzlers also did not have differential contact with criminal norms from which they had learned their embezzling behavior and attitudes. Although Cressey generally supported differential association theory, he recognized that embezzlement was an exception to it.

While Clinard (1946), too, found support for differential association theory in his study of wartime price regulations, he recognized its limitations. Specifically, he thought that it was inadequate for explaining individual differences in involvement in the violation of these regulations, and that personality factors needed to be taken into account.

Other limitations soon became apparent as well. There was the problem of correlation and causation. Just because criminals or delinquents tend to associate with one another does not mean that that association causes the criminality. There are other possible interpretations of this differential association, including the possibility that persons with similar interests and values simply tend to associate with one another (Vold and Bernard, 1986: 220). Perhaps the most serious of the criticisms is that differential association theory is so abstract and ambiguous in its formulation that its concepts are difficult, if not impossible, to operationalize and to test (Vold and Bernard, 1986: 220–221); Martin, Mutchnick, and Austin, 1990: 164). It was also a theory that emphasized the process by which individuals become criminal and did not take into account macro-level variables pertaining to social structure, except to acknowledge that communities vary in their social organization and in the degree to which they experience culture conflict.

Strain Theory

In the development of explanations of white-collar crime, one of the main tendencies was to apply or reformulate existing theories. As case studies of white-collar crime accumulated, one of the traditional theories that was employed was strain theory. Unlike differential association, which was conceived as a general theory of all criminal behavior,[4] strain theory originated as an explanation of lower-class crime and as an explanation of urban gang delinquency.

In strain theory, crime and delinquency are the consequence of socially structured pressures. Robert K. Merton's (1938) early statement of this theory argued that strain is produced in society by the unequal distribution of legitimate means by which to achieve widely shared cultural goals and aspirations. In Albert K. Cohen's (1955) version of strain theory, delinquent subcultures arise in urban, working-class neighborhoods as a response to the common problems of disadvantage experienced by lower-class youth. In still another statement of strain theory, Richard A. Cloward and Lloyd E. Ohlin (1960) saw the sources of gang delinquency in the unequal distribution of both legal and illegal opportunities in society. The common denominator in all of these variants of strain theory is that the socially structured pressures—the strain—converge on the urban lower class in the form of blocked opportunities for advancement.

Because strain theory has been traditionally a class-based (lower-class) theory, it seems an unlikely candidate to explain white-collar crime. However, the core concept of the theory that is applicable is the idea that aspects of social structure produce stressful conditions that, in turn, generate crime. William N. Leonard and Marvin Glenn Weber's (1970) analysis of fraudulent auto repairs in the automobile industry is in this strain tradition, even though they do not explicitly acknowledge the connection. They argued that the oligopolistic market structure of the automobile industry exerts pressure on dealers—who must maintain high sales and low profit margins—to increase profits in the nonsales areas of their business where they have more control, especially in their service departments. One response of dealers to this "coercion" from the manufacturers is to overcharge in the service and parts end of their business, to make phony repairs, and to engage in other illicit practices.

Similarly, Diane Vaughan's (1983: 54ff.) study of Medicaid fraud in the Revco Drug Store chain relied upon strain theory, particularly Merton's means/goals framework, to understand unlawful organizational behavior. She explained that corporations are constantly striving to maintain or improve their position relative to others in the stratification of the corporate world. The competition to obtain scarce resources, maximize profit, and achieve other organizational goals is the result of pressures induced by social structure. Vaughan pointed out, however, that these pressures toward unlawful behavior are also a function of opportunity and the ability of social control agencies to impose costs on such unlawful behavior.

In their study of the Fortune 500 companies in 1975–1976, Clinard and his associates hypothesized that poor financial performance—financial strain— would be related to law violations. Their findings, however, were only slightly supportive of this relationship in that only a small proportion of the corporate crime of these firms could be accounted for by this financial strain (Clinard et al., 1979: 163–168), meaning that other factors are involved in the explanation.

A limitation of strain theory in explaining white-collar crime is that although it offers a plausible source of motivation for criminal conduct, it does not explain why all individuals (or organizations) who are "strained" in the same fashion do not also respond in the same way; some choose crime, and others do not (Green, 1990: 77). In addition, strain theory accepts the social-structural sources of crime as given. It does not question, for example, why legal or illegal opportunities are unequally distributed in society, nor does it question the market structure or goals of corporate capitalism that produce pressures that sometimes result in white-collar crime. A theory that raises such questions would also need to explain these aspects of social structure, a macro-level theory.

Neutralization Theory

A theory that addresses one of the limitations of strain theory is neutralization theory. It explains why some persons who are motivated toward criminal conduct will in fact commit crimes, and others will not. The critical factor is whether individuals who are predisposed to crime can also rationalize or justify their actions. Presumably there are individual differences in either ability or willingness to employ such rationalizations. It is this redefinition of one's actions so as not to experience guilt that makes crime possible for those who are otherwise committed to conventional values—this is the process of neutralization.

Like the previous theories, neutralization theory derives from explanations of conventional crime—in this instance from Gresham M. Sykes and David Matza's (1957) theory of delinquency, which was later elaborated in Matza's *Delinquency and Drift* (1964). They envisioned a process by which most delinquents, because of their drift between conventional and delinquent values, employ various "techniques of neutralization" that allow them to engage in delinquency by releasing them from the "moral bind of law" (Matza, 1964: 98).

In his study of embezzlers, Cressey (1953) recognized the importance of neutralization. In addition to opportunity, he noted that a necessary condition for embezzlement was the individual's ability to rationalize the "stealing" as "borrowing." Gary S. Green (1990: 81–83) provided other examples of occupational criminals' use of neutralization techniques: Employee theft is justified because "It's not really hurting anybody—the store can afford it," or "The store owed it to me," and "I felt I deserved to get something additional for my work since I wasn't getting paid enough." Clinard and Peter C. Yeager (1980) also noted the rationalizations available to corporate executives, particularly the rationalization that cites the perception that an illegal or unethical practice is widespread in the business world as a justification for one's own wrongdoing—"Everyone is doing it."

Neutralization theory is distinct from differential association theory in that such rationalizations are necessary when the individual's primary commitment is to conventional values. Neutralization techniques are not required if there is already a commitment to a criminal pattern of behavior. In Sutherland's theory, the differential association leads to the internalization of criminal or delinquent values and norms that, in turn, produce the illegal conduct. But Sutherland's theory presupposes the existence of such subcultures or criminal patterns without accounting for their formation. This is the void filled by our next major traditional theory.

Cultural and Subcultural Theories

The starting point for a theory of subcultures is to account for the formation of such a subculture, which also means identifying the conditions that produce the withdrawal from the dominant culture. In this respect the formation of a subculture is the collective counterpart to neutralization techniques, which temporarily release individuals from the moral bind of conventional values. Subcultures provide a collective basis for a more enduring release from the dominant culture, in effect neutralizing the moral grip of that culture. In a subculture of deviance or crime, neutralization techniques are elaborated into a larger world view that is shared by a particular group.

Cohen's (1955) general theory of subcultures was one of the first to systematically deal with these issues, although he is clearly indebted to the earlier work of the "Chicago School."[5] Cohen (1955: 59) identified individuals with "similar problems of adjustment" as the crucial condition for the emergence of a subculture. In applying his model to the formation of delinquent subcultures (urban, working-class gangs), Cohen argued that the delinquent subculture represents a collective solution to common status problems experienced by working-class boys. Because these boys are at a disadvantage when growing up because they are judged against the "middle-class measuring rod," as he puts it, the delinquent subculture is constructed so that these boys have an alternative status system in which they can achieve and succeed on their own terms, not those of the middle class.

Walter B. Miller (1958) also relied upon a cultural explanation to account for gang delinquency, but he saw the roots of delinquency in what he called the "focal concerns" of lower-class culture. In his view gang delinquency did not develop as a separate delinquent subculture, as Cohen maintained, but was instead an extension of lower-class culture itself. In addition, Miller asserted that this cultural system of the lower class has a long history and is becoming increasingly distinctive.

Our concern here is not with assessing the relative merits of these two subcultural/cultural explanations of delinquency, but simply with considering their relevance to white-collar crime. As we noted, Sutherland's theory, which preceded the work of Cohen and Miller, included the concept of "culture conflict." Although Sutherland did not attempt to explain the formation of such conflicting cultures, their existence did help to explain the differential association and learning of crime by his individual offenders.

The concepts of subculture and culture have made their way into the white-collar crime literature. James W. Coleman (1989: 100), for example, characterized the police corruption in the New York City Police Department of the 1960s, which was investigated by the Knapp Commission, as so ingrained in police practice that it had become a subculture of corruption: "it was the honest cops, not the crooked ones, who were the deviants." Twenty years later, the Mollen Commission, investigating corruption in the New York City Police Department of the 1980s, again uncovered a departmental culture supportive of corruption along with "institutional resistance" to combating it (Raab, 1993: A1). It requires, however, a rather extreme form of occupational or organizational crime for it to become so embedded in a separate and distinct subculture. More commonly such crimes are viewed as deriving from broader cultural patterns, such as those of the business world in general or of a particular industry. In this respect Miller's cultural explanation seems to have more support.

Consistent with Miller's approach is the work of Clinard and Yeager (1980), which points to the important role of the cultural environment of the modern corporation. They emphasized how corporate culture may encourage or discourage unethical or illegal practices. Moreover, they noted the variation that exists among corporations and among industries in the normative standards that they set. In their study of the Fortune 500 companies, for example, they found corporate crime most concentrated in the oil, automobile, and pharmaceutical industries. Although corporate crime varied by firm within these industries as well, almost all of the firms in these industries had at least one law violation in 1975–1976 (Clinard and Yeager, 1980: 119–120). Clinard and Yeager's explanation of this variation in corporate crime focused on the ethical tone set by top management. The influence of top management is pivotal in creating the ethical climate of the corporation, where law violations may be encouraged or discouraged. This influence can spread throughout the corporation, and eventually even diffuse throughout the industry (Clinard and Yeager, 1980: 60ff.). Clinard and Yeager, however, are not clear on the source of the ethical tone of the organizational elite. Because top managers have themselves been selectively recruited by a given organization as well as socialized in the context of the wider business culture, it is difficult to separate out the managerial elite from their subcultural setting in attributing cause and effect. Which is the cause, and which is the effect? It is akin to the chicken/egg problem.

Control Theory

Still another traditional theory that has been applied to explaining white-collar crime is control theory. The basic assumption of control theory is very different from the strain or the subcultural/cultural theories. While these latter theories hold that crime stems from either social-structural pressures or subcultural patterns of behavior, control theory maintains that crime is rooted in human nature, and unless these internal drives and impulses are curbed by external social forces, criminal behavior will result. Conformity is maintained by the social bond that individuals establish with their society, including family, peers, church, school, and neighborhood. As the bonds to these groups and institutions are weakened, the likelihood of crime or delinquency increases (Vold and Bernard, 1986: 232ff.). Neutralization theory may also be seen as an offshoot of control theory insofar as neutralization focuses on one aspect of the process whereby the social bonds are loosened: the rationalization of criminal acts.

Travis Hirschi and Michael Gottfredson (1987: 959) extended the control theory of delinquency to a general theory of crime, including white-collar crime. They maintained that human behavior is "motivated by the self-interested pursuit of pleasure and the avoidance of pain." Crimes are events where force or fraud is used to achieve immediate gratification. Crimes, including white-collar crimes, therefore have the same underlying motives as other forms of behavior, but the means employed to achieve them differ. They also claimed that the correlates of crime (such as age, gender, and race) are no different for white-collar crime than they are for conventional crime, and, therefore, crime is a unitary phenomenon, not requiring separate explanations for each type of crime. Because of this commonality in crimes, as they saw it, the search for the causes of criminality lies in individual differences.

According to control theory, those individuals who are more likely to resort to force or fraud to achieve their goals are also more likely to have weak social bonding to friends, family, neighborhood, and the like. It is this weakening of ties and this lack of a stake in one's community that give rise to nonconformist behavior. Because white-collar offenders are assumed to have greater attachments and commitments to society than ordinary offenders, Hirschi and Gottfredson (1987; 1989) accordingly predicted a lower rate of offending among white-collar offenders. In a response to Hirschi and Gottfredson's view of the "causes" of white-collar crime, Darrell Steffensmeier (1989) questioned their claim as to the essential similarity of conventional and white-collar crime as well as their assertion that white-collar crimes are relatively rare.

We have come full circle. Sutherland began the search for explanation with a general theory of crime, and now Hirschi and Gottfredson have returned to that quest. All three dismissed the supposition that you could explain crime by only focusing on specific types of crime, including white-collar crime. In between, as we have seen, there have been numerous efforts at applying older, traditional theories to white-collar crime. But the story is not yet complete. There are still other theoretical developments that we must consider.

FROM PERSONS TO ORGANIZATIONS AND BEYOND

Until the late 1970s, theories of crime and deviance focused largely on explaining the misconduct of individuals: Why will one person smoke marijuana, and another will not? Why do some people embezzle? Why do some boys join delinquent gangs, and others do not? These questions call our attention to individual traits that might account for the different outcomes. Even theories that point to social-structural or cultural sources of crime almost always have the individual as their unit of analysis. In strain theory, for example, the blocked opportunities of lower-class youth are experienced and responded to in individual terms although, as Cohen maintained, these frustrations can lead to group formations.

The recognition that much individual behavior takes place in an organizational context is more recent and adds a new dimension to the quest for explanation. James S. Coleman (1974; 1982) traced this development in modern society. He showed how over the centuries society has been transformed from a system of social relationships with individuals as the key building blocks to a society where organizational actors are increasingly the dominating force. One need only consider the rapid growth in the number and size of corporations during this century. In 1918, there were approximately 300,000 corporations in the United States; by 1987, the number had increased to about 3.6 million (Coleman, 1982: 96; U.S. Bureau of the Census, 1991: 525). Moreover, the amount of assets controlled by the largest firms increased at the same time. In 1981, the 200 largest corporations controlled 60 percent of the manufacturing assets, up from 47.7 percent in 1950 (Currie and Skolnick, 1984: 27). In its heyday in 1965 as the world's largest industrial corporation, General Motors' annual sales exceeded the revenue of every foreign government except the United Kingdom and the Soviet Union. Its $20.7 billion in sales, when translated into profits, amounted to $242,649 per hour (Mintz and Cohen, 1971: 27).

Paralleling these trends in the private sector has been the growth of government, especially at the local and state levels. Between 1950 and 1987, government employment (at all levels) increased from 6.4 million to 17.3 million, accounting for approximately 16 percent of the civilian labor force (Currie and Skolnick, 1984: 41, 43; U.S. Bureau of the Census, 1991: 305). In the twentieth century, employment in large organizations has become the norm, whether in the private sector or in government.

Coleman also traced changes in the law that relate to this rise of organizational actors. Beginning around the fifteenth century, the concept of "juristic person" developed to take into account these emerging organizational entities. Juristic person denotes the rights and responsibilities that now inhere in organizations such as churches, corporations, towns, and other kinds of collective entities. "Natural persons," in contrast, are basically physical individuals (humans) who are recognized by the law as having rights and responsibilities of their own (Coleman, 1974: 22). In the transformation Coleman described, natural persons have become marginal to organizational actors in modern society, with individuals essentially replaceable in the positions they occupy in those organizations.

The application of organizational theory to crime and deviance developed in the late 1970s and is largely rooted in the work of M. David Ermann and Richard J. Lundman (1978a,b; 1992), Laura Schrager and James F. Short (1978), and Edward Gross (1980). The core idea of their work is that not only do organizations have a life of their own, separate and distinct from biological persons, but also they act on their own. Clearly the ultimate actors in an organization are individuals, but the argument is that the structure and culture of organizations transcend the persons who occupy given positions. Patterns of activities become institutionalized in organizational behavior, and it is this ongoing quality of certain practices that allows us to attribute the action to the organization (and its structure) rather than to the individual.

Ermann and Lundman have been perhaps the foremost advocates of the "organizational deviance perspective" in the study of crime and deviance. They emphasized that organizations, and not just individuals, can be deviant. In order to differentiate organizationally deviant actions from individual deviance, at least two conditions must be met. There must be a norm violation, as judged by an outside authority. The action must also be supported by the internal norms of the organization. This internal support takes two forms: peer support and elite support. Peer support occurs when one's colleagues or fellow workers also participate in or tolerate the deviance in question. Elite support occurs when the top level of management or administration of the organization supports the activity.[6] Without such elite support the deviance within the organization remains either individual or subcultural deviance.

Ermann and Lundman's criteria also serve to delineate the difference between occupational and organizational crime or deviance. In the former, individuals are committing crimes in the course of their occupational activities, but the gain is a personal one, as in employee theft or embezzlement. In an organizational crime, individuals are also committing crimes in the course of their occupational activity, but in this case it is the organization that benefits from the crime, although there may be some personal gain as well. This brings us to a third defining criterion for organizational crime: It is primarily the organization's goals, and not the individual's, that are being advanced by the criminal enterprise (Edelhertz, 1970: 19–20); Coleman, 1989: 8–10). Thus, price-fixing in the electric industry, illegal marketing practices by pharmaceutical firms, and the "daisy chain" operations of the domestic oil companies were all implemented in pursuit of organizational goals to expand markets, profits, or both. Let us consider how these criteria apply in a particular case.

The Federal Bureau of Investigation's (FBI's) secret counterintelligence program (COINTELPRO), which was aimed at disrupting domestic political groups from 1956 to 1971, is an example of this kind of organizational deviance. It involved FBI intelligence operations that went beyond simply monitoring the activities of groups such as the Black Panthers, the Ku Klux Klan, and the antiwar movement to actually disrupting their activities.[7] Although the FBI has legal authority to conduct intelligence operations, many COINTELPRO activities exceeded that authority. The Petersen Committee, which conducted an internal Justice Department inquiry in 1974, found that several statutes may have been violated, some activities interfered with First Amendment rights, and in certain "isolated instances" practices were involved that "can only be considered abhorrent in a free society" (U.S. Senate, 1976: 8, 73–74). However, charges were never brought against any agents or officials because of the statute of limitations.

COINTELPRO also meets Ermann and Lundman's second condition of organizational deviance: that there be internal support, particularly elite support, for ongoing organizational deviant activities. COINTELPRO was authorized in 1956 at the highest levels of the Bureau, by J. Edgar Hoover and his top officials, when it appeared to them that the battle against communism was being lost in the public arena, and that a new strategy was necessary. The Communist Party USA was the first domestic political group targeted under COINTELPRO. It was two years later before any higher-level officials in Dwight Eisenhower's administration were informed of COINTELPRO's existence (U.S. Senate, 1976: 10–11, 15, 64ff.).

But what about organizational benefit? What did the FBI have to gain by conducting such counterintelligence operations? In corporate crime we are accustomed to thinking of gain in financial terms, but this is not always the case. Other kinds of organizational goals may be advanced as well. The FBI's domestic intelligence activities in the post–World War II era, including COINTELPRO, were at the heart of the Bureau's expanding appropriations and organizational power. The growth of FBI powers in the 1950s and 1960s is very much linked to its achievement of a monopoly position in the domestic intelligence arena and to its ability to define the national security threats that the nation faced (Poveda, 1990: 31ff.). Although many of the Bureau's intelligence activities were secret, its image as a bulwark against communism and subversion was widely promoted.

Whether the focus is organizational deviance or organizational crime (Schrager and Short, 1978), the critical contribution of the organizational perspective is to move the understanding of deviance and crime to the organizational level of analysis. By recognizing that some actions represent ongoing organizational practices and not just individual misconduct, an additional dimension of understanding is provided. Ermann and Lundman (1992: 18ff.) also discussed this in the context of three stages in the development of organizational deviance: introduction, institutionalization, and termination. The first stage refers to how deviant solutions to organizational problems get introduced. In the institutionalization stage these deviant solutions are incorporated into the organizational fabric as routine practices. Such organizational practices typically continue until challenged by insiders (whistleblowers) or outsiders (media, victims, prosecutors) and may be terminated following such disclosures.

In the third or termination stage whether a practice is actually terminated depends upon the outcome of the "organizational-deviance defining process" (Ermann and Lundman, 1992: 26). This concept is derived from the labeling theory of deviance and asserts that no behavior, individual or organizational, is intrinsically deviant. Deviance is instead a function of who has the power to define or label the conduct as deviant. The CIA's activities in attempting to assassinate foreign officials or in overthrowing foreign governments are deviant only when organizations with sufficient power can define them as such (Waegel, Ermann, and Horowitz, 1981). Unlike conventional criminals, who are relatively powerless to counter the stigmatizing labels of the criminal justice system, large organizations may use their enormous resources to respond to accusations of crime or deviance. The response may be to terminate the organizational practice, to repudiate the allegations of deviance or illegality, or to redefine the action in a more favorable light. The CIA, for example, may deny that these actions took place or claim that they were justified on national security grounds. In Ermann and Lundman's view deviance is relative to who has the power to define the meaning of the questionable organizational practices. The competing claims of accuser and accused are the essence of the organizational-deviance defining process. Whichever organizational actor, accuser or accused, prevails will determine the meaning of the organizational conduct in question: criminal, unethical, or legitimate.

It is on this very point that conflict theorists[8] typically depart from the views of labeling and traditional theorists, who accept the official or legal definition of crime as the standard for defining crime. Conflict theorists are critical of the legal definition and view it as an imposition of those groups who have the power to influence and even to control the state; state power in conflict theory encompasses a range of institutions, including the government, the administration, the military and the police, and the judicial branch (Schwendinger and Schwendinger, 1970; Miliband, 1969: 50). Therefore, to accept the state's official label of crime is tantamount to accepting the viewpoint of the dominant interests in society. The idea that crime is relative to those who have the power to define it is antithetical to the conflict perspective.

David R. Simon and D. Stanley Eitzen (1993: 34ff.) attempted to resolve this problem in the area of white-collar crime by essentially rejecting this relativist view of deviance and crime. They also rejected the term "white-collar crime" itself because its meaning has become so ambiguous. Instead, Simon and Eitzen favored "elite deviance" as the term and concept of choice. As the term implies, it is concerned exclusively with the immoral, unethical, or illegal actions of economic and political elites.[9] Furthermore, Simon and Eitzen (1993: 38–39, 307–309) argued that these unethical or illegal actions of elites are deviant regardless of their legal status at the historical moment. They are intrinsically deviant based on moral principles that are deeply rooted in Western (and non-Western) traditions, including the recognition of basic human rights that are the foundation of much international law. Drawing upon C. Wright Mills's concept of the "higher immorality," Simon and Eitzen (1993: 49ff.) contended that many of these unethical, corrupt, or illegal practices have become institutionalized in contemporary U.S. society; they have become a "normal" part of the way in which economic and political elites conduct their business. This higher immorality was epitomized in the 1980s by the Iran-Contra affair and the savings and loan scandal,[10] where national security and greed became rationalizations for wrongdoing at the highest levels of government and business.

Conflict theorists also depart from the organizational perspective by their emphasis on broader institutional forces, such as the political economy, that produce white-collar crime. While organizational theory broadens our understanding of behavior by locating individual actions in terms of the structure and culture of organizations, conflict theorists extend that to include the social, economic, and political environment of those organizations.[11] The starting point for conflict analysis is the stratification system in which persons and organizations find themselves, along with the power relations in society that maintain those structured inequalities. Harold C. Barnett's (1981) analysis, for example, showed how the political economic structure of corporate capitalism generates corporate crime. This view is echoed in Simon and Eitzen's (1993: 311) work as well: "Perhaps the most basic cause of elite deviance is the structure and intraworkings of the contemporary political economy." The nature of the political and economic institutions is central because they are regarded in conflict theory as the dominant institutions in industrial societies. It is the political economy that shapes the secondary institutions in the society, such as the family and education. It is also of primary interest in conflict theory to understand the elites who control these two key institutions.

To illustrate conflict theory, let us return to our previous discussion of the FBI's COINTELPRO as an example of organizational deviance and see how it would be approached from a conflict perspective. In his study and analysis of the conviction of Leonard Peltier, a leader in the American Indian Movement (AIM) in the 1970s, Jim Messerschmidt (1983) explicitly pointed to the role of the FBI in the repression of AIM in general, and Peltier in particular. Messerschmidt detailed the FBI's and the prosecution's misconduct in the investigation, trial, and conviction of Peltier for the murder of two FBI agents on the Pine Ridge Reservation in South Dakota in 1975. This misconduct included tampering with witnesses and evidence, committing perjury, and carrying out various COINTELPRO-type activities (Messerschmidt, 1983: 37ff.). Messerschmidt maintained that the FBI functioned as a "colonial police force" on reservations, keeping American Indians in their colonial status. In Messerschmidt's (1983: 141ff.) view the subordination of native peoples was necessary for corporate expansion, especially to expropriate energy resources on Indian land.

In the conflict perspective FBI organizational behavior, including its lawless activities, may be understood in political economic terms. The FBI's domestic intelligence activities are aimed at "neutralizing" and "disrupting" individuals and groups who not only threaten national security, but also threaten corporate capitalism and its expansion. The targeting of the American Indian Movement, not unlike the rounding up of the anarchists and radical aliens in 1919 and 1920 and communists during the McCarthy era of the early 1950s, points to a broader pattern in the FBI's role as a secret political police force in our nation's history (Perkus, 1975; Poveda, 1990). By targeting various dissident individuals, groups, or movements, the FBI's domestic intelligence operations have put it on the side of the status quo and in opposition to those who advocate social change outside mainstream political opinion. In conflict terms, this means that the role of the FBI has been to serve the interests of political and economic elites, which include maintaining the existing unequal distribution of wealth and resources in society, the prevailing majority-minority relations between groups, and the political economic system that maintains those inequalities.

Organizational goals, whether corporate or governmental, must be understood in this wider context of the environment of organizations. Conflict theory offers one way of conceptualizing this environment, by emphasizing the role of political and economic institutions and the stratification system that exists in society. This emphasis on the environment of organizations thus introduces a third level of analysis, the institutional or societal level. This dimension and the individual and organizational dimensions comprise the three levels that must be taken into account in a comprehensive explanation of white-collar crime.

INTEGRATING THEORIES: THREE VERSIONS

In the quest to understand white-collar crime, one of the more recent developments has been the integration of existing theories into a comprehensive theoretical framework. These efforts at integration consider not only the different levels of analysis, but also the several questions that a comprehensive theory must address: What is the source of motivation for lawlessness? How does this motivation get translated into actual illegal behavior? Why do some individuals become involved and not others? Are there subcultural factors that facilitate illegal behavior? What is the role of social control agents? And, finally, who controls or shapes the process of criminalizing or legitimating the conduct in question? The answers to these questions are at the heart of understanding any criminal behavior and are the core questions that a theory should attempt to explain. We shall consider three integrated theories of white-collar and organizational crime.

Box's Synthesis

Steven Box's (1983: 34–64) theory focused on understanding corporate crime. He located the basis for corporate motives of criminal conduct in the contradictions created when corporations attempt to achieve their goals (especially profits) in an environment filled with uncertainties. These uncertainties in the corporate environment stem from competitors, government, employees, consumers, and the public. Drawing from Merton's anomie/strain theory, Box cited this "motivational strain" as the source of corporate crime. This strain in the achievement of corporate goals may be resolved by illegally reducing or eliminating the environmental uncertainty through price-fixing, bribery of public officials, fraudulent advertising, air pollution, and the like.

Although such motivational strain is a necessary condition, it is still not a sufficient condition to produce illegal conduct. Box emphasized that it is ultimately individuals who act and think. Therefore, there must be individuals, especially high-level ones, who are willing to translate these motives into illegal acts. He considered the selective recruitment and promotion process that seems to favor certain personality characteristics in the rise to the top of the corporate ladder—ambition, shrewdness, loyalty, and moral flexibility. Box also considered the psychological consequences of this success. Drawing upon Emile Durkheim's (1951) original formulation of the concept of anomie and upon William Simon and John H. Gagnon's (1976) "anomie of affluence," Box saw anomie as a condition of those at the top of the corporate hierarchy. It is expressed in the tendency of the corporate elite to view itself "above the law" and not bound by the same rules as everybody else. Ironically, it is the upward mobility of the elite that provides the basis for its neutralizing the social and moral bind of conventional values and the law. Unlike traditional criminological theory, this formulation of anomie explains the normlessness of those on the top rather than on the bottom rungs of society's ladder. These are the ingredients, according to Box, that make some individuals willing to engage in corporate crime.

Box also enlisted control and subcultural theories as part of his explanation. In the context of corporate personnel contemplating illegal behavior, he asked, "What stands in the way?" (Box, 1983: 43). In his assessment of social control factors such as deterrence, his answer seems to be "not much." The risk of disclosure and punishment is so low that it does not particularly jeopardize the high stake in conformity that typically characterizes corporate executives. Perhaps just the opposite is the case.

Moreover, Box (1983: 54) argued that, like C. Wright Mills's higher immorality, there is a "subculture of 'structural immoralities' " that facilitates corporate crime. This subculture utilizes a variety of neutralization techniques, not unlike the strategies that Sykes and Matza's (1957) delinquents employ, that serve to release corporate executives from the moral bind of the law. These techniques may involve shifting the blame to others, including higher officials; attributing the act to accident or ignorance; or denying that anyone was injured.

The final component to Box's theoretical framework consists of the opportunity structure of corporate crime. There are three parts to it, each of which serves to facilitate corporate crime. The leniency with which law enforcement and regulatory agencies handle white-collar crime constitutes a kind of opportunity. Second, the tendency of public law to respond to corporate crime as a regulatory violation rather than as a criminal act comprises another type of opportunity. But, according to Box, the most critical aspect of the illegal opportunity structure is the ability of corporations to legitimate their own conduct, that is to say, to keep the harm that they produce out of the law in the first place.

In this manner Box combines strain theory for the origins of corporate motives with anomie, control, neutralization, and subcultural theories for the conditions that translate these motives into illegal conduct. Moreover, the role of corporate power is incorporated as part of the process by which illegal opportunities are created, in terms of both lax law enforcement and the legitimation of harmful corporate conduct.

Coleman and the Culture of Competition

James W. Coleman (1987; 1989: 199–242) offered a second version of how existing theories can be combined into a broader theoretical framework. Unlike Box's version, Coleman's integration of theory provides a general theory of white-collar crime, not just corporate crime. In other respects, however, he is dealing with the same set of questions that a comprehensive theory must address.

The starting point in Coleman's analysis is the identification of the two levels of explanation that must be combined: the social-psychological and the structural levels. Corresponding to these two levels are two theoretical problems that must also be explained: motivation and opportunity. In approaching the problem of motivation, Coleman first considered the role of personality factors in the decision to commit white-collar crime. Although he conceded that a particular personality type might facilitate white-collar crime in some instances, on the whole, such psychological factors play a minor role in his theoretical formulation.

Much more significant as a source of motivation is what he called "the culture of competition" (Coleman, 1989: 204). This culture is characterized by an intense desire for wealth and success along with an underlying fear of failure. Although this cultural pattern is played out in social-psychological motives, its origins are structural—in the political economy of industrial societies, where enormous surplus wealth has been generated. This culture of competition is nevertheless more ingrained in some industrial countries than others. Western capitalist nations, and especially the United States with its frontier tradition and strong ethic of individualism, are most imbued with this competitive drive. But Coleman emphasized that this spirit of competition is also restrained by ethical standards. In order to commit white-collar crime, it is still necessary for these ethical standards to be neutralized. Drawing from Sykes and Matza (1957), Coleman discussed the role of rationalizations and the various neutralization techniques that white-collar offenders employ to redefine the criminality of their actions in a more acceptable way.

The second element of Coleman's theory that needs to be incorporated is the distribution of illegal opportunity. He pointed out that the legal system, through its criminalizing or legitimating of certain kinds of conduct, is the ultimate source of criminal opportunities. These opportunities, however, vary according to certain factors, and they account for some of the variation that occurs in white-collar crime by gender, the type of industry, the ethical tone set in an organization, and the occupational subculture.

In Coleman's integrated theory, three conditions are therefore necessary in order for white-collar crime to occur. The motivation to commit crime must be present. The individual must be able to neutralize any ethical standards that inhibit criminal behavior. And, third, the criminal opportunities must be available.

Braithwaite's Theory of Reintegrative Shaming

John Braithwaite's (1989a: 125–151; 1989b) theory also integrates some of the major theoretical traditions in criminology. Unlike the other two versions, Braithwaite's formulation began as a general theory of crime, including conventional and white-collar as well as organizational crime. The pivotal concept in his theoretical framework, derived from labeling theory, is the idea of shaming. Shaming includes a wide spectrum of expressions of social disapproval by significant others, ranging from mild rebuke to extreme punitive measures.

Perhaps the critical distinction in Braithwaite's theory is the distinction between two types of shaming: stigmatization and reintegrative shaming. Stigmatization, in Braithwaite's view, is a counterproductive type of shaming where offenders are treated as outcasts, with the likely consequence that criminal subcultures are formed. In reintegrative shaming a "family model" of discipline is employed, where not only is punishment administered, but also, and most important, such measures of disapproval are followed by "gestures of reacceptance into the community of law-abiding citizens" (Braithwaite, 1989a: 55). Societies that emphasize this latter type of shaming, the reintegrative variety, will have the lowest crime rates, in terms of both conventional crime and white-collar crime.

In applying his theory to organizational crime, Braithwaite (1989b) began with propositions that derive from strain/opportunity theory. Organizational crime is likely to occur when the legitimate opportunities for attaining an organization's goals are restricted or blocked, and, at the same time, illegitimate opportunities for achieving those goals are available. Braithwaite further maintained that this blockage of legitimate opportunities also tends to foster the formation of a criminal subculture within the organization. This could be a subculture of corruption within a police department or an ongoing illegal organizational practice within an entire industry, such as the price-fixing behavior of the electric companies. Braithwaite raised the question as to the point at which social control efforts tip organizational behavior in the direction of law compliance versus noncompliance and subcultural formation. This is the challenge that he presented for organizational theory. He argued that a "theory of tipping points" is needed, and that central to understanding this process is the role of differential shaming (Braithwaite, 1989b: 339ff.). In this differential shaming, stigmatization affects offenders according to the tenets of labeling theory, by reinforcing them in their criminality, and reintegrative shaming operates according to the tenets of control theory, by attempting to enhance the offenders' stake in conformity and their bonds to the community.

This tipping point of an organization, from a culture of compliance to a subculture of resistance, is at the heart of Braithwaite's theory of organizational crime. He developed this idea in relation to different regulatory styles of policing business activities. A regulatory style that relies upon punitive, adversarial relationships with business is more likely to produce subcultures of resistance. A cooperative, but firm, regulatory style, in contrast, is more likely to maintain an organization's stake in compliance with the law. Braithwaite contended that most organizations have a greater stake in complying with the law and in projecting a legitimate reputation (control theory) than in maintaining criminal subcultures, and that our methods of social control should be more reflective of that. A greater reliance upon the reintegrative shaming of individuals and organizations by peers and professional colleagues, as well as by the state, would go a long way toward reducing white-collar and organizational crime.

All three integrated theories draw upon existing criminological theories to provide their own synthesis. Without introducing a new theory *per se*, they combine levels of analysis and address the several questions that a comprehensive theory of white-collar crime must incorporate. What is not clear, however, is the degree to which these several theories are successful in their task. Do they really explain white-collar and corporate/organizational crime? This question addresses their validity, and we can only answer it by testing these theories against the data or facts of white-collar crime. As we saw in the last chapter, our knowledge of variation or patterns of white-collar crime is still quite limited.

NOTES

1. In 1986, Ivan Boesky pleaded guilty to a felony count of insider trading and was sentenced to three years in federal prison. In the civil case brought by the Securities and Exchange Commission, Boesky agreed to pay $100 million. Much of Boesky's multimillion-dollar fortune from his financial activities on Wall Street was the result of illegal inside information he had obtained about upcoming corporate takeovers (Green, 1990: 222; Vise and Coll, 1991: 6).

In 1990, Michael Milken was sentenced to 10 years in prison and fined $600 million for a variety of securities violations. The actual time Milken served in prison was closer to two years. His salary and bonus in 1984 for selling junk bonds, which were risky but high-yield securities, totaled $45.7 million. By 1988, his annual compensation at Drexel Burnham Lambert, an investment firm, was estimated at $500 million (Vise and Coll, 1991: 6). Milken, like Boesky, had achieved much of his fortune from illegal securities activities.

2. In June 1992, California's Department of Consumer Affairs initiated action to revoke Sears's license to perform automobile repairs. An 18-month undercover investigation by the agency revealed a pattern of unnecessary auto repairs in Sears's shops across the state, with an average overcharge of $223. This resulted in civil actions involving 42 states, and Sears agreed to refund $50 each to nearly 1 million customers for the unnecessary auto repairs (Patterson, 1992).

In July 1990, the U.S. Justice Department brought criminal charges against Eastern Airlines and its high-level managers for falsifying safety and maintenance records in order to avoid flight delays and cancellations. The alleged violations took place at several eastern airports between 1985 and 1989 (Marcus and O'Brian, 1990).

In April 1989, it was disclosed that several generic firms had engaged in illegal activities in order to expedite Food and Drug Administration (FDA) approval of their drugs; these

illegal activities included bribery of FDA officials and fraud on their bioequivalence studies. The seven drug firms implicated in these activities have been essentially shut down
by the FDA, and the 57 drugs that had been fraudulently approved were taken off the
market ("Generic Drugs," 1990: 310ff.).

3. Hearings conducted in 1975 by select committees in the U.S. House of Representatives and Senate, sometimes known as the Pike and Church Committees, respectively,
revealed widespread lawless practices among the intelligence agencies, including the FBI
and the CIA. For example, the FBI's counterintelligence program (COINTELPRO) went
beyond monitoring and collecting intelligence on domestic political groups and sought
to disrupt and "neutralize" them. With respect to the CIA, the hearings disclosed that it
had engaged in attempts to assassinate foreign leaders and had been engaged in spying on
domestic political groups (Halperin et al., 1976; U.S. Senate, 1976).

4. Prior to applying differential association theory to white-collar crime, Sutherland
had originally employed his theory to explain the behavior of the professional thief. In
his manuscript on the professional thief, Sutherland described the criminal underworld
of the period 1905–1925, as related to him by a professional thief of that era, "Chic
Conwell" (Sutherland, 1937).

5. The "Chicago School" refers to the program of research that developed in and
around the Department of Sociology at the University of Chicago in the 1920s and 1930s.
Many of these studies in the city of Chicago involved research on subcultures of various
kinds, including Frederic Thrasher's study of gangs and Clifford Shaw and Henry McKay's
study of delinquency areas (Madge, 1962: 88ff.). The term "subcultures" was not used in
sociology until later to refer to some of these same phenomena.

6. Both peer support and elite support may be either active or passive. Active support
refers to direct involvement in deviant activities. In the case of elites this means that they
have initiated, authorized, or in some way encouraged the deviant actions. Passive support
refers to knowledge and toleration of the deviant activities, but no direct participation
(Ermann and Lundman, 1978a: 7–9).

7. The disruption techniques employed by the FBI were and are the counterintelligence techniques used in wartime against enemies. They included the use of propaganda
and disinformation against the targeted groups. Attempts were made to promote faction-
alism within and between groups, sometimes even encouraging violence between rival
groups. Targeted individuals were sometimes made to appear as if they were FBI informants
("snitch jacket" technique). Sometimes derogatory information was sent to family, friends,
or associates. If the targeted groups could not be disrupted, efforts were made to disrupt
the personal lives of group leaders (U.S. Senate, 1976: 33–61).

8. In sociology and criminology, conflict theory refers to a broad perspective or paradigm for viewing the nature of society, including the interrelationships among law, society, and crime. Conflict theorists see conflict between groups as the primary dynamic in
understanding society. This conflict can be based on inequalities of political or economic
power and resources or, in the Marxist version, on social-class struggle. Both crime and
criminal law are viewed as byproducts of this larger struggle as well as of conflict between
groups, where the dominant groups seek to maintain or expand their position of privilege
and the subordinate groups assert their claim to some power and resources (Chambliss,
1988: 156–158).

9. The economic elite consists of those persons and families who possess most of the
nation's income and wealth—the upper class—and who control the major corporations
and financial institutions. The political elite, which overlaps with but is independent of

the economic elite, is comprised of those persons who occupy the top positions in the federal government, including the executive, legislative, and judicial branches (Simon and Eitzen, 1993: 14–17).

10. Refer to Chapter 1 for an account of the savings and loan (S&L) scandal. The S&L scandal was made possible by legislation passed in the early 1980s that deregulated savings and loans, and that changed the traditional mission of these financial institutions. In this new context, coupled with lax regulatory enforcement, there was widespread fraud that contributed to the collapse of hundreds of the S&Ls. By late 1990, 331 executives, accountants, lawyers, and others had been convicted and sentenced to prison (Simon and Eitzen, 1993: 50ff.). Perhaps more than any single individual, Charles Keating, the chair of Lincoln Savings and Loan, personified the S&L scandal. Lincoln's bankruptcy cost taxpayers $2.6 billion, and Keating was indicted for defrauding investors of more than $250 million. He was convicted of 17 counts of fraud and, in April 1992, was sentenced to 10 years in prison (Kurtz, 1992: 7, 9). A few months later, in January 1993, Keating and his son were found guilty of 72 counts of federal fraud and racketeering charges. These included fraudulently diverting about $1 million for personal use—to buy a fleet of private jets and a vacation home in Florida—and paying excessive salaries to family members and himself (Sims, 1993).

The Iran-Contra scandal, which began to unfold in late 1986, involved the illegal sale of arms to Iran along with the diversion of funds from those sales to illegally aid the Contras in Nicaragua. Early in the 1980s, Ronald Reagan's administration helped to create the Contras, a group of insurgents whose aim was to overthrow the Sandinista government in Nicaragua. By the mid-1980s, Congress passed legislation (the Boland Amendments) to prohibit such aid to the Contras. The Iran-Contra affair involved a variety of illegal schemes contrived by Reagan administration officials to circumvent these statutes. The U.S. Senate held hearings in the summer of 1987 on Iran-Contra and on the "secret government" that had emerged in the executive branch to handle such questionable activities (Simon and Eitzen, 1993: 275, 318). In the waning days of his administration in late 1992, President George Bush pardoned six principals in the Iran-Contra scandal, including former Defense Secretary Caspar Weinberger, who was about to be tried for his alleged law violations (Johnston, 1992: 1).

11. Organizational theory does take the environment of organizations into account (Perrow, 1979: 200; Gross, 1980: 65), but in the development of the organizational de-viance perspective, much of the emphasis has been on the internal structure and culture of particular organizations.

Part Three

THE SOCIAL CONTROL OF WHITE-COLLAR CRIME

■ CHAPTER 7 ■

Traditional Approaches to the Problem

Over the last 100 years white-collar crime has taken expression in various forms. At the turn of the century it took the form of monopolistic abuses of corporate power wielded by the large trusts that emerged on the national scene, with Rockefeller's Standard Oil Company perhaps the most notable. Around the same time there were national scandals in the meatpacking and patent-medicine industries, which raised questions about the safety of the nation's food supply and over-the-counter remedies. Since then there have been periodic accidents and scandals where white-collar crime has surfaced in the form of unsafe or defective consumer products, unsafe work conditions, environmental pollution, securities violations, the defrauding of financial institutions, and various types of governmental corruption and abuses of authority. And, of course, there are the uncelebrated cases, committed by more ordinary citizens (i.e., non-elite persons), comprising such offenses as fraud, forgery, and embezzlement, which are also an enduring, but less visible, part of the white-collar crime landscape.

During the twentieth century various approaches have been taken to control white-collar crime. Typically they have involved the passage of legislation to correct an ongoing practice or problem. Often, too, an administrative agency may be established to handle recurring aspects of the problem. As we noted in Chapter 4, the legal basis for most white-collar crime is the administrative law, where the offenses of business and professional groups are handled by regulatory agencies. If such violations are serious enough, they may also be handled as criminal matters. This, however, is rare. The criminal justice system, for the most part, is concerned with a very limited group of white-collar crimes: fraud, forgery, counterfeiting, bribery, and embezzlement. An additional remedy for an individual victimized by white- collar crime is a civil lawsuit against the offender, where monetary damages are sought for the injury. In a given case, all or some of these options may be employed: administrative, criminal, and/or civil actions. In this chapter we shall examine these traditional mechanisms for the social control of white-collar crime; in the final two chapters of this volume we shall consider their limitations.

LAW AS SOCIAL CONTROL

A common response to crime of any sort is to enact laws, or to increase the penalties in existing laws, that will ostensibly correct the problem. This kind of legislative response has often been in evidence in the history of white-collar crime. There is often a disaster or tragedy that generates public outrage. This outrage leads to the mobilization of public opinion on the issue by various interest groups. If successful, the mobilization of opinion is translated into legislation. This scenario has been repeated in many scandals during this century where white-collar crimes have been disclosed.

In the 1960s, for example, auto safety had been a simmering issue for many years, with the annual death toll on the nation's highways mounting each year—nearing 50,000 in the early 1960s. The auto safety issue came to the fore in the mid-1960s as publicity centered on the unsafe features of General Motors' Chevrolet Corvair. Although promoted as a "sporty car" and a "family sedan," it was plagued with numerous handling difficulties that often caused its drivers to lose control of the vehicle and be involved in one-car accidents. As of October 1965, more than 100 Corvair owners who experienced such accidents had sued General Motors (Nader, 1966). Due in large part to the efforts of consumer advocate Ralph Nader, whose congressional testimony and 1966 book *Unsafe at Any Speed* documented the built-in design flaws of the Corvair, Congress passed the National Traffic and Motor Vehicle Safety Act of 1966. Nader (1966) showed how the "tuck-under" and "oversteer" problems of the Corvair contributed to these one-car accidents, and he argued that General Motors was well aware of the unsafe design of the Corvair before it was even manufactured.[1] The Safety Act of 1966 established what is now the National Highway Traffic Safety Administration, which has authority to set automobile safety standards and may require manufacturers to recall defective vehicles. Prior to this law, it was neither illegal for an automobile manufacturer to knowingly sell a vehicle with safety-related defects nor illegal to fail to notify consumers after such a defect was discovered. In the first three years following passage of the Safety Act, some 12 million vehicles were recalled (Mintz and Cohen, 1971: 322).

The passage of the Safety Act of 1966 is a textbook version of how laws are created. The government acts as a neutral arbiter among competing interests, in this case automobile manufacturers and consumers, and fashions a compromise that presumably resolves the conflict between those parties. This, at least, is the conventional wisdom of what transpires in the creation of laws. In a later chapter we will consider the several theories of law creation, but for now we will simply identify some key white-collar crime laws that historically have attempted to control some segment of the problem. We will begin with laws that are aimed at protecting property, particularly those that protect against violations of trust, which is at the core of much of white-collar crime.

Law of Theft, Embezzlement, and Fraud

It is common to think of most laws as fair, even-handed, and generally protecting the public welfare. Certainly laws against stealing seem to fit into this category. A law against theft protects all of us equally. Or does it? It all depends upon how you define theft. At common law, theft involved a trespass against the possession of another's property with the intent to permanently deprive him or her of it (Wingersky, 1958: 706). It does not matter whether you steal from your neighbor or vice versa, whether your neighbor is rich or poor, white or black; permanently depriving others of their property is theft. Suppose, however, that you hire someone to deliver a parcel to a friend who lives on the other side of town. En route to making the delivery the transporter of your parcel decides to abscond with it and make your parcel his. Is that theft? It most surely is by today's legal definition, but that was not always the case.

This case was problematic in fifteenth-century England when a very similar case—the Carrier's case—occurred in 1473 (Hall, 1952: 3ff.). The common law definition required that theft necessarily involve a trespass upon someone else's property. If someone is already in legal possession of property (including someone else's), by definition such a trespass could not occur. Common law placed a considerable burden on the owners of property to choose trustworthy people for such tasks.

Social and economic conditions in England were changing, however. There was an emerging merchant class that relied upon commerce, including the increasing use of carriers to transport goods. The law of theft was eventually modified to take into account this new social and economic reality, and to protect the interests of this new merchant class. This modification, which took about 50 years, entailed making a distinction between custody and possession of property. By the sixteenth century it was maintained that servants and carriers were merely entrusted with the custody of property, and not in possession of it, and therefore if they converted it for their own use, they committed a trespass upon that property (Hall, 1952). Jerome Hall's classic work on the law of theft and society clearly showed how laws change to accommodate new political and economic conditions. His analysis also made clear that such changes protect certain segments of society over others.

Another major development in the law of theft was the first English embezzlement statute, enacted in 1799. The problem posed by embezzlement relates to the status of property received by an employee from a third person; that property, however, is intended for the possession of the employer. The earlier changes in the law of theft had already established that when property is received directly from the employer, the employee has custody, and not possession, of the property.

However, when it is received from a third person for the employer, the employee is regarded as having legal possession of the property. Therefore, no theft (or trespass) is involved if the employee decides at that point (prior to possession by employer) to keep the employer's property.

The Bazeley case in 1799 highlighted this problem in the law of theft. As a bank teller, Bazeley frequently received deposits from customers. On one occasion he received a 100-pound note for deposit. Rather than depositing it with the bank's funds, Bazeley deposited it in his own pocket for personal use. Because the customer's note was appropriated by Bazeley prior to the bank's possession, there was no trespass and therefore no theft, and the charges had to be dismissed. It did not take Parliament long to remedy this omission in the law. In the same year, it passed the first embezzlement statute, covering initially only servants and clerks, but the statute was later extended to include other kinds of employees who are in positions of trust (Wingersky, 1958: 799). This change in the law of theft clearly protects certain kinds of employers from thievery by their employees. Again, this change corresponds to the commercial revolution and the growth in banking during this period.

Fraud (or false pretenses), like embezzlement, was not a crime at common law. The law of criminal fraud also did not develop until the eighteenth century. The early fraud statutes were intended to correct two gaps in the common law: (1) that obtaining someone's property by deception or false pretenses was not a crime unless it involved the use of some kind of objective device (false weights, measures, or tokens), and (2) that it was not a crime if someone willfully parted with their property (Wingersky, 1958: 816). The first English statute to make criminal (a misdemeanor) the use of false pretenses without the use of any objective device in obtaining another's property was the statute of 30 Geo. II in 1757 (Hall, 1952: 40). Closely related to false pretenses was larceny by trick. In a landmark 1779 case Pear was charged with stealing a horse. He hired the horse from a person (Finch), representing that he intended to travel to a nearby community. Instead, Pear sold the horse on the same day in which he had received it from Finch. The jury decided that because the hiring was fraudulent from the outset, Finch had retained possession of the horse, and that Pear was guilty of larceny, a felony (Wingersky, 1958: 836–837). These eighteenth-century developments further extended the traditional meaning of theft to now encompass fraud, although it was still narrowly conceived in terms of false pretenses and larceny by trick.

The transformation of the law of theft beyond its common law definition is critical to understanding the history of white-collar crime legislation. It is important to recognize that the changes in definition reflect legislative or judicial efforts to protect the economic interests of the propertied classes, whether it be from unscrupulous carriers, embezzlers, or others bent on stealing through trickery or deceit. As new social and economic conditions arose, such modifications became necessary. It is equally important to recognize, however, that other kinds of changes in the law were not as forthcoming. Historically the state was much more reluctant to intervene in the marketplace on behalf of consumers, workers, and the general public. The dominant ideology of the eighteenth century was a combination of *laissez faire* ("hands off" by government) and *caveat emptor* ("let the buyer beware").[2] Again, Hall (1952: 45) captured the prevailing eighteenth-century view in Hawkins's writing:

It seemeth to be the better opinion, that the deceitful receiving of money from one man to another's use, upon a false pretense of having a message and order to that purpose, is not punishable by a criminal prosecution, because it is accompanied with no manner of artful contrivance, but wholly depends on a bare naked lie; and it is said to be needless to provide severe laws for such mischiefs, against which common prudence and caution may be a sufficient security.

Similarly, writing about the same time, Justice Dennison stated, "It is not indictable, unless he came with false tokens; we are not to indict one man for making a fool of another" (Hall, 1952: 47). This remained the prevailing view until well into the twentieth century. The burden of liability relating to product safety and fraud in the marketplace rested with the general public.

The history of white-collar crime legislation during the twentieth century may be understood as a reversal, or at least an erosion, of the *laissez faire* and *caveat emptor* doctrines. It also represents a belated response to the same social and economic conditions that produced the Carrier's case in the fifteenth century and the other legal developments of the eighteenth century. The local trade economies, which were at their height in the fourteenth to the sixteenth centuries, gave way to the commercial and industrial revolutions, where production was increasingly on a large scale, banking was growing rapidly, and the marketing of goods was increasingly on a national scale. The collapse of local trade economies, in which producers, merchants, and buyers knew each other on a more personal basis, meant that consumers of commodities no longer had the kind of protections and safeguards against fraud in the marketplace that had traditionally existed (Hall, 1952: 69–70). The burden of liability, whether it pertained to fraud in the patent-medicine industry, occupational safety, consumer product safety, or pollution of the environment, gradually shifted to corporations in the twentieth century.

Antitrust Law

In the United States it was the antipathy toward big business and the trusts, which emerged in the late nineteenth century, that gave rise to the first wave of reform efforts to hold corporations accountable. At the turn of the century more than 300 industrial trusts had been established, which exemplified not only the shift in the U.S. economy from agriculture to manufacturing, but also a rapid concentration in the ownership of these monopolistic enterprises (Faulkner, 1971: 28–29). The dissatisfaction with bigness and concentration in the U.S. economy began in rural America with the Populist movement of the 1890s and continued in the early 1900s with the Progressive movement, which was the result of a more broadly based disenchantment among the urban middle class (Hofstadter, 1955).

The reform impulse took many expressions, but one of its early apparent successes was Congress's passage of the Sherman Antitrust Act of 1890. The Sherman Act had two main sections, which prohibited two types of corporate practices. Section 1 prohibited overt cooperation between firms that was in "restraint of trade." The main target of this provision was price-fixing agreements between corporations that, in theory, are competing with each other in the same market. Section 2 was a prohibition against the formation of monopolies in a given market (Wilcox and Shepherd, 1975: 113). The underlying rationale for both provisions was to prevent corporate practices that would seriously undermine economic competition, whether it be in the form of illegal conspiracies between firms or in the dominance of a single firm in one market.

Although there is debate about whose interests were actually served by the Sherman Act, it is reasonably clear that in the decades following its enactment the Sherman Act's objectives were not achieved. Its passage did little to curb the first major wave of mergers in U.S. history, from 1897 to 1904. Moreover, nearly three-quarters of the trusts in existence in 1904 were formed after 1898, well after the Sherman Act became law (Hofstadter, 1955: 169). Furthermore, the Sherman Act was not seriously enforced against business until 1904. Two of the most celebrated cases of antitrust enforcement occurred in 1911, when both the Standard Oil Trust and the American Tobacco Trust were ordered dissolved into several smaller, but still regionally dominant, firms, This, however, was one of the rare instances when the provisions of the Sherman Act were used to break up monopolies. Historically, the emphasis of antitrust enforcement has been on Section 1 of the Sherman Act, overt collusion between firms that is anticompetitive. Ironically, the disuse of Section 2 (against monopolies) and the emphasis on Section 1 have meant in practice the targeting of relatively small- and medium-sized firms, who are more likely to resort to such collusion. The consequence of this pattern of antitrust enforcement is that the positions of dominant firms are reinforced (Wilcox and Shepherd, 1975).

An additional legacy of antitrust and its enforcement is that they contributed to the distinctive structure of the U.S. economy. By permitting mergers between corporations, including those between competitors, and by prosecuting cooperative kinds of behavior between firms, antitrust law was in effect encouraging corporate mergers. Because monopolies were illegal, the tendency was to form oligopolies[3] in various manufacturing markets. The case of the automobile industry is illustrative. In 1904, there were 35 companies producing automobiles; this peaked at 88 firms in 1921. Largely due to mergers and heightened entry barriers in the industry, the number of companies in the auto industry declined rapidly after 1923. By 1926, there were 43 firms, and by 1935, the number was down to 10. After 1935, until the 1970s, the Big Three domestic auto makers (General Motors, Ford, and Chrysler) accounted for 90 percent of domestic auto sales. Moreover, there were no successful domestic entrants in the U.S. auto market during this period (Green, Moore, and Wasserstein, 1972: 242–244). It is estimated that two-thirds of the manufacturing sectors in the U.S. economy are oligopolies, and that much of this structure was set by the 1920s. Furthermore, as the national economy has become part of a global economy, this oligopolistic structure has been challenged, as has the nature of antitrust enforcement. Our focus at this point, however, is the historic task of antitrust, which was to help preserve the nineteenth-century free-market economy.

In the Clayton Act of 1914, Congress extended antitrust law by prohibiting four additional corporate practices that were viewed as anticompetitive: price discrimination, exclusive and tying contracts, intercorporate holdings, and interlocking directorates. Price discrimination was concerned with predatory pricing practices, which might unfairly drive a competitor out of the market. Exclusive and tying contracts involved agreements between sellers and buyers that would prevent the buyer from doing business with a competitor. Intercorporate holdings referred to corporations that buy shares in a competing firm. And interlocking directorates related to those who serve on the boards of directors of more than one competing corporation. None of these practices is absolutely prohibited by the Clayton Act; they are unlawful only if they "substantially lessen competition or tend to create a monopoly" (Wilcox and Shepherd, 1975: 113).

Two amendments were subsequently made to the Clayton Act, the Robinson-Patman Act of 1936 and the Celler-Kefauver Act of 1950. The former act limited various kinds of price cutting, especially to protect small business. The 1950 amendment was aimed at preventing certain anticompetitive mergers (Wilcox and Shepherd, 1975). The basic core of antitrust law was, however, set in the Progressive era. On the whole, the antitrust movement did not basically alter the bigness or the consolidation of corporations that occurred at the turn of the century. In a few celebrated cases the movement did seem to symbolically strike at the capitalists and trusts who were the objects of disdain, but the mergers and abusive practices continued. Nevertheless, antitrust law is important because it represents an early legislative effort at remedying some of the problems created by the commercial and the industrial revolutions.

Consumer Protection

Another expression of the Progressive era reform impulse was the journalism of exposure, of the muckrakers who brought to national attention the corporate abuses of the day (Hofstadter, 1955: 186ff.). In *McClure's* magazine there was a famous series of articles by Ida Tarbell on the history of Standard Oil and the work of Lincoln Steffens on municipal corruption. Also memorable was the publication of Upton Sinclair's *The Jungle* in 1906. In his undercover writing assignment, for which he infiltrated the meatpacking district of Chicago, Sinclair discovered to everyone's shock that sausage and processed meats sometimes contained dead rats, poisoned bread, and miscellaneous other distasteful ingredients, including the remains of dead workers. Around the same time Samuel Hopkins Adams wrote a series of articles in *Collier's* magazine entitled "The Great American Fraud." He revealed to the public what it was consuming in patent medicines, which were widely available at the turn of the century. Their contents often consisted of large amounts of alcohol, opiates, and narcotics, and a wide assortment of other harmful chemicals. Patent medicines not only were sold on the basis of false claims, but also were often harmful, such as "medicines" for babies that contained morphine and opium (Faulkner, 1971: 112–114, 237–238). These public revelations led to enactment of the Pure Food and Drug Act and the Meat Inspection Act of 1906. Both were impressive legislative achievements and represent the major consumer protection laws of the Progressive era.

During the New Deal of the 1930s, a second wave of consumerism gave rise to yet another series of disclosures about dangers in the marketplace. There was Arthur Kallet and Frederick Schlink's *100,000,000 Guinea Pigs* in 1933 and Ruth Lamb's *American Chamber of Horrors* in 1936; both warned consumers about the hazards of drugs and cosmetics. However, it took a tragedy in 1937 to generate outrage and the demand for additional legislation to protect the public. In that year one of the drug companies marketed a new sore throat remedy, Elixir Sulfanilamide. More than 100 people, including children, died after taking the drug before it was discovered that one of its ingredients, diethylene glycol (a component of antifreeze), was highly toxic. A new Food, Drug, and Cosmetic Act was passed in 1938, requiring more adequate testing of new drugs and improved labeling (Faulkner, 1971: 277–279; Braithwaite, 1984: 110). The consumerism of the 1930s also produced two consumer organizations that would scientifically test a wide range of products for their safety and effectiveness: the short-lived Consumers' Research, Inc., and Consumers Union ("Fifty Years Ago . . . ," 1986a; "Fifty Years Ago . . . ," 1986b). For the first time the public would have an independent source of information about the thousands of products that were part of the growing consumer culture of the twentieth century.

It was, however, in the affluence of post–World War II America that the consumer culture flourished, with televisions, freezers, air conditioners, and frozen foods making their way into the homes of millions of Americans (Satin, 1960: 16–17). It took yet another tragedy, again involving the unsafe manufacturing practices of the pharmaceutical industry, to arouse public outrage. This involved the drug Thalidomide, which was first manufactured by a German drug company in the 1950s and marketed for "morning sickness" during pregnancy. It is estimated that 10,000 babies in 20 countries were born severely deformed because their mothers had been prescribed Thalidomide (Green, 1990: 127). The drug was never marketed in the United States largely because of the efforts of Dr. Frances Kelsey of the Food and Drug Administration (FDA), who resisted pressures from Richardson-Merrell, Inc., the U.S. pharmaceutical company. The bitter lessons of Thalidomide were learned from the mothers who had taken it in Canada and Europe. The outcome was a 1962 law that amended the Food, Drug, and Cosmetic Act of 1938. This 1962 law required that all new prescription drugs undergo pre-market testing for safety and effectiveness, and that all drugs approved between 1938 and 1962 be similarly reviewed (Braithwaite, 1984; Mintz and Cohen, 1971: 33; Wolfe and Coley, 1981).

The consumer movement of the 1960s was further galvanized by the auto safety issue, with Nader's campaign to publicize the dangers of General Motors' Corvair. As we previously noted, this resulted in passage of a federal law that, for the first time, regulated automobile safety. The consumerism of the 1960s continued into the 1970s. One of its most important achievements, the Consumer Product Safety Act of 1972, created a regulatory agency with the authority to set safety standards and even to recall hazardous consumer products in the marketplace (besides drugs and automobiles). In 1971, the National Commission on Product Safety estimated that 20 million Americans were seriously injured annually by consumer products, with 30,000 of the injuries fatal (Box, 1983: 29; Coleman, 1989: 141).

Occupational Safety

Paralleling the erosion of the *caveat emptor* doctrine in the area of consumer protection was a mounting concern for safety in the workplace. In his history of the Progressive era, Harold U. Faulkner (1971: 77) maintained that "the United States was the last great industrial nation to recognize the principle that responsibility for occupational accidents should rest upon the industry rather than the individual." Under pressure from both unions and the muckrakers of the Progressive era, considerable legislation was passed after 1900 pertaining to working conditions—the labor of women and children, minimum wages, and industrial accidents (Faulkner, 1971: 77; Hofstadter, 1955: 242). Most of this legislation was enacted at the state level, and the Progressive solution to occupational safety was workers' compensation laws, which offered some protection to injured workers and at the same time limited employer liability in industrial accidents. While these workers' compensation laws addressed accidents in the workplace, they did not initially cover occupational disease—illnesses acquired years later from conditions that workers had been exposed to on the job (Coleman, 1989: 139).

In the New Deal era, unions successfully focused their energies on establishing workers' rights to organize and to bargain collectively, but there was not much legislative action concerning occupational safety *per se*. Consumers Union, the major consumer organization of the last 50 years, was itself founded as a result of a strike against its forerunner, Consumers' Research, during this period. The striking workers were never able to come to terms with Consumers' Research and instead formed their own organization, Consumers Union, in 1936. Included in the mission of the new consumer organization was the idea that not only would it report on the safety and effectiveness of consumer products, but also it would report on the labor conditions that produced those products ("Fifty Years Ago . . . ," 1986a; "Fifty Years Ago . . . ," 1986b). Thus, the issues of consumer protection and worker safety were briefly joined, but it was the former concern that has received the attention of Consumers Union over the years.

In the 1960s, occupational safety issues again came to the fore. The plight of asbestos workers (and their families), who had been exposed to asbestos in a variety of occupations, was just beginning to unfold. Although the causal link between asbestos and lung cancer and asbestosis was established as early as 1935, this relationship was concealed from workers by asbestos producers and company doctors (Coleman, 1989: 35). However, the scientific studies linking asbestos with disease mounted. One of the most prominent of these studies was that conducted by Dr. Irving Selikoff of the Mt. Sinai School of Medicine in the mid-1960s; he studied the high incidence of asbestosis, mesothelioma, and lung cancer among insulation workers. In a subsequent 1982 study, commissioned by the U.S. Department of Labor, Dr. Selikoff estimated the magnitude of the damage to asbestos workers from occupational exposures in the preceding 40 years. Selikoff's study estimated that 27.5 million Americans had been significantly exposed to asbestos in the workplace and projected that two hundred thousand of them would die from that exposure by the year 2000. Furthermore, the Selikoff study surveyed the families of 1,000 insulation workers who died of asbestos-related diseases to see how they had fared in terms of workers' compensation. Even though probably eligible for disability benefits, most of these workers did not apply. Those who did apply received benefits (about $74 a week on the average) in 89 percent of the cases, but nearly half of the claims were still pending at the time of the worker's death (Bale, 1983: 413–419). The full scope of the asbestos problem was only slowly surfacing in the 1960s.

By the end of the decade a combination of worker activism and party politics generated legislative activity in Congress. Along with the emerging asbestos scandal, there were strikes and protests regarding safety conditions by workers in various sectors of the economy, including the auto workers, teamsters, steel workers, and mine workers. The outcome was passage of the Occupational Safety and Health Act of 1970, which, according to Patrick G. Donnelly's (1982) thesis, was part of an attempt by Richard Nixon's administration to expand the Republican political base to working-class voters.

The Act created the Occupational Safety and Health Administration (OSHA) in the Department of Labor, whose jurisdiction initially included some 55 million workers in 4.1 million workplaces. It is responsible for setting standards in the workplace and for enforcing those standards. OSHA represents a major expansion of federal authority in the workplace, with the government having the right to inspect work sites and to penalize employers for safety violations (Donnelly, 1982).

Environmental Protection

Although the movement to protect the environment can also be traced to the Progressive era, the modern concern with environmental and ecological issues is a much more recent development, stemming from the 1960s and early 1970s. In the Progressive era the issue was one of better managing our natural resources. President Theodore Roosevelt established a federal program to conserve public lands, including forests, minerals, and oil (Shenton, 1964: 184–185). During the New Deal period, the focus continued to be on the management of natural resources, with the conservation of oil one of the major issues. In 1935, an Interstate Compact to Conserve Oil and Gas was established to reduce the wasteful production of these resources. But, as John M. Blair (1978: 152–163) pointed out, the commission that was formed by this act also served as a mechanism by which the oil companies could limit production and thus control petroleum prices. It is in the modern era (around 1960) when the policy focus shifted from conservation to the effects of industrial development on the environment.

Rachel Carson's *Silent Spring*, in 1962, provided the early, eloquent warning that "man's war against nature," particularly against pests and weeds, was wreaking havoc on the environment. She documented the dangers of pesticides, like DDT, which were believed to be harmless at the time. Carson also pointed to the role of the chemical industry in the proliferation of pesticides and herbicides in the post–World War II era; production of synthetic pesticides in the United States increased fivefold between 1944 and 1960. For Carson, this contamination of the environment was "the central problem of our age" (Carson, 1962: 8, 17).

A central concern of the environmental movement is the pollution of the air, water, and ground, and, more broadly, the effects of industrial development on humans, wildlife, and the ecosystems of the planet. Both intentional acts of pollution and accidents, such as oil spills or nuclear accidents, are encompassed in the movement's concern for protecting the environment.

There is no lack of examples to underscore the damage that has been done to the environment as a byproduct of industrial activity. In the notorious Love Canal case an entire housing development near Niagara, New York, was built on an industrial dump, where Hooker Chemical Company had disposed of hundreds of tons of chemicals and waste for more than 10 years. In 1953, Hooker sold its dumpsite to the local school board for $1. An elementary school, a playground, and hundreds of houses were eventually built on or around the dumpsite. In 1977, black sludge began seeping to the surface, and tests later showed the presence of 82 chemicals, including 12 known carcinogens. More than 200 families had to leave their homes, now worthless, in order to avoid even further exposure to this highly toxic environment (Green, 1990: 135; Simon and Eitzen, 1993: 9–10).

In 1907, the Chisso Corporation built a factory in Minnamata, Japan, a small fishing village. The chemical wastes from the Chisso plant were dumped into Minnamata Bay, and eventually local villagers began to experience varying symptoms of brain damage. It was not until about 1960 that researchers were able to definitively link these mysterious symptoms (Minnamata disease) to mercury poisoning from Chisso's waste. The Chisso Corporation responded by attempting to suppress additional research and continued dumping mercury into Minnamata Bay until 1968 (Ermann and Lundman, 1982: 11–13).

Over the last quarter century oil spills have produced extensive damage to the environment. Between 1969 and 1988, there was an annual average of 43 accidental oil tanker spills worldwide, amounting to 1.3 million barrels of annual spillage (U.S. Department of the Interior, 1989: 99). Among these was the 1969 oil spill in the Santa Barbara Channel, resulting from offshore drilling, which seriously damaged beaches and wildlife on the California coast (Molotch, 1970). But the largest U.S. oil spill to date occurred in 1989 when the oil tanker Exxon *Valdez* ran aground, and 11 million gallons of oil leaked into Prince William Sound, extensively harming the pristine coastline of Alaska (W. Stevens, 1993).

Crucial to the environmental debate is the question of locating responsibility for the hazardous effects of our industrial system. Does it rest with individuals, corporations, government, or some combination of the three? Nader's (1966) analysis of the air pollution problem showed how this responsibility has gradually shifted from individuals to corporations and to government. In particular, Nader traced the 15-year struggle between air pollution authorities, especially those in Los Angeles, and officials in the automobile industry over smog and the role of the automobile in producing it. The traditional position of the automobile industry (before 1950) was that there was no relationship, and if there was one, it would have to be proved. From the standpoint of the auto industry, the burden of proof rested with others to spend money and produce the data indicating that automobiles pollute; the industry would then judge whether the threshold of proof had been met.

In 1950, Dr. Arlie Haagen-Smit, a California biochemist, conclusively established the link between automobile exhaust and smog. In addition, about the same time the research of the Los Angeles Air Pollution Control District showed that more than half of the air pollution in Los Angeles was attributable to automobiles. These findings could not be disputed by the auto industry because they had not conducted research of their own. The industry continued to maintain, however, that automobiles at best played only a minor role in pollution, and that was probably due to consumers who did not properly maintain their vehicles. Nevertheless, in 1953, the industry announced the formation of an industrywide research group, the Vehicle Combustion Products Committee, to look into the problem.

At the same time the Automobile Manufacturers Association warned that reducing vehicle emissions is a highly technical problem that will probably take years to solve. Indeed, it was not until the mid-1960s that automobile exhaust control devices were installed on new models, but only after California passed a law requiring such devices, and after other companies, outside the major auto companies, had developed exhaust control devices. As it turned out, the devices the auto industry installed on its 1966 models required no major scientific or technological breakthrough, but were based on old engineering and chemical principles. The position of the industry throughout this period was one of "show me"; the burden of proof was on others to show first that there was a link between automobile exhaust and air pollution, and later that there was a solution to the problem (Nader, 112–128).

A grand jury investigation (1966–1967) of the auto industry's delaying tactics concluded that there was an agreement among auto makers not to compete with each other in the development of exhaust control devices, and that any discovery and installation of such devices would be done in concert and delayed as long as possible. This conspiracy was conducted through the industrywide research committee that had been established by the Automobile Manufacturers Association back in 1953. Although the Justice Department decided against a criminal case, it did file a civil suit in this matter in January 1969. The suit was settled a few months later by a consent decree that in effect said, "Don't do it again" (Green, Moore, and Wasserstein, 1972: 255–260).

In 1970, authority for protecting the environment was entrusted to a new federal agency, the Environmental Protection Agency (EPA). Its mission is to enforce laws and set standards regarding air, water, solid waste, pesticide, noise, and radiation pollution (Clinard et al., 1979: 234). Among the EPA's first responsibilities was enforcement of the Clean Air Act of 1970, which required the auto industry to reduce engine emissions (hydrocarbons, carbon monoxide, and nitrogen oxide) by 90 percent over six years. The law also provided for development of national air quality standards for 10 major pollutants (Naughton, 1971).

The enactment of laws in the several areas that we have considered (antitrust, consumer protection, occupational safety, and environmental protection) reflects a historical trend in the twentieth century of shifting the responsibility and the burden of proof from individuals to corporations. The enlisting of the government, through the passage of laws, to control various forms of white-collar crime marks one of the traditional approaches to the problem.

THE REGULATORY APPROACH

As we have seen, the legislative response to white-collar crime has often been accompanied by the creation of regulatory agencies. These agencies have ongoing authority and responsibility for controlling a given segment of business and/or professional activities: food labeling, securities transactions, occupational safety, advertising, and so on. The vast majority of regulatory agencies originated in three distinct eras: the Progressive era in the early part of the twentieth century, the New Deal era of the 1930s, and the consumer era of the 1960s and early 1970s (Frank and Lombness, 1988). In the Progressive era the task of regulation was to create a countervailing government force to match the private, unchecked power of the trusts, whose resources overshadowed those of government. The Federal Trade Commission and the Food and Drug Administration were among the agencies established during this period. During the New Deal era, regulation focused on creating a role for government in the regulation of financial institutions, especially banks and the stock exchange, and on fostering economic recovery following the Great Depression. The Securities and Exchange Commission and the Federal Deposit Insurance Corporation were formed during this era. In the more recent period of the 1960s, regulation came in response to the consequences of industrial development—environmental, health, and safety issues. The Environmental Protection Agency, the Occupational Safety and Health Administration, and the Consumer Product Safety Commission all derive from this era (Frank and Lombness, 1988; Hofstadter, 1955).

The accumulated effect of these regulatory agencies is the creation of a body of public law, the administrative law. One of the key functions of these federal and state agencies is rule-making, a task delegated to them by Congress or state legislatures, respectively. The regulatory rules that these agencies issue have the effect of law. These rules may sometimes prohibit certain harmful business or industrial practices, but, more typically, they will limit the risk of harm—by, for example, establishing the absorption standard on automobile bumpers, the allowable emissions of certain pollutants from factories, and the number of hours that airline pilots can fly. Also, such regulatory rules are not concerned with the intent or state of mind of rule violators (as in the criminal law), but rather they tend to hold violators strictly liable for their conduct.

One of the unique aspects of regulatory agencies is that they combine all three functions of government. Besides having legislative (rule-making) authority, most agencies have executive and judicial functions (Frank and Lombness, 1988). In other words, the same agency that makes rules may also have investigative authority to detect potential rule violations, and it may even have authority to take certain legal actions against the offender. For example, the National Highway Traffic and Safety Administration not only issues automobile safety standards, but also has responsibility for seeking compliance with those standards from the auto industry and, if necessary, ordering recalls of unsafe vehicles.

The Federal Trade Commission

In order to better appreciate how regulatory justice works in terms of white-collar crime, let us consider the workings of one such regulatory agency, the Federal Trade Commission (FTC), whose origins were in the Progressive era. The FTC consists of five commissioners (including a chair) appointed by the president for seven-year terms (Cox, Fellmeth, and Schulz, 1969). In fiscal 1991, the Commission's staff numbered about 950, with a budget of $76 million (Potts, 1991).

When it was established by Congress in 1914 (the same year the Clayton Act was passed), the FTC was conceived primarily as an antitrust agency. Its main task was to prevent the use of unfair methods of competition in the marketplace. It had investigative powers to gather information on specific business practices and enforcement powers to take legal action against conduct that it judged to be unfair. The FTC's main enforcement tool was the cease and desist order, which required a company to terminate a particular unfair practice, but would not impose penalties for any past misconduct. Since 1938, with the passage of the Wheeler-Lea Act, which made "deceptive acts and practices" illegal, the FTC also has become a consumer protection agency, particularly concerned with false advertising and questionable sales techniques (Cox, Fellmeth, and Schulz, 1969: 215–220).

In the late 1960s, a Nader task force investigated the Federal Trade Commission to determine whether it was living up to its historical mandate, especially in the consumer protection area. Its report, issued in 1969, found the agency seriously lacking in this regard. The report categorized the FTC's failures into four areas: (1) failure to detect violations, (2) failure to establish priorities, (3) failure to enforce, and (4) failure to seek effective resources and authority. In short, it found that the FTC had not been aggressive in monitoring deceptive practices in the marketplace. The violations it did detect and pursue typically involved small companies. Large corporations were avoided unless the violation was a minor one.

An example of the FTC's failure to enforce was the Geritol case. During the 1960s, the J. B. Williams Company, the manufacturer of Geritol, had advertised Geritol as a remedy for fatigue. Apparently Geritol had this effect on only a tiny minority of its users. In 1967, after years of investigation, the FTC ordered the company to stop representing Geritol in this manner. In a follow-up investigation the FTC concluded that the J. B. Williams Company was "flouting" the FTC's cease and desist order in its advertising. The agency ordered the company to file a compliance report, which would explain to the Commission how it had modified its commercials pursuant to the order. Geritol's compliance report was still found to be inadequate by the FTC's staff, but the commissioners took no further legal action even though the matter could have been referred to the courts for civil action (Cox, Fellmeth, and Schulz, 1969: 65–67).

In the aftermath of the Nader report on the Federal Trade Commission, President Nixon asked the American Bar Association (ABA) to look into the report's allegations. The ABA task force essentially agreed with the Nader evaluation and concluded that Nixon should "Get the FTC to focus on important issues or abolish it" (Cohen, 1980: 216). As new leadership was appointed to the FTC, the agency took the former course and entered perhaps its most activist phase during the 1970s. The FTC challenged major advertisers and took on major industries in terms of both deceptive practices and unfair competition. Whole categories of advertisers (autos, drugs, etc.) were ordered to submit documents substantiating their ad claims. The FTC encouraged comparative advertising in which companies would compare their products with those of a competitor rather than brand X. It sometimes also required corrective ads when advertisers were found to have made inaccurate statements in earlier ads. At one point in the 1970s, the FTC also considered banning all children's advertising on the grounds that it was inherently unfair (Cohen, 1980). Moreover, in the early 1970s, the FTC filed antitrust suits against the eight largest domestic oil companies for utilizing anticompetitive practices during the Arab oil embargo of 1973–1974, and against the cereal industry for overcharging consumers through its "shared monopoly" (Blair, 1978; "Monopoly on the Cereal Shelves?" 1981).[4] Although neither of these lawsuits was successful, the agency that the Nader report had criticized in the preceding decade had clearly emerged from its passivity and "do nothingness."

By the late 1970s, the backlash to this activist FTC, and to other regulatory agencies, had set in. There was mounting pressure on Congress to rein in the regulatory agencies, which business groups believed had exceeded their authority. When Congress held appropriation hearings on the FTC in the fall of 1979, the FTC became the first of these agencies to receive the brunt of the antiregulatory attack. By the time a compromise bill had been worked out in May of 1980, the FTC had some of its powers restricted, with the prospect of Congress now being able to veto any of its industrywide rulings. On one day during that same month the FTC even had to close its doors because of Congress's failure to appropriate funds to the agency (Miller, 1980; Sulzberger, 1980a; 1980b). The message was clear to the FTC and to the other regulatory agencies as well: The decade of activism was over, and Congress would act to limit the authority and independence of these agencies.

Deregulation

The backlash to the FTC was part of a broader antiregulation movement that began in the late 1970s and reached its peak during Ronald Reagan's administration of the 1980s. Its objections to regulation were both pragmatic and philosophical. On the pragmatic side was the argument that regulations are not cost effective. If you calculate the costs and the benefits of regulation, the costs generally outweigh the benefits. Murray Weidenbaum's 1979 study of the costs of regulation ($102.7 billion) was one of the most widely cited at the time, although critics challenged this figure and said that he had ignored many benefits of regulation as well (Green and Waitzman, 1979). During the 1980s, cost effectiveness became one of the central principles guiding whether a given regulation was necessary. It was the basis for eliminating or modifying many regulations. As a result, for example, the collision speed that an auto bumper would be required to absorb was reduced from 5 m.p.h. to 2.5 m.p.h.; the regulation that would make hot dog manufacturers inform consumers if their products contain bone was canceled; and the *Car Book*, a government publication that informed consumers of safety features (including crash tests) on some 80 domestic and foreign automobiles, was discontinued (Isaacson, 1981).

The philosophical basis for the antiregulation movement was the "Chicago School" of economics, which espoused the classical economic doctrine of the free market. The underlying principle is that the free market will regulate itself, and that any outside interference, especially by government, is anticompetitive and not in the public interest (Isikoff, 1984). One 1980s political slogan, "Get government off the backs of the people," reflected this hostility toward government intervention. Deregulation was viewed as a solution to many social and economic ills. This was also reflected in the dramatic personnel reductions experienced by regulatory agencies during this era. Between 1980 and 1983, the total staff of the federal agencies with responsibility for consumer protection, workplace safety, and antitrust enforcement was cut by 19 percent; from 1983 to 1986, the staff of these agencies was reduced by another 7 percent (Coleman, 1989: 189). In short, the regulatory apparatus that handles violations of the administrative law was sharply curtailed during this deregulation period.

In 1981, when James C. Miller was appointed by President Reagan as the new chair of the Federal Trade Commission, he brought deregulation to the FTC. In one of his early speeches, Miller contended that the FTC should get out of the consumer protection business. He went on to defend the availability of what he called "imperfect products" for consumers who cannot afford better-quality merchandise. In Miller's view, defective products should be part of consumer choice, and competition in the marketplace is the regulating mechanism that looks after the safety and effectiveness of products. About the same time, Miller was volunteering his agency for an 18 percent cut in appropriations ("Consumer Defection," 1981).

This public policy of deregulation continued into George Bush's administration.[5] Near the end of his term President Bush in fact had a moratorium on new federal regulations. At a White House ceremony in 1992, Bush argued for the need for such a moratorium using an anecdote referring to stepladders. He claimed that if ladders became too expensive because of regulations, consumers would turn to cheaper alternatives, such as chairs or stools, which are less safe (Rosenthal, 1992). Ironically, in this view, safety regulations are dangerous.

Resurgence in the 1990s

The antiregulation movement peaked in the Reagan years of the 1980s. By the early 1990s, there were indications of a regulatory resurgence, not to the level of the 1970s, but to a more middle ground of enforcement activity. This was in evidence at the Federal Trade Commission, with stepped-up activities in both antitrust and consumer protection; these included a flurry of new price-fixing cases (kitchen appliances and infant formula) and investigations on advertisers' claims (Mufson, 1990; Potts, 1991). At the Food and Drug Administration a crackdown on deceptive food labels was an early sign of this resurgence (Gladwell, 1991). In both instances a new chair (Janet Steiger at the FTC and David

Kessler at the FDA) provided leadership that was less ideological than in the Reagan era, and that was more in keeping with the traditional mandates of those agencies.

It should be apparent that even though regulatory agencies have existed since the Progressive era, this approach to controlling corporate misconduct has had its vicissitudes. There have been three distinct periods of regulatory activism during this century, and for the most part they have been short-lived. The first period coincided with the Progressive era (1906–1920), the New Deal period from 1938 to 1952 saw the second wave of activism, and the third period, focusing on consumer concerns, occurred during the 1960s and 1970s (Wilcox and Shepherd, 1975). To understand the limits of this regulatory approach, we must appreciate the ebbs and flows of regulatory justice in these different historical eras.

THE USE OF CRIMINAL SANCTIONS

Many regulatory agencies have the authority to refer administrative violations to the courts for either civil or criminal actions. Typically, however, a criminal action is a last resort rather than a first response in the regulatory justice system. Historically there has been controversy over the appropriateness of criminal penalties for corporate misconduct. As we noted in Chapter 4, certain white-collar offenses—embezzlement, forgery, bribery, and criminal fraud—are routinely handled as criminal matters. These are offenses where individuals are the main perpetrators, and where intentionality (*mens rea*) can be relatively easily determined. The use of criminal sanctions to control corporate or organizational offenses is viewed as more problematic. Let us consider some of the arguments in this debate.

Sanford Kadish (1963) outlined the key arguments from the standpoint of those who view criminal sanctions as inappropriate for controlling corporate misconduct. Although he recognized the difficulty in pinpointing corporate criminal responsibility, especially among high-level officials, perhaps his main objection to using criminal sanctions is that they would be applied to "morally neutral" conduct. Corporate offenses, Kadish maintained, are by and large regulatory offenses that are not inherently harmful (*mala en se*). They do not involve behavior that is widely regarded as "morally reprehensible." Corollary to this is the idea that by applying criminal penalties for this purpose, we will undermine their effectiveness in terms of traditional crime control.

Critics of this position argue not only that criminal sanctions are appropriate, but also that they could be even more effective in deterring corporate offenders than they are in deterring conventional criminals if applied with certainty and sufficient severity—because of the more rational, deliberative nature of much white-collar crime (Yoder, 1978; Braithwaite and Geis, 1982). Furthermore, the research of Francis T. Cullen and his associates (1987: 43) demonstrated that the public is far from indifferent to the consequences of white-collar crime and does not view it as "morally neutral," and that public concern over white-collar crime has increased in recent years.

Whatever the merits of these arguments, it is clear that the immunity from criminal liability that corporations traditionally enjoyed has been radically eroded in the twentieth century. Historically *mens rea*, or criminal intent, was regarded as an attribute of individuals, not organizations. But early in this century courts held that the criminal intent of corporations may be established by the intentions of high-level officials who act on behalf of their corporations (Bernard, 1984; Moran, 1992). Once this precedent was set, the evolution of including more and more corporate conduct within the scope of the criminal law had begun.

By the late 1970s, even the barrier to the criminal prosecution of corporations for homicide was removed. The 1980 criminal trial of the Ford Motor Company for reckless homicide in the Pinto case marked the first time a corporation was prosecuted for criminal homicide—although it was acquitted in the deaths of three Indiana girls who died in their Pinto after being struck from the rear (Cullen, Maakestad, and Cavender, 1987). Just a few years later another barrier came down when three officials of Film Recovery Systems, Inc., were prosecuted and convicted for the murder of one of their workers; he had been exposed to toxic fumes on the job. The president, plant manager, and foreman were all found guilty and sentenced to 25 years each. An Illinois appeals court, however, overturned the conviction five years later ("Employers Found Guilty," 1985; "Illinois Court Overturns Conviction," 1990).

In spite of a growing number of celebrated criminal prosecutions of corporations or their top executives, it should be emphasized that these cases are still atypical of how such violations are handled. Even in the famed Indiana Pinto case, the prosecutor, Michael Cosentino, indicated that normally this kind of case should be handled as a regulatory or civil matter (a product liability case). It is only when these other remedies are not available, he argued, that criminal sanctions should be considered, and that was the case in Indiana (Cullen, Maakestad, and Cavender, 1987: 176).

THE RESORT TO CIVIL LAW

The use of the civil law constitutes another of the traditional approaches to white-collar crime. It is a remedy where the person victimized sues the offender with the aim of obtaining monetary damages for an injury. There are compensatory damages, by which the plaintiff is reimbursed for expenses incurred from the injury, and punitive damages, which provide an additional monetary award reflecting the wrongful behavior of the offender.

There are certain advantages to pursuing a civil rather than a criminal case, although the two are not mutually exclusive. A lower level of proof is required in a civil case (a "preponderance of the evidence") in contrast to a criminal one ("beyond a reasonable doubt"). The monetary award in a lawsuit goes to the injured party whereas in a criminal case any fines accrue to the state. The disadvantage, of course, is that a civil action places an enormous burden of risk and expense on the victim to get justice done. The plaintiff commonly encounters a corporation with considerable resources, which can contribute to numerous legal obstacles and lengthy proceedings drawn out over several years. To more fully explore the lawsuit as a response to white-collar crime, let us consider a recent celebrated case involving the tobacco industry.

The Case of Rose Cipollone

To date, the tobacco companies have defended themselves against more than 300 lawsuits over four decades; they have yet to pay out any damages in any of these cases. The Cipollone case, which represented a small chink in the tobacco industry armor, reached the U.S. Supreme Court and was eventually dropped by the plaintiff's family (Strum, 1992).

Rose Cipollone died in October 1984 after a near lifetime of smoking cigarettes; it was estimated that she smoked 370,000 cigarettes (a pack a day) between 1942 (at age 16) and 1981, when she quit after developing lung cancer. The year before her death, Rose Cipollone and her husband sued three cigarette manufacturers (the Liggett Group, Lorillard, and Philip Morris), arguing that these companies had contributed to her death by not warning her and the public about the hazards of smoking. What was unique about the Cipollone case was evidence from internal company documents that showed the industry knew about the health hazards of cigarettes long before the warning labels were first placed on cigarette packs in 1966. This included testimony from a former assistant research director for Liggett and Meyers who asserted that he concluded in the late 1950s that smoking contributes to lung cancer. There were also internal research reports that found links among cigarettes, cancer, and other detrimental health effects. Cipollone's lawyer argued that there has been a conspiracy among the tobacco companies to conceal these health effects, to glamourize their product, and, in fact, to deny any causal connection between their product and cancer to the present day (Margolick, 1988; Clayton, 1988).

There was a four-month trial in Newark, New Jersey, ending in June 1988. The three tobacco companies were defended by nine lawyers from three different law firms. In addition, there were a large number of supporting clerical staff that required the law firms to rent 40 hotel rooms to accommodate them. On the Cipollone's side were their lawyer, Marc Edell, and his law firm, who at the time of the trial had spent five years and $2.5 million on the case. Also, public interest groups, such as the Tobacco Liability Project, had taken a strong interest in the case. When the federal jury reached its verdict in June 1988, the result was a mixed one for both sides. Only one of the companies, the Liggett Group, was held partially liable for Rose Cipollone's death. The Liggett Group manufactured Chesterfields and L&Ms, which Mrs. Cipollone had smoked before 1966. The jury concluded that the company had not warned her and the public about the dangers of smoking prior to 1966, but it also found Mrs. Cipollone 80 percent responsible for her own death. The jury awarded $400,000 in damages to Mrs. Cipollone's husband, Antonio (Margolick, 1988; Greenhouse, 1992).

In 1990, a federal appeals court set aside the $400,000 award and ruled that smokers could not sue tobacco companies for injuries resulting from their smoking after January 1, 1966—the day that the warning label was required on cigarette packages and advertising. The Cipollones appealed this ruling to the U.S. Supreme Court. In a 7–2 decision in June 1992, the Court rejected industry arguments (and the appeals court ruling) that warning labels automatically shield tobacco companies from lawsuits; the decision paved the way for a new Cipollone trial on these issues. In the Court's decision, Justice Stevens argued that such federal laws (requiring warning labels) did not give companies a license to commit fraud and deception. The Court, however, did not address the issue of tobacco industry liability before 1966. Several months later the Cipollone family decided not to pursue the case, after 10 years of litigation (Greenhouse, 1992; Strum, 1992).

Confidentiality Agreements

Perhaps one unintended consequence of lawsuits is that they serve as a kind of early warning to the public that there may be a defective product on the market. In recent years, however, there has been a new development that prevents such information from being released to the public. A growing number of lawsuits are settled in secrecy. A court-imposed confidentiality order prohibits the disclosure of evidence in the case to any outside parties, including regulators. For example, in a Florida case, a U.S. district court judge ordered a lawyer suing Pfizer Laboratories not to disclose to any government agency (including the FDA) evidence in the case. Ironically, one of the issues in the suit was whether Pfizer had withheld information from the FDA regarding a prescription painkiller, Feldene (Walsh and Weiser, 1988).

The impact of secrecy orders is even more evident if we consider the General Motors (GM) strategy of handling lawsuits in the 1970s and 1980s in contrast to that of the Ford Motor Company. During the 1970s, many GM cars suffered from some of the same safety problems as the Ford Pinto, with the gas tank under the trunk and close to the rear bumper. The vast majority of lawsuits involving these automobiles were settled with confidentiality agreements, which means that few internal GM documents reached the public domain—except in cases that went to trial or documents that were leaked. One of those documents that surfaced was the Ivey analysis, a two-page memo (dated June 29, 1973) prepared by GM engineer Edward Ivey, who did a cost-benefit analysis of the gas-tank problem. Like the Pinto cost-benefit analysis about the same time, it put a value on human life ($200,000) and estimated how much it would cost to correct the problem on new models. An earlier GM analysis had concluded that a design change would be too expensive (Walsh and Weiser, 1988). Of course, the implication of these analyses is that GM management was aware of the problem. The Ivey analysis was illegally disclosed by a lawyer in one of the GM lawsuits in the early 1980s; the lawyer was fined $8,000 for violating the secrecy order. In contrast, many of the Pinto lawsuits (as well as the Indiana criminal case) were settled in a very public way. The upshot of all of this is that most people learned of the flawed gas-tank location of the Pinto, but were largely oblivious to a similar problem in GM automobiles.[6]

Why are confidentiality agreements suddenly popular? Ironically, it is often in the interest of all of the parties to settle in this manner. Corporations keep embarrassing information about their products out of the public record. Judges see it as an efficient way to get out-of-court settlements and avoid lengthy trials, involving perhaps thousands of documents. Victims, too, see it as an opportunity to get a quick settlement (Walsh and Weiser, 1988). Lost in this process is the public's right to know about defective products in the marketplace.

Although large corporations sometimes consider lawsuits a part of the cost of doing business, the threat of the occasional large civil suit, with its accompanying publicity, undoubtedly gives corporate policymakers some pause in their decision-making. Brent Fisse and John Braithwaite (1983) have written extensively on the financial and nonfinancial impacts of adverse publicity. They found that the fallout from a celebrated case, such as the Pinto case, can go beyond the sales and profitability of the product in question. It can impact on the overall image of the corporation, lower the personal reputations of executives, reduce sales of other products made by the same firm, and have implications for legislative actions.

CONCLUSION

Since the Progressive era there has been a gradual erosion in the doctrines of *caveat emptor* and *laissez faire*, with the burden of liability relating to product safety and fraud in the marketplace slowly shifting to corporations. Nevertheless, different eras have emphasized different strategies for the control of white-collar crime. During the three reform eras of this century (the Progressive, New Deal, and consumer eras), activists advocated a regulatory approach, where government agencies would assume a more activist role *vis-à-vis* the corporate sector. During the 1980s (the "Reagan revolution"), deregulation became the solution: Less regulation rather than more would make for a safer, fairer marketplace.

Throughout this century the civil and administrative laws have comprised the major mechanisms for the social control of white-collar crime, with the criminal law (and criminal justice system) an avenue of last resort. In the remaining chapters we shall consider the limitations of these traditional approaches and what that implies for our rethinking of white-collar crime.

NOTES

1. The "tuck-under" problem was due to the swing-axle suspension of the rear wheels in the 1960–1963 models. This caused the rear wheels to assume a rather sharp angle to the pavement when the car was cornering, which, in turn, on occasion caused the car to roll over, even at moderate speeds. The "oversteer" problem was caused by the weight distribution of the Corvair. As a rear-engined vehicle, most of the Corvair's weight was in the rear. This produced a tendency for the rear end to swing around to the front when making turns. The combination of these two properties made the Corvair difficult to handle (Nader, 1966: 3–14). Although Nader, as an outsider to GM, could only make inferences about General Motors' internal decisions on the Corvair design, a decade later a former GM vice-president, John DeLoren, confirmed that there had been a vigorous internal debate between GM engineers and management over these very same design features. Thus, it was clear that GM management was well aware of these design flaws prior to the manufacture of the Corvair (Wright, 1979: 65).

2. *Laissez faire* is the economic doctrine that the economy is best regulated by the "invisible hand" of market forces, and that the government should not intervene or tamper with these "natural" laws of regulation. The notion of *caveat emptor* clearly derives from this philosophy, with its presumption that government should not intervene on behalf of consumer interests. Presumably market forces will look after the interests of both consumers and producers.

3. An oligopoly, sometimes also called a shared monopoly, occurs when four or fewer firms control 50 percent or more of a given economic market.

4. The FTC dropped its suit against the major oil companies in 1981, when the anti-regulation movement was becoming politically dominant, and when it became clear that the case was depleting the agency's diminishing resources (Coleman, 1989: 185). The FTC case against the cereal industry charged the major firms (Kellogg, General Mills, and General Foods) with acting as if they were a single company. The agency's analysis of industry pricing decisions showed a coordinated effort on the part of the major firms to act together when making pricing decisions between 1950 and 1972; 94 percent of the price changes during this period were price increases. Product proliferation and expensive advertising also created barriers for companies considering entering the cereal market. The FTC argued that the cereal market constituted a "shared monopoly" and was therefore in violation of the antitrust laws. In January 1982, the FTC dropped its suit against the three cereal manufacturers following a recommendation by an administrative law judge that the case be dismissed ("Monopoly on the Cereal Shelves?" 1981; "Snap, Crackle, Flop!" 1982).

5. When George Bush was vice-president, during the Reagan administration, one of his responsibilities was to head the president's special task force on regulations; its aim was to reduce the burden that government regulations impose on business.

6. General Motors also had a fuel-tank design problem in 4.7 million full-sized pick-up trucks produced between 1973 and 1987. The "sidesaddle" design made these trucks vulnerable to fire and explosion during side collisions. In February 1993, the parents of 17-year-old Shannon Moseley were awarded $105 million in damages for his death in one of those truck fires in 1989 (Levin, 1993). Although these GM pickup trucks were on the market for many years, national media publicity surrounding the fuel-tank design only

occurred in the fall of 1992. Furthermore, the National Highway Traffic Safety Administration did not ask GM to recall the vehicles until April 1993. Over the years many lawsuits regarding these pickups were settled with confidentiality agreements; secrecy undoubtedly played a role in concealing this problem.

CHAPTER EIGHT

Is White-Collar Crime Enforcement More Symbolic Than Real?

In order to examine the limitations of the traditional approaches to white-collar crime, we need to place these approaches in theoretical perspective. How do we account for the creation of laws to control white-collar crime? Are such laws a departure from the traditional double standard of justice in which conventional crime is regarded as synonymous with *the* crime problem? Are recent white-collar crime enforcement efforts an exception to this double standard? Is the punishment of white-collar offenders more symbolic than real? These are some of the questions we shall explore in this chapter.

THEORIES OF LAW CREATION

The problem of explaining the origins of laws to control white-collar crime is a special instance of the broader problem of explaining the source of all laws. Explanations of law creation are rooted in differing assumptions about the nature of society.[1] Such explanations are typically divided into consensus and conflict theories. Consensus theories assume that there is widespread acceptance in society as to what constitutes right and wrong behavior (moral consensus), with laws simply a reflection of that consensus. The state, in this view, is value-neutral in the passage and administration of the law. In the pluralist version of consensus theory, there are a large number of interest groups in society that lobby to get their particular agenda legislated. No single interest group is dominant, and a different constellation of interest groups is associated with each issue. The state remains a neutral arbiter of these diverse interests in pluralist theory.

In contrast, conflict theory begins with the assumption that the major dynamic of society is struggle, dissensus, and turmoil between groups. In this view law is created to maintain and enhance the position of the dominant groups in society's hierarchy of power and privilege. William Chambliss and Robert Seidman (1982: 306–309) distinguished two versions of conflict theory: the instrumentalist and the structuralist perspectives. In the instrumentalist view there is a single, dominant interest group, a capitalist or ruling class, whose interests are always served in the creation of law. The state is no longer value-neutral; its interests coincide with those of the capitalist class. As a direct agent of this ruling class the state makes laws that benefit the economic and political elites. Sometimes this takes the form of laws that control the behavior of the lower classes; other times it may take expression in legitimating questionable conduct of the wealthy and politically powerful.

Structuralist theory departs from the instrumentalist view by granting some autonomy to the state from the capitalist class. Although the state typically reflects capitalist interests, it does so because of the institutionalized relations that are embedded in the activities of the state, not simply because of those who occupy elite positions (Beirne and Messerschmidt, 1991). Furthermore, structuralists distinguish between the long-term and the short-term interests of the capitalist class. They argue that the state will pass laws that are in the long-term interests of capitalism, although in the short run its actions may appear to depart from those interests. This is because in order to resolve the contradictions or crises of capitalist society, the state must sometimes take measures to ensure its immediate stability and legitimacy. In doing so it may have to make symbolic concessions to non-elite interests. In this manner the law is a mechanism by which the state legitimizes existing political and economic arrangements (Michalowski, 1985: 164).

This does not provide a detailed treatment of these theories, but simply points out the major currents in the explanation of the origins of law. Our task here is to relate these theories specifically to the creation of law for the control of white-collar crime. In this chapter we shall consider two recent developments and their implications for these theories: (1) the emergence of white-collar crime as a top federal investigative priority in the 1970s and (2) the federal response to the savings and loan scandal in the late 1980s and early 1990s. Through these two examples we gain insight into these theories as well as into the limitations of traditional strategies of white-collar crime control.

THE JUSTICE DEPARTMENT'S "DISCOVERY"

In Chapter 3 we noted the assimilation of the concept of white-collar crime into the mainstream of criminology during the 1970s along with a wider renewal of interest in white-collar crime, which some have likened to a social movement. Paralleling this was the U.S. Justice Department's sudden "discovery" in the mid-1970s of white-collar crime as a top investigative priority. This is particularly noteworthy given the traditional avoidance of white-collar crime by the criminal justice system and the historical reliance upon regulatory agencies and the administrative law to control white-collar crime (Poveda, 1992).

It is important to locate this "discovery" in the social and political context of the 1970s. Katz (1980) saw the sudden interest in white-collar crime in terms of the political crisis that accompanied and followed the Watergate scandal, when crime at the top became a major public issue. Others viewed it as part of a wider decline in public confidence in major U.S. institutions that began in the late 1960s and continued into the 1970s. The national crises over civil rights, the Vietnam War, and Watergate all contributed to the erosion of public trust in government and big business (Lipset and Schneider, 1978; Cullen, Maakestad, and Cavender, 1987; Kramer, 1989; Simon and Eitzen, 1993). The numerous disclosures of wrongdoing in the higher circles of government and business created a climate favorable for pursuing corporate and governmental misconduct.

However, more than just an "anti-establishment" climate was required to reorder the Department of Justice (DOJ) priorities. One of the unintended consequences of the Watergate scandal was the disclosure of abuses of authority by the Federal Bureau of Investigation (FBI) (part of the Justice Department) and the intelligence agencies. For example, as part of his Watergate defense, President Richard Nixon argued that past presidential administrations had engaged in similar practices. In defending his administration Nixon unwittingly revealed that the FBI had committed surreptitious entries (burglaries) in previous administrations "on a very large scale." This and other revelations, the death of J. Edgar Hoover, and congressional inquiries caused a rethinking of the FBI and its investigative priorities. The outcome was a dramatic decline in FBI domestic intelligence activities, the main source of the disclosed abuses, and the elevation of white-collar crime, organized crime, and foreign counterintelligence to top investigative priorities. Thus, organizational scandal and reform, coupled with the post-Watergate political climate, were necessary ingredients in the "discovery" of white-collar crime (Poveda, 1990).

Additionally, Justice Department and FBI officials themselves needed to be convinced of the importance of pursuing white-collar crime. The underlying concern in the targeting of white-collar crime was explicitly stated by a variety of FBI and DOJ officials during the 1970s. In a speech to a business advisory panel of the U.S. Chamber of Commerce, U.S. Attorney General Griffin Bell (1979) developed the idea that "white-collar crime erodes respect for the justice system" (Bell, 1979: 2). He further observed, "Each time that such a crime is successfully perpetrated, the public will begin to doubt the integrity of our criminal justice apparatus." In a similar vein FBI Director William Webster (1980: 279) noted, "White-collar crime had to be placed high on the list of priorities because it strikes at the very fiber of our society by undermining trust and confidence in our political, governmental, and financial systems." This linkage between white-collar crime and erosion of respect for the law and the integrity of our institutions was a recurrent theme throughout the mid- and late-1970s. It was repeatedly expressed by high-level FBI and DOJ officials and by government publications of that period.

Transforming the Definition of White-Collar Crime

In large part the task of transforming white-collar crime from a sociological to a legal concept fell upon the Justice Department. In order to institutionalize white-collar crime as an investigative priority in the 1970s, white-collar crime had to be translated into legal terminology. In early 1977, the Attorney General's White-Collar Crime Committee adopted the following working definition: "White-collar offenses shall constitute those classes of non-violent illegal activities which principally involve traditional notions of deceit, deception, concealment, manipulation, breach of trust, subterfuge or illegal circumvention" (U.S. Department of Justice, 1980: 5). The FBI's working definition, not surprisingly, closely followed the DOJ definition: "Those crimes that are committed by non-physical means to avoid payment or loss of money or to obtain business or personal advantage where success depends upon guile or concealment" (Webster, 1980: 276).

In their transformation of white-collar crime into a legal concept, both the DOJ's and the FBI's definitions fundamentally altered Edwin H. Sutherland's concept of white-collar crime by including the criminal acts of non-elite persons within their scope. The Justice Department had also adopted an offense-based rather than an offender-based definition. The defining criterion was not who committed the act (elite or non-elite), but the nature of the act itself. In his testimony before the House Subcommittee on Crime, Deputy Attorney General Benjamin Civiletti explained the DOJ's rejection of the historic definition of white-collar crime:

Our definition markedly departs from the traditional view held by many sociologists who have in the past stressed the social characteristics of the offender or the relationship between offenders and their occupations. That traditional academic approach does not accurately reflect the type of offenses and offenders encountered by the criminal justice system. Our experience has demonstrated that white-collar offenses are regularly committed by members of all social classes and are not the exclusive domain of the rich and powerful. . . . The traditional approach was further rejected because it implicitly raises the specter of large enforcement agencies targeting whole segments of society for special enforcement emphasis. . . . (U.S. House, 1979: 65)

Similarly, the Justice Department report on national priorities for white-collar crime rejected the traditional view: "we conclude that for purposes of defining national law enforcement priorities, most of the ways in which offenses have been traditionally defined by law enforcement agencies and the public are not workable" (U.S. Department of Justice, 1980: 6).

Herein lies the basic dilemma in translating white-collar crime from a sociological concept into a legal one. Its operationalization into a legal definition for investigative purposes ironically loses the historic meaning of the concept. Sociologist Donald Cressey, at a hearing before the House Subcommittee on Crime, also recognized the transformation in the meaning of white-collar crime that was taking place. Not unlike Sutherland, he said that we should focus on the crimes of businessmen themselves and not simply crimes against business. In pointing out that white-collar crime is not a legal category, Cressey asserted, "It seems to me that we now are witnessing the 'politics of definition' in the United States" (U.S. House, 1979: 31).

The definition of white-collar crime that has prevailed in law enforcement circles since the 1970s is the DOJ view, where white-collar crime is a nonviolent illegal activity that is not linked to any particular social class. This, perhaps unwittingly, serves to deflect attention away from the distinctive crimes of the wealthy and powerful. It implies that white-collar crimes do not produce physical harm and injury, only economic losses. Moreover, it emphasizes the crimes of individuals, which tends to obscure the organizational nature of much white-collar crime.

Operationalizing White-Collar Crime as a Priority

In the fall of 1974, shortly after President Nixon's resignation in the Watergate scandal, FBI Director Clarence Kelley (1974: 1) identified white-collar crime as a "serious problem" in his "Message from the Director" column in the *FBI Law Enforcement Bulletin*. Fiscal year 1974 marked the first year that white-collar crime was explicitly mentioned and provided with a separate subheading in the Bureau's annual report. Closer examination of the FBI's annual reports from 1974 to 1976 reveals that the kinds of investigations included under white-collar crime consisted of bank fraud and embezzlement, bribery, antitrust, perjury, conflict of interest, and fraud against some government programs. Bank fraud and embezzlement alone accounted for 35 percent of the white-collar crime cases investigated in 1974 (U.S. Attorney General, 1974–1976).[2] There is, of course, nothing new about any of these investigative areas; they have all been part of the FBI's investigative responsibilities for many years. What is new is that they have been combined under a new crime category: white-collar crime.

This reclassification of traditional FBI crimes into a white-collar crime category does not necessarily discredit Kelley's claim that he was taking white-collar crime seriously and making it a top priority. The Bureau's seriousness can also be measured by examining its allocation of resources to this new crime program. In fact, in the immediate post-Watergate period an increasing proportion of FBI investigative resources was allocated to white-collar crime. In 1975, 11.7 percent of the total investigative matters received were in the white-collar crime program; this amount increased to 22.3 percent by 1979 (U.S. House, 1980b).

Moreover, by 1978, public corruption began to emerge as the distinguishing feature of this new white-collar crime program. A survey of FBI field offices in 1980 found corruption of public officials to be the top-ranked priority within the white-collar crime program in 54 percent of the field offices (U.S. Department of Justice, 1980: 12a). This corruption focus reflected some of the continuing public concerns of the post-Watergate period.

In the late 1970s, in spite of the FBI's and the Justice Department's apparent pursuit of white-collar crime, some congressional representatives raised concerns as to the adequacy of the federal response to white-collar crime. In 1978, the Conyers Subcommittee on Crime held hearings where evidence was presented that the federal response was "underfunded, undirected, uncoordinated, and . . . in need of the development of a national strategy and national priorities" (U.S. House, 1979: 2). It was to some extent in response to these concerns that President Jimmy Carter's Justice Department and Webster's FBI more carefully delineated a strategy and national priorities for investigating white-collar crime. These were issued in a 1980 report (U.S. Department of Justice, 1980), which listed the seven priority white-collar crimes:

1. Crimes against federal, state, or local government by public officials
2. Crimes against the government by private citizens
3. Crimes against business
4. Crimes against consumers
5. Crimes against investors
6. Crimes against employees
7. Crimes affecting the health and safety of the general public

Writing about the same time, FBI Director Webster (1980: 284) identified these same priorities and proceeded to outline the FBI strategy for combating white-collar crime, what he described as a "five-pronged, coordinated approach" that involved prevention, detection, investigation, prosecution, and sentencing.

By 1980, the process of institutionalizing the concept of white-collar crime in the Justice Department was more or less complete. A legal definition had been formulated to serve the purposes of investigation and prosecution. A separate white-collar crime program had been established, with a growing share of investigative resources allocated to it. And, finally, a national strategy and set of priorities had been put in place.

Theoretical Implications

What did the Justice Department's pursuit of white-collar crime in the 1970s imply for the several theories we reviewed at the beginning of this chapter? Did this mean a reversal of the traditional double standard in the handling of conventional and white-collar crime? What was the impetus for this change—interest groups, the state, a ruling class? Was it the outcome of an underlying struggle or conflict? The DOJ's "discovery" of white-collar crime is most problematic for conflict theory, which generally views the origins of law in terms of the interests of economic and political elites. The targeting of white-collar crime for investigation and prosecution would appear to contradict conflict explanations, especially insofar as it involves upper-class and corporate offenders (Poveda, 1992).

In both the instrumentalist and the structuralist versions of conflict theory it is difficult to account for the enactment of laws that are contrary to elite interests. This is especially the case with the instrumentalist perspective where the state is viewed as a direct agent of the ruling class. Instrumentalists resolve this issue by maintaining that such legislation is actually supported and sometimes initiated by elite interests. Gabriel Kolko's (1963) research on the meatpacking industry supported this view, where the largest meatpackers, to the detriment of their smaller competitors, sought regulation of the industry during the Progressive era. Similarly, Albert E. McCormick's (1979) research on the Sherman Antitrust Act of this same era found that antitrust legislation was actually designed to protect the dominant class interests.

Structuralists, on the other hand, do allow for short-term concessions to non-elite interests. In their view the state must sometimes make symbolic concessions to non-elites in order to maintain the stability and legitimacy of the political and economic system. McCormick's analysis of antitrust legislation also supported this view. By passing a moderate bill, by failing to provide enforcement resources, and by co-opting anti–big business sentiment, the Sherman Act not only was consistent with elite interests, but also accomplished its symbolic and legitimating purposes with regard to non-elites.

There is also the pluralist version of consensus theory, which is more consistent with laws reflecting non-elite interests. While its strength is in its recognition of a diversity of interest groups in the creation of law, including non-elite ones, it is less credible in accounting for the consistently dominant influences of the wealthy and powerful in shaping white-collar crime legislation. The basic dividing point of pluralist and conflict theory is the question of how concentrated political power is in society. Conflict theorists adopt an elite view of political power; pluralists contend that political power is widely dispersed in a variety of interest groups. This is a long-standing debate in sociology and political science, and will not be settled by one illustrative example. Nevertheless, the emergence of white-collar crime enforcement in the 1970s is useful in showing the strengths and weaknesses of the several theoretical approaches.

There are several aspects to the DOJ's "discovery" of white-collar crime that should be highlighted and that will add to our analysis. First, it should be noted that during the 1970s high-level FBI and DOJ officials repeatedly acknowledged the existence of a crisis of public confidence in institutions, some of it engendered by the Watergate scandal. These same officials explicitly linked the FBI's and the Justice Department's responses to white-collar crime as an attempt to restore trust and confidence in the criminal justice system as well as governmental and economic institutions (Kelley, 1974; Bell, 1979; Webster, 1980). A second consideration was the DOJ's transformation of the definition of white-collar crime to include offenders from all social classes, not just the economic and political elites. In fact, the vast majority of white-collar offenders prosecuted by the Justice Department are non-elite offenders (Weisburd et al., 1991). Finally, it appears that the DOJ's response to the crisis of confidence of the 1970s was not part of a centrally coordinated effort initiated at the highest levels of government (Poveda, 1992). Katz (1980), for example, argued that within the Justice Department the movement against white-collar crime came from prosecutors in the field rather than from policy shifts in Washington.

All of these elements are supportive of structuralist theory. Although the structuralist perspective does provide for symbolic, and perhaps even some measure of real, concessions to non-elite interests by the state in responding to societal crises, overall it subscribes to the idea of an elite power structure (unlike pluralist theory). The disclosures of wrongdoing in the higher circles of government and corporations during the 1970s made it necessary for the state to respond to the legitimation problems that were raised. However, as we saw, the vast majority of those targeted by the Justice Department's white-collar crime program were non-elite offenders. There were the occasional celebrated cases involving elite offenders, as in the Wall Street insider-trading cases of the 1980s, but these were exceptional rather than the rule. In this respect the DOJ's pursuit of white-collar crime may have been more of a symbolic solution to the crisis of confidence than a real one, which would require more enduring structural or institutional reforms.

THE CASE OF THE SAVINGS AND LOAN SCANDAL

In what was perhaps the crime(s) of the century, the massive stealing from savings and loans (S&Ls) during the 1980s, we shall further consider the extent to which white-collar crime enforcement is more symbolic than real. Because of the government-insured deposits that were involved, U.S. taxpayers will pay several hundred billion dollars over the years to cover the losses.[3] How this happened and what punishments were meted out to the offenders constitute the focus of this section.

What Happened

In the 1930s, savings and loans (or thrifts) were established to promote home construction and to provide home loans to consumers. The deposits in these financial institutions were federally insured by the Federal Savings and Loan Insurance Corporation or FSLIC, not unlike banks which were insured by the Federal Deposit Insurance Corporation or FDIC. However, the thrifts were limited in the interest rates they could pay on deposits and in the kinds of commercial investments for which their funds could be used. These restrictions proved to be a serious handicap for the S&L industry during the 1970s, when other, more profitable kinds of investments were available and S&L deposits declined (Calavita and Pontell, 1991; Pizzo, Fricker, and Muolo, 1991).

In response to this S&L crisis of the 1970s, the federal government took several measures. In 1980, Congress passed the Depository Institutions Deregulation and Monetary Control Act, which increased insurance coverage on deposits from $40,000 per account to $100,000 and phased out interest rate controls. In October of 1982, President Reagan signed the Garn-St. Germain (Depository Institutions) Act, which further deregulated the thrift industry. It permitted S&Ls to invest in riskier commercial loans and investments and did away with the cap on interest rates on its deposits. In 1982, thrift regulators also made it easier for a single shareholder to own a thrift, without the controlling influence of other shareholders (Pizzo, Fricker, and Muolo, 1991: 21–29). In short, the deregulation of the savings and loan industry allowed thrifts to move away from their traditional role as the provider of home mortgages and to engage in riskier investments with fewer controls, all insured by the federal government.

To the advocates of deregulation this seemed like the solution to the thrift crisis of the 1970s—indeed, at the signing of the Garn-St. Germain Act, President Reagan was quoted as saying, "I think we've hit the jackpot" (Pizzo, Fricker, and Muolo, 1991: 12). These deregulatory measures instead provided the conditions and opportunity for massive fraud and embezzlement throughout the industry. A new breed, what Ed Gray, chair of the Federal Home Loan Bank Board (FHLBB) in the 1980s, called the "high fliers," moved in and operated savings and loans as if they were their own personal piggy banks. Bank deposits were used to support extravagant life-styles, to make loans to friends, and to invest in questionable ventures. In the extreme case of Vernon Savings and Loan in North Dallas, 96 percent of all of its loans were in default at the time of its failure in March 1987, and it would eventually cost the federal government $1.3 billion to bail out this one institution (Pizzo, Fricker, and Muolo, 1991: 298). Although these losses were not all due to fraud, a substantial portion was. Officials of the FDIC and the Resolution Trust Corporation (RTC), who are responsible for resolving the assets of failed banks and thrifts, estimate that wrongdoing was present in 75 to 80 percent of the failed banks and thrifts; this involved wrongdoing by directors, officers, accountants, attorneys, securities brokers, appraisers, etc. (U.S. Senate, 1992: 8). Moreover, this insider abuse and fraud significantly contributed to the failure of these financial institutions (U.S. House, 1990: 9).

Don Dixon, owner of Vernon Savings and Loan, was an example of one of the entrepreneurs of the 1980s who thrived on deregulation. At the time he acquired Vernon in 1982, he was already head of his own successful construction company. Ownership of Vernon now gave him access to millions of dollars to finance commercial real estate projects. Dixon funneled Vernon funds into 30 subsidiary companies, which he controlled or owned; these were created to bypass regulations that prohibited large loans to "affiliated persons." In addition, Dixon used Vernon's deposits to finance his own lavish life-style. In the four years after acquiring Vernon, Dixon purchased a $1.9 million chalet in the exclusive Beaver Creek community in Colorado. He also had a $1 million home in Solano Beach, just north of San Diego. He commuted weekly between Southern California and Dallas on Vernon's jet. To go along with skiing and the Southern California sun, he acquired a $2.6 million yacht, docked in Florida. There were also "business" trips to Europe, more airplanes, a hunting club in West Texas, expensive shotguns, and the list goes on. In December 1990, a Dallas jury found Don Dixon guilty on 23 counts of defrauding Vernon Savings and Loan (Pizzo, Fricker, and Muolo, 1991: 246–265, 490).

In 1989, President Bush signed the 371-page S&L bailout bill (the Financial Institutions Reform, Recovery and Enforcement Act or FIRREA), which reregulated the thrifts, provided the initial $50 billion to close bankrupt S&Ls, and created the Resolution Trust Corporation to manage and dispose of the assets of the failed thrifts (Pizzo, Fricker, and Muolo, 1991: 442–444). In June of 1990, President Bush also announced his initiative against financial institutions fraud, proclaiming "we will not rest until the cheats and the chiselers and the charlatans spend a large chunk of their lives behind the bars of a federal prison" (U.S. Senate, 1991b: 105). This initiative included the appointment of a special counsel for financial fraud within the DOJ, a 27-city task force, and a list of the 100 top priority criminal cases the DOJ would pursue. In the following section we shall examine the federal government's claim that it was going to "get tough" with the S&L crooks.

The Punishment: Myth and Reality

Testifying before the Senate Judiciary Committee in August 1990, the newly appointed special counsel for financial institutions in the Justice Department, James Richmond, assured the senators that the DOJ regarded financial institution fraud as a serious matter, and that it was vigorously pursuing these cases on both criminal and civil enforcement fronts. Included in his statement was a statistical summary of major thrift cases to date.[4] At that time the Justice Department was prosecuting approximately 243 failed savings and loan cases, involving losses of $2.5 billion. There were 328 defendants who had been charged, 213 convicted, and 5 acquitted. Those who received prison sentences were serving 415 years; another $975,000 in fines and $56.6 million in restitution had been ordered by the courts. Richmond also mentioned two cases where lengthy prison sentences had been imposed on owners of thrifts—12 years in one case and 15 years in the other. Both owners were also ordered to pay over $6 million in restitution (U.S. Senate, 1991b: 43–46).

In spite of the initial promise of the Bush administration initiatives to pursue and punish the S&L offenders, criticism of these efforts mounted—from the House Committee on Government Operations, the General Accounting Office, the Senate Banking Committee, public interest groups, and the media. The shortcomings in the war against S&L fraud and embezzlement lay on both the criminal and the civil sides of enforcement.

On the criminal side the Justice Department was accused of allocating insufficient resources to the problem. Although FIRREA had authorized the Justice Department to spend an additional $75 million a year for the next three years on law enforcement efforts in this area, the Bush administration requested only $50 million a year in additional spending, which Congress appropriated (U.S. Senate, 1991b: 110). Meanwhile, there was a growing backlog of criminal referrals in S&L fraud and embezzlement. John Downey of the Office of Thrift Supervision (OTS) estimated that there were 18,000 criminal referrals between 1987 and 1990, one of the reasons the OTS, the RTC, and the DOJ had to prioritize and limit the criminal investigations to 100 major cases in the summer of 1990 (U.S. Senate, 1991b: 70–71). Even in these prioritized criminal cases, the Justice Department strategy was to focus on specific, discrete criminal acts that could more easily be prosecuted and simplified for a jury to understand. The more complex conspiracies that were typically part of the S&L frauds would not be pursued (Knight, 1990; LaFraniere, 1990). By the end of 1991, the number of convicted offenders in major S&L cases (losses of $100,000 or more) increased to 661 (since Oct. 1, 1988); these included some 200 presidents, CEOs, directors, and officers. The courts also ordered $12 million in fines and over $372 million in restitution.

Approximately 60 percent of these offenders (401) were sentenced to prison, with an average sentence of 3.3 years (U.S. Attorney General, 1992: 9). Although these penalties may seem severe by white-collar crime standards, keep in mind that these are the court-ordered sentences and not the actual times served. Nevertheless, these penalties pale when compared to the sentences received by those who rob banks from the outside (conventional crime). In 1990, 99 percent of those convicted of bank robbery in federal courts went to prison for an average sentence of 8.3 years. These sentences were for crimes involving substantially smaller amounts of money than the losses incurred from S&L fraud; the FBI estimated the average economic loss in bank robberies in 1990 at $3,244 (Flanagan and Maguire, 1992: 396, 532).

There is no denying that there were S&L convictions and that perhaps two-thirds of these offenders spent some time in prison. There were also celebrated cases, such as that of Charles Keating, where lengthy prison sentences will be served.[5] Because of the complexity of the S&L frauds, many cases, however, were either not pursued or not pursued to their full extent, given limited enforcement resources. We must also not lose sight of the enormity of the crimes that were committed. Stephen Pizzo and his associates (1991: 486–487) stated this most graphically. They estimated that 1,700 S&Ls failed during this period, costing U.S. taxpayers around $500 billion. This is more than the $60 billion (in today's dollars) that the federal government spent rebuilding Western Europe after World War II. It is also more than the $167 billion (in today's dollars) that the

United States spent in 10 years of fighting the Vietnam War. Put still another way, it amounts to about $2,000 for every man, woman, and child in the United States.

What about the civil side of the ledger? Was the federal government able to recoup some of the billions of dollars in losses incurred as a result of the massive fraud in the thrift industry? One manner of reclaiming these losses is through restitution payments that courts order convicted defendants to pay. A subcommittee of the House Banking Committee investigated the restitution collection practices of the FDIC and the DOJ, and found them to be seriously wanting (U.S House, 1992). In the subcommittee staff report that focused on 15 major S&L criminal cases, it was found that less than 1 percent of the restitution payments had been collected. For example, Ted Musacchio, former president of Columbus Marin S&L Association in San Rafael, California, was convicted of bank fraud, and on January 1, 1990, he was sentenced to five years' probation and ordered to pay $9.3 million in restitution to the FDIC. Although this was due immediately, none of this had been collected by either the FDIC or the DOJ at the time of the staff report. In a second case, Woodrow Brownlee, former president of Commodore Savings Association, was sentenced on October 30, 1990, to five years' probation and ordered to pay $1 million in restitution; 18 months later only $500 had been collected.

In the DOJ's own accounting of its success at collecting court-ordered restitution in 584 major S&L cases, it reported that about 4 percent ($16.9 million of $403.2 million) of the payments had been collected as of January 13, 1992. The FDIC had only a slightly better success rate at 6.3 percent ($19.8 million of $296.2 million)—as of January 31, 1992. The subcommittee report attributed this failure to collect millions of dollars to inadequate collection efforts by both the DOJ and the FDIC, and to the unwillingness of judges to require immediate restitution at sentencing (U.S. House, 1992).

Still another recourse for the federal government in the recovery of funds lost due to financial institution fraud is civil litigation. As part of their regulatory function the FDIC and the RTC can initiate civil suits against individuals who defraud failed banks and thrifts. In June 1992, the General Accounting Office (GAO) reported on the success of FDIC and RTC efforts in this area. Although the GAO report indicated that wrongdoing was present in more than 75 percent of financial institution failures, it also pointed out that the FDIC filed claims against only about 20 percent of the failed banks and the RTC against about 41 percent of the failed thrifts. In his testimony before the Senate Banking Committee, the associate director of the GAO, Harold Valentine, was quite critical of the FDIC's and the RTC's performance in pursuing these liability claims. Although they had recovered nearly $1 billion in such claims since 1989, Valentine (and the GAO report) argued that both the FDIC and the RTC had not given high priority to these liability cases. The key shortcomings were staffing shortages, inadequate procedures for tracing assets, and inadequate management information systems to keep track of their investigations. Meanwhile, the three-year statute of limitations was running out on these cases, so that if they were not pursued within that time frame, the government would lose by default—60 percent of the RTC's claims were filed within one week of the expiration of the statute of limitations (U.S. Senate, 1992).

To make matters worse, about this same time the RTC was investigating its own legal department because of allegations by three of its attorneys that they were disciplined for aggressively pursuing certain cases, and that the RTC was "going easy" on people with political connections ("RTC Asks for Investigation," 1992). Furthermore, the general counsel of the RTC's legal department was himself barred from considering S&L lawsuits while his own ties to a failed savings and loan were being investigated ("RTC Curbs Aide's Duties," 1992).

Again, in the example of massive fraud in the savings and loan industry during the 1980s, we are confronted with the disparity between the initial promise— that the federal government would "get tough" with the S&L crooks—and the reality of the punishment that was meted out to these offenders, in terms of both criminal and civil penalties. While the jury may still be out on some of these cases, the statute of limitations in both criminal and civil matters means that the vast majority have already been decided.[6] In broader terms, what does this imply for white-collar crime enforcement? Does this mean that white-collar crime enforcement efforts are intended more for symbolic purposes than for the serious pursuit of white-collar offenders? For legitimating existing institutions rather than punishing elite crime? If so, the two examples that we have focused on in this chapter highlight some of the limitations of pursuing crime when it is committed by the wealthy and politically powerful. These limitations are of critical importance to both theory and social policy.

THE LIMITS OF WHITE-COLLAR CRIME ENFORCEMENT

In the 1970s, when the Justice Department made white-collar crime one of its top investigative priorities, one of the officially stated purposes of the program was to restore public trust and confidence in U.S. political and economic institutions. Similarly, as Francis T. Cullen and his associates (1987: 13) noted in their analysis of the Ford Pinto case, prosecutions of white-collar criminals "reassert the ideology of equal justice and the neutrality of law." In other words, when wrongdoing in high places is publicly revealed to the extent that it challenges the very integrity of institutions—whether it be the public corruption of Watergate or widespread fraud in the savings and loan industry, it becomes imperative for the justice system to respond to such elite misconduct. Failure to do so exposes the double standard with which we treat conventional and white-collar offenders, and this, in turn, raises questions about the neutrality and even-handedness with which the justice system operates. This, of course, is the symbolic function of white-collar crime enforcement.

Is white-collar crime enforcement necessarily limited to such symbolic and legitimating functions, as structuralist theory maintains? Can such enforcement efforts deter white-collar offenders or, more fundamentally, help to reform the underlying conditions that produce elite misconduct? This is the problem we shall take up in the final chapter.

NOTES

1. The typology of theories set forth in this chapter is generally informed by the work of William Chambliss and Robert Seidman (1982), Chambliss (1988), and Piers Beirne and James Messerschmidt (1991). Moreover, it should be noted that in sociological theory the use of state or state power encompasses a range of institutions and is not synonymous with the term "government," which refers mainly to the legislative bodies and elected officials. The state system is comprised of several elements, including the government. These other elements are the administrative apparatus of the state (e.g., executive departments, regulatory commissions, public corporations), the military and the police, and the judicial branch (Miliband, 1969: 46ff.).

2. As of February 1, 1980, the FBI used some 70 existing statutes to group white-collar offenses for investigative and reporting purposes (U.S. Department of Justice, 1980: 1a).

3. Estimates of the amount of the S&L bailout vary. As of March 17, 1993, Congress had approved $149 billion for the bailout; an additional $26.3 billion was approved by the U.S. House in November 1993 (Karr, 1993: A2; "S&Ls," 1993: B8). When the interest on this money (which contributed to the federal deficit) is taken into account, the amount is around $500 billion.

4. These were DOJ savings and loan prosecutions from October 1, 1988, to July 12, 1990. "Major" is defined as cases where the fraud or loss totals $100,000 or more, or where the defendant was an officer, director, or owner (U.S. Senate, 1991b: 46).

5. On July 8, 1993, Keating was sentenced in federal court to a 12.5-year sentence, which he will serve concurrently with a 10-year state prison sentence. Keating was the former owner of Lincoln Savings and Loan; in January 1993, he was convicted of 73 counts of fraud and racketeering charges. It is likely that he will actually serve close to 10 years on both the state and the federal convictions (Sims, 1993; A. Stevens, 1993).

6. As we noted, the statute of limitations in civil litigation involving bank and thrift failures is three years. The statute of limitations for bank fraud was increased in 1989 from 5 to 10 years (Pizzo, Fricker, and Muolo, 1991: 301).

■ CHAPTER NINE ■

Is There a Solution?

During this century, as we have seen, the predominant response to the discovery of white-collar crime was a regulatory approach, employing administrative and civil laws through government agencies to control the lawlessness that was exposed in each of three eras (the Progressive, New Deal, and consumer eras). By the late 1970s, dissatisfaction with this traditional approach mounted. Those opposed to regulation argued that there was too much regulation, and that it was both costly and anticompetitive. Moreover, in the 1970s, this regulation, it was claimed, had become too adversarial and accusatory. The result was a conservative backlash that led to the deregulation movement of the 1980s.

Accompanying this backlash was the sense that the traditional regulatory approach was a failure (Frank and Lombness, 1988: 121ff.). Ironically, the idea that "nothing works" in white-collar crime enforcement, as Laureen Snider (1990: 387) noted, led to the opposite policy direction than when the identical discovery was made regarding conventional crime in the 1970s. The "nothing works" controversy in conventional crime control policy was linked to the failure of liberal crime policies, especially rehabilitation, to curb violent crime.[1] It was also part of the ideological basis for emerging conservative crime control policies in the 1970s and 1980s, which sought a more punitive, "get tough" approach to conventional offenders—more aggressive law enforcement, more prisons, and weakened procedural safeguards (Walker, 1989). In contrast, the major policy thrust regarding corporate crime that derived from the apparent failure of the traditional regulatory justice system was less regulation, fewer resources, and voluntary compliance for corporate offenders—in short, the deregulation of white-collar crime.

The ongoing debate about white-collar crime policy is the focus of this chapter. It is a debate not only about the proper policy models (cooperative versus adversarial), but also about the limits of regulatory reform, given the structural constraints of corporate capitalism. We begin by examining the link between theory and social policy.

THEORY AND SOCIAL POLICY

The question of "solving" the white-collar crime problem is closely related to the theory of society and political power to which one subscribes. In the previous chapter we considered the several theories of law creation. Clearly if one views the state as a neutral arbiter among numerous, more-or-less equal interest groups (pluralist theory), there is some reason for optimism in terms of mobilizing public opinion in order to get one's interests legislated. However, if one views political power as concentrated in a dominant economic class, with the state tightly under its control (conflict theory), the prospect of reining in the misconduct of political and economic elites is not so promising.

The differing theoretical orientations reflected in the work of various students of white-collar crime, of course, have implications for what policy options are possible. Richard Quinney (1977), for example, argued that crimes of domination (corporate and governmental crimes) are a necessary and intrinsic part of capitalism, and, therefore, it is unlikely that any measures to reduce or eliminate such crimes would be successful within the existing institutional framework (instrumentalist theory).

Harold C. Barnett (1981), taking a more middle ground, argued that some reduction of corporate crime is possible, but that any fundamental change in the extent of corporate crime would probably require a transformation of the U.S. political economy. Some response to corporate crime is necessary because of the legitimating and stabilizing function of the state, but there are structural limits to this response because of the nature of corporate capitalism (structuralist theory).

Francis T. Cullen and his associates (1987: 343, 347) sounded a still more optimistic note, challenging the notion of the corporation as an "invincible criminal." They argued that measures can be taken to reduce corporate crime that go beyond simply symbolic gestures; their view has elements of both pluralist and structuralist perspectives. These three positions do not exhaust the spectrum of theory and policy possibilities, but they should make clear the linkage between theoretical perspective and social policy. Ultimately underlying any policy debate regarding the control of white-collar crime is a debate about social and political theory. This should be kept in mind in our ensuing discussion of the limits of regulatory reform and the controversy over policy models.

WHERE THE LAW ENDS

Two decades ago Christopher Stone (1975) wrote a book, with the same title as this section's subheading, where he succinctly outlined the flaws in the traditional regulatory strategy for controlling corporate crime—the limits of the law. Overall, he characterized this traditional approach as a deterrent strategy, attempting to control corporate conduct by threatening corporate profits—what he called "pocketbook control." It was also a reactive strategy, sanctioning offenders after the fact, rather than a preventive approach. Stone then proceeded to divide his criticism of the traditional approach into two categories: (1) measures aimed at corporations and (2) measures aimed at key individuals.

In terms of the measures aimed at corporations, Stone argued that the traditional strategy assumes that corporate behavior is totally based on maximizing profits. This is not entirely true. He observed that corporations, at different stages of development, may value other goals as well: growth, market share, control over corporate environment. He further noted that there are numerous subgoals within a corporation that may be even more critical in influencing corporate behavior than the overall profits of the company. Each administrative unit within the firm (marketing, finance, production, research and development, product testing, etc.), will have subgoals that are the important reality that shapes the conduct of individuals. Stone's point here is that if traditional sanctions are based on pocketbook control, and if the actual behavior of individuals within the corporation is based on a different set of factors, then the pocketbook measures will not work.

It is also sometimes argued that if existing sanctions (especially fines) do not work, we simply need to increase the penalties—hit the corporation with a bigger stick, so to speak. Stone concluded that this "bigger stick" approach has its limits as well, arguing that judges would not allow companies to be bankrupted or seriously financially threatened by fines. The 1967 Roginsky case was used to illustrate this, when Judge Henry Friendly limited the civil damages Richardson-Merrell, the pharmaceutical company, would pay to a plaintiff, taking into account what the company could afford to bear (Stone, 1975: 55–56).[2]

Stone then turned his attention to the measures aimed at key individuals in the corporation. He observed that threats to the corporate pocketbook do not necessarily threaten top executives because their salaries are not indexed to corporate profits or losses. He also pointed out that when executives' own pocketbooks are threatened by fines, most major firms carry liability insurance, which reimburses their top officers when fined in civil or criminal proceedings. Corporate executives are thus shielded from the deterrent effect of the law when corporations relieve them of financial responsibility in this manner (Stone, 1975: 64).

Stone also considered the effect of laws that establish the criminal liability of corporations by the wrongdoing (active or passive) of their top officers. An unintended consequence of this is to discourage the awareness of corporate officials of wrongdoing in the company. Such awareness by top officers establishes not only their liability, but also that of the corporation itself. Stone argued that this affects the flow of information in a firm by keeping "bad news" from rising in an organization.

Given the limitations of the traditional regulatory strategy, what then did Stone propose? He did not advocate abandoning regulation, but instead argued that it should be supplemented by measures that encourage corporate responsibility. His overall strategy was more proactive (preventive) than the traditional regulatory approach. His proposals were based on two key ideas: (1) The corporation's information network needs to be restructured so that it will get feedback on the harm it may cause ("bad news"), and (2) it is necessary to develop measures that are more intrusive into the corporation's internal decision-making processes in order to minimize the possibility of harm occurring in the first place.

To illustrate the feedback mechanism, Stone proposed that companies be required to collect information that makes them aware of certain practices or the effects of their products. For example, pharmaceutical companies might be required to conduct not only pre-market testing, but also post-market testing in order to detect the incidence of side effects in a larger population after the marketing of their product. These data might also have to be reported to the Food and Drug Administration (FDA). This is analogous to current affirmative action practices where we require certain companies and government agencies to keep records of their recruitment practices. In this manner organizations are at least sensitive to the profile of women and minorities that they employ and the hiring practices that produce that result. Such feedback measures are attempts to increase corporate awareness of their conduct and the effects of that conduct. This also means that top executives are made aware of corporate practices, and this knowledge establishes their liability as well as that of the firm. They cannot later deny knowledge of such practices or their effects (Stone, 1975: 203–204).

In regard to intrusions into corporate decision-making, Stone proposed specifying the composition of the board of directors of companies. Each corporation that manufactures consumer products, for example, would be required to have someone who represents consumer interests sitting on its board. A chemical or petroleum corporation might similarly be required to have a director who speaks for environmental interests. Every corporation might be required to have a director who represents workers. In this manner issues that might not ordinarily be considered by a board of like-minded individuals would be aired at the highest levels of the corporation.

Stone also advocated appointing special directors or trustees for corporations that habitually violate the law. These "outside" personnel would be court-appointed and would have powers to inspect records, suspend or fire employees, and take other measures necessary to bring the company back into line. There is some precedent for this in bankruptcy proceedings, where courts may appoint special directors, or in prisons operating under unconstitutional conditions, where "special masters" have been appointed by the courts (Stone, 1975: 179).

The main thrust of Stone's proactive regulatory approach is to establish a structure whereby corporate responsibility is encouraged. This is achieved by making corporations sensitive to certain issues (consumer safety, environment, occupational safety, etc.) by reforming their internal decision-making process or

by using a feedback mechanism that produces awareness of the harmful consequences of their products and practices—pollution, defective products, unsafe
drugs, unsafe work conditions, and so on. This is in contrast to the traditional
approach that delegates considerable autonomy to corporations in their decision-
making and then reacts, after the fact, to the harmful consequences of that decision-making with sanctions (fines, recalls, warnings).

Stone's work offers a useful critique of the traditional regulatory strategy and
shows the limitations of sanctions aimed at top executives or the corporation
itself. Whether his proposals for reform are viable or not in terms of existing
political and ideological realities is another question. This will be taken up as
we consider the current debate over cooperative and adversarial policy models.

COOPERATIVE VERSUS ADVERSARIAL MODELS

It has often been observed that regulatory agencies tend to have different
enforcement styles. Some are more oriented toward seeking voluntary compliance from the business community. This entails a close relationship between the
regulator and the regulated industry, with negotiation and cooperation between
the two the central feature of the relationship. One of the dangers in this close-
ness is the corruption or capture of regulators by those they are regulating. In the
other regulatory style agencies seek to maintain their independence from the
regulated parties. They are more bent on detecting violations and punishing
offenders with the appropriate sanctions. The relationship between agency and
industry in this style is typically accusatory and adversarial, and may even involve
calling for the criminal sanctioning of white-collar offenders (Frank and Lombness, 1988: 77). In recent years these differing enforcement styles among regulatory agencies have been elevated to a major policy debate between those who
advocate a more "cooperative" or "compliance" strategy and those who seek a
more "adversarial" or "sanctioning" approach. There are also those who argue
for an intermediate position.

Reintegrative Shaming

Although his position is difficult to classify, John Braithwaite's (1989a; 1989b)
reintegrative shaming most closely fits the cooperative or compliance model.
Central to his argument is the idea that punishment that stigmatizes is counterproductive. It fosters the development of criminal subcultures or, in the context
of organizational crime, subcultures of resistance to law and regulation. In terms
of his theory of tipping points, stigmatization pushes offenders to the criminal
side of the equation and tends to make them outcasts. It is not that Braithwaite
opposes punishing offenders, but that the punishment (shaming) must be done
in such a manner that the offender is ultimately reintegrated into the community.
In Braithwaite's words,

Reintegrative shaming means that expressions of community disapproval, which may range from mild rebuke to degradation ceremonies, are followed by gestures of reacceptance into the community of law-abiding citizens. These gestures of reacceptance will vary from a simple smile expressing forgiveness and love to quite formal ceremonies to decertify the offender as deviant. (Braithwaite, 1989a: 55)

Braithwaite's reintegrative shaming approach is an attempt to restore the role of informal sanctions in the rehabilitation of offenders and to make the community part of that process. Reintegrative shaming is also unique in that it is one of the few theories/policies that apply equally to conventional and white-collar crime.

In accordance with his theory, Braithwaite (1989a: 125) noted the important effect of adverse publicity on corporate offenders, particularly how this impacts their reputation and that of their company. In an earlier study Braithwaite and Brent Fisse studied the impact of adverse publicity on large corporations. They found that the public disclosure of misconduct in all 17 cases they examined produced some corporate reform. They also concluded that such adverse publicity had a greater nonfinancial impact (loss of reputations, personal and corporate) than financial impact (loss of sales, earnings, stock prices) on corporations (Fisse and Braithwaite, 1983).

This illustrates the more general theory that Braithwaite is advancing, which is that more effective crime control is achieved not only when we punish and show disapproval to an offender, but also when that process seeks to reincorporate the offender into the community. In this case the adverse publicity seems to threaten the corporation's (and the executives') reputation, and the corporate reforms, even though they may be symbolic, are attempts to restore the shamed corporation's standing in the community. Thus, the adverse publicity serves both to shame the offender and to produce some reform/rehabilitation. This, again, is in contrast to current crime control policies. In the case of conventional criminals those policies are driven by retribution and deterrence along with the desire to remove criminals from society; with regard to white-collar offenders, contemporary policies not only do not stigmatize, but also fail to shame or to show community disapproval to any degree.

As a further criticism of the traditional regulatory approach, Braithwaite (1989a: 147–149) pointed to the dilemma of who guards the guardians. If the regulatory strategy is to create agencies (guards) to police the marketplace, who will guard these guardians? If the solution to this problem is to create still another level of guardians, then we get caught up in an infinite regress, with more and more levels of guards and their guardians. There will always be ways that these guardians can be corrupted, requiring still more guardians to protect against such abuse. According to Braithwaite, this is the crisis that we face in attempting to control white-collar and organizational crime. The way out of this quandary, he argued, is through the reintegrative shaming model, where social control relies more strongly on informal and community mechanisms than on an "ultimate" guardian who metes out formal punishments.

Snider's Critique

Laureen Snider (1990) offered an important criticism of cooperative models, such as Braithwaite's reintegrative shaming. Such models, she argued, are developed in response to the apparent ineffectiveness or inappropriateness of criminal sanctions and more adversarial forms of regulation in controlling corporate crime. In fact, Snider pointed out, cooperative approaches have always dominated regulatory strategy, with voluntary compliance between regulator and regulated industry the norm. Moreover, they have been no more successful than criminalization.

What is new about the cooperative models of the 1980s is that they legitimate the existing imbalance of power between regulatory agencies and corporations by accepting the current limits of regulatory power. It is this disparity of power, with corporations the dominant of the two actors, that makes for regulatory failure and, in Snider's view, this is the core of the problem. Unless policy models address this unequal distribution of power, the specific regulatory measures employed (criminal, administrative, civil) will be irrelevant. She is vague, however, on just how to accomplish this.

The Hawkins and Pearce/Tombs Debate

In an exchange in the *British Journal of Criminology*, Frank Pearce and Steven Tombs (1991) argued that advocates of cooperative or compliance models of regulation, such as Keith Hawkins (1991), are part of the deregulation backlash of the 1980s. Such compliance models create an even more conciliatory style in the regulation of corporate misconduct and, in doing so, further limit state control over the private sector. Instead, Pearce and Tombs favored an adversarial policy model that gives regulatory agencies more power to administer severe sanctions against corporate offenders. However, such an empowerment of regulatory agencies could be achieved only by a shift in the current imbalance between regulatory power and corporate power—precisely Snider's argument. Again, there is no clear plan on how to restore that imbalance.

In defense, Hawkins questioned the dichotomy between compliance and sanctioning schools that Pearce and Tombs made in their discussion. Real-life law and regulatory enforcement involve elements of both styles. Moreover, what Pearce and Tombs proposed, Hawkins argued, is not that different from the so-called compliance school they are so critical of.

This debate over policy models clearly shows the limitations of cooperative and adversarial models, but it is not so clear on what the alternatives are. Snider readily recognized this in her closing comments: "What we should not do, however, is much clearer than what we should do" (Snider, 1990: 386).

THE OBSTACLES

While policy models must consider the limitations of other approaches, they must also appreciate the obstacles in the path to reform. Such obstacles typically entail ideological and political elements. Ideological obstacles are those that pertain to the way in which we think about a particular problem or issue—the shared beliefs, concepts, and ideas that are dominant in an era, and that may interfere with new solutions to a problem. Political obstacles relate to the barriers presented by those with entrenched interests in old solutions. Such obstacles are matters of power politics, which includes law creation, the allocation of resources, and ultimately who has the power to mobilize public opinion on an issue. Throughout this text the ideological obstacles to our rethinking of white-collar crime have been highlighted. We shall return briefly to those obstacles and their implications for policy.

The Traditional Dualism

In the opening chapters we discussed the dualistic fallacy in our thinking about crime and crime control, and the role of conventional wisdom in masking the crimes of the wealthy and powerful. We also noted that to the extent such white-collar crimes are even recognized, there is a tendency to handle them differently than conventional crime—using the administrative law and regulatory agencies rather than the criminal law and the police. This differential handling gives rise to the double-standard issue: the idea that white-collar offenders are treated not only differently, but also more leniently than conventional offenders. Permeating much of our thinking about crime and crime control is this dualism in our thought about white-collar and conventional crime and criminals. One of the major themes of this volume is the need to rethink this traditional dualism. This dualism, wittingly or unwittingly, contributes to the tendency to minimize the harmfulness of white-collar crime and therefore to our ability to control it through shame and stigma. How we resolve this is at the core of the social control of white-collar crime.

The Dilemma of Shaming and Stigma

Retribution in crime control runs deep in the history of punishment and corrections. It is expressed in our desire to harshly punish, to seek revenge on, and to banish criminal offenders. This has been the dominant policy ethos of the last 20 years with respect to conventional crime. As Snider (1990) observed, during much of this same period the main policy response with respect to white-collar crime was just the opposite, one of deregulation and *laissez faire*. Although research shows that public concern over white-collar crime has increased since the 1970s, prevailing official policies continue to handle white-collar crime, particularly regulatory offenses, in a manner distinct from conventional crime. While there have been some celebrated cases involving the criminal prosecution of white-collar offenders—Boesky for insider trading, Keating for S&L fraud—the basic legal and administrative framework for handling such offenses has not changed.

The dilemma, however, for all crime control, as Braithwaite understood, is how to strike a balance between policies that isolate and further alienate offenders and those that are too lenient and do not appropriately convey a community's disapproval of the offending act. Clearly traditional policies intended to control white-collar crime have erred in the latter direction, failing to appropriately shame white-collar offenders. Crime control policies for conventional crime have erred in the opposite direction, being too stigmatizing. Additionally, both kinds of policies have been historically ineffective in controlling crime.

So where does this leave us? Braithwaite's reintegrative shaming seems to offer a middle ground, where not only are offenders shamed, but also measures are taken to reincorporate offenders into the community. Braithwaite's work also stands out as one of the few in the criminology literature to provide an integrated framework for thinking about both white-collar and conventional crime in terms of theory and policy. Stone's proposals also provide a different model for encouraging corporate responsibility in the marketplace. But, as Barnett (1981) argued, such policy measures assume a political economy that is amenable to such a transformation. And, as Snider (1990) argued as well, measures aimed at reducing corporate crime can be effective only if they address the disparity in power that exists between the corporate sector and regulatory agencies.

The Political Dimension

Besides the ideological obstacles, there are political barriers on the road to reform. As we noted at the beginning of this chapter, what political obstacles we see depends on our view of political power, with elite theorists more pessimistic about controlling white-collar crime than those who subscribe to a pluralist view. In the elite view (conflict theory) white-collar crime (especially corporate crime) will not be substantially reduced without fundamental change in the current political economy (corporate capitalism). Punishments administered to white-collar offenders are largely symbolic. Moreover, the prosecution of individual cases, even when it does occur, does not necessarily result in broader institutional change (Cullen, Maakestad, and Cavender, 1987). The solution to white-collar crime from this perspective is nothing less than transforming society as a whole. Because crimes of the economic and political elites are rooted in social structure, particularly the capitalist economy, it is this structure that must be altered. David R. Simon and D. Stanley Eitzen's (1993) program for economic democracy is one such proposal for eliminating what they call "elite deviance."

Although the political obstacles for pluralists are less forbidding, they still require interest-group political activity and the mobilization of public opinion in order to achieve legislative ends. The solution to the white-collar crime problem from this perspective is achievable within the limits of contemporary society. It involves finding and implementing the measures or sanctions that will be effective in crime control. Such measures are possible within the existing political-legal framework.

This volume cannot begin to resolve these basic questions of social and political theory that have divided scholars for decades, if not centuries. It should be clear, however, that the solution to the white-collar crime problem is linked to how these fundamental issues are settled. If anything, our awareness of white-collar crime, especially the crimes of the wealthy and powerful, should make us more sensitive to questions of power, privilege, and inequality. This was an observation Donald J. Newman (1958) made over 35 years ago. It should also make us more sensitive to understanding the nature of crime, law, and criminal justice in a way that studying conventional crime alone cannot. Rethinking white-collar crime means addressing these basic questions about the nature of law and society.

NOTES

1. The "nothing works" controversy stems from a 1974 report by Robert Martinson and his associates to the New York Governor's Special Committee on Criminal Offenders. They surveyed 231 correctional programs in operation between 1945 and 1967 that had previously been evaluated for their effectiveness. Their conclusion that very few of these rehabilitation programs had much effect in reducing recidivism was soon translated into "nothing works," even though they did not actually say this. These findings came at a time when the rehabilitation ideal was already being challenged, and advocates of correctional programs were increasingly on the defensive. The Martinson Report fit into this changing policy climate, as the pendulum swung from liberal to conservative ideologies (Walker, 1989: 202–204).

2. In the 1950s, Richardson-Merrell developed a drug, MER/29, which it believed would repress cholesterol. Prior to marketing, the pharmaceutical company made false statements to the FDA about its pre-market testing results, which showed adverse blood changes in rats and monkeys. Once marketed (1960–1962), users of MER/29 experienced alarming side effects, including the development of cataracts. Roginsky was one of these unsuspecting consumers. His civil suit netted $17,500 in compensatory damages (medical expenses for his cataracts) and $100,000 in punitive damages. Although the company's liability was established, Judge Friendly indicated that the potential of hundreds of plaintiffs suing Richardson-Merrell could financially threaten the firm, and he probably limited the amount of the award in the Roginsky case because of this (Stone, 1975: 55–56).

References

Bale, Tony. (1983). "Breath of Death: The Asbestos Disaster Comes Home to Roost." *Health Pac Bulletin* 14 (May-June). In Jerome H. Skolnick and Elliott Currie, eds., *Crisis in American Institutions*, 413–427. 6th ed. Boston: Little, Brown, 1985.

Bancroft, Tom. (1989). "Two Minutes." *Financial World* 158 (June 27): 28–32.

Barnett, Harold C. (1981). "Corporate Capitalism, Corporate Crime." *Crime and Delinquency* 27 (Jan.): 4–23.

Becker, Howard S. (1963). *Outsiders.* New York: Free Press.

Beirne, Piers, and James Messerschmidt. (1991). *Criminology.* San Diego: Harcourt Brace Jovanovich.

Bell, Griffin. (1979). "White-Collar Crime Erodes Respect for the Justice System." *LEAA Newsletter* 8 (Jan.): 2, 11.

Bernard, Thomas J. (1984). "The Historical Development of Corporate Criminal Liability." *Criminology* 22 (Feb.): 3–17.

"Big Lie About Generic Drugs." (1987). *Consumer Reports* 52 (Aug.): 480–485.

Blair, John M. (1978). *The Control of Oil.* New York: Vintage Books.

Bloch, Herbert, and Gilbert Geis. (1962). *Man, Crime, and Society.* New York: Random House.

Blumstein, Alfred. (1993). "1992 Presidential Address: Making Rationality Relevant." *Criminology* 31 (Feb.): 1–16.

Box, Steven. (1983). *Power, Crime, and Mystification.* London: Tavistock.

Brace, Charles Loring. (1967). *The Dangerous Classes of New York.* Montclair, NJ: Patterson Smith.

Braithwaite, John. (1989a). *Crime, Shame, and Reintegration.* Cambridge: Cambridge University Press.

———. (1989b). "Criminological Theory and Organizational Crime." *Justice Quarterly* 6 (Sept.) 333–358.

———. (1984). *Corporate Crime in the Pharmaceutical Industry.* London: Routledge and Kegan Paul.

Braithwaite, John, and Gilbert Geis. (1982). "On Theory and Action for Corporate Crime Control." *Crime and Delinquency* 28 (Apr.): 292–314.

Brennan, Troyen A., Lucian Leape, Nan Laird, Liesl Hebert, Russell Locallo, Ann Law-thers, Joseph Newhouse, Paul Weiler, and Howard Hiatt. (1991). "Incidence of Adverse Events and Negligence in Hospitalized Patients—Results of Harvard Medical Practice Study I." *New England Journal of Medicine* 324 (Feb. 7): 370–376.

Cahalan, Margaret W., and Lee Anne Parsons. (1986). *Historical Corrections Statistics in the U.S., 1850–1984*. Rockville, Md.: Westat, Inc.

Calavita, Kitty, and Henry N. Pontell. (1991). " 'Other's People's Money' Revisited: Col-lective Embezzlement in the Savings and Loan and Insurance Industries." *Social Problems* 38 (Feb.): 94–112.

———. (1990). " 'Heads I Win, Tails You Lose': Deregulation, Crime, and Crisis in the Savings and Loan Industry." *Crime and Delinquency* 36 (July): 309–341.

Caldwell, Robert G. (1959). "Book Reviews." *Journal of Criminal Law, Criminology and Police Science* 50 (Sept.-Oct.): 281–283.

———. (1958). "A Reexamination of the Concept of White-Collar Crime." *Federal Pro-bation* 22: 30–36.

Carson, Rachel. (1962). *Silent Spring*. Boston: Houghton Mifflin.

Chambliss, William J. (1988). *Exploring Criminology*. New York: Macmillan.

Chambliss, William, and Robert Seidman. (1982). *Law, Order, and Power*. 2d ed. Reading, Mass.: Addison-Wesley.

Clayton, Mark. (1988). "Documents Boost Smokers' Claims Against Tobacco Firms." *Christian Science Monitor* (Apr.): 1, 32.

Clinard, Marshall. (1990). *Corporate Corruption: The Abuse of Power*. New York: Praeger.

———. (1946). "Criminological Theories of Violations of Wartime Regulations." *Amer-ican Sociological Review* 11 (June). In Gilbert Geis and Robert Meier, eds., *White-Collar Crime: Offenses in Business, Politics, and the Professions*, 85–101. New York: Free Press, 1977.

Clinard, Marshall B., and Richard Quinney. (1973). *Criminal Behavior Systems: A Typol-ogy*. 2d ed. New York: Holt, Rinehart and Winston.

Clinard, Marshall B., and Peter C. Yeager. (1980). *Corporate Crime*. New York: Free Press.

Clinard, Marshall B., Peter C. Yeager, Jeanne Brissette, David Petrashek, and Elizabeth Harries. (1979). *Illegal Corporate Behavior*. Washington, D.C.: GPO.

Cloward, Richard A., and Lloyd E. Ohlin. (1960). *Delinquency and Opportunity: A Theory of Delinquent Gangs*. New York: Free Press.

Cohen, Albert K. (1955). *Delinquent Boys: The Culture of the Gang*. New York: Free Press.

Cohen, Stanley E. (1980). "Advertising Regulation: Changing, Growing Area." *Adver-tising Age* 50 (Apr. 30): 213.

Coleman, James S. (1982). "The Asymmetric Society." In M. David Ermann and Richard J. Lundman, eds., *Corporate and Governmental Deviance*, 95–104. 2d ed. New York: Oxford University Press.

———. (1974). "Power and the Structure of Society." In M. David Ermann and Richard J. Lundman, eds., *Corporate and Governmental Deviance*, 21–27. New York: Oxford University Press.

Coleman, James W. (1989). *The Criminal Elite*. New York: St. Martin's Press.

———. (1987). "Toward an Integrated Theory of White-Collar Crime." *American Journal of Sociology* 93 (Sept.): 406–439.

Congressional Quarterly. (1975). *Watergate: Chronology of a Crisis.* Washington, D.C.: Congressional Quarterly.

"Consumer Defection." (1981). *The Nation* 233 (Nov. 7): 460.

Cox, Edward F., Robert C. Fellmeth, and John E. Schulz. (1969). *The Nader Report on the Federal Trade Commission.* New York: Grove Press.

Cressey, Donald R. (1953). *Other People's Money: A Study in the Social Psychology of Embezzlement.* Glencoe, Ill.: Free Press.

Cullen, Francis T., Bruce G. Link, and Craig W. Polanzi. (1982). "The Seriousness of Crime Revisited." *Criminology* 20 (May): 83–102.

Cullen, Francis T., William J. Maakestad, and Gray Cavender. (1987). *Corporate Crime Under Attack: The Ford Pinto Case and Beyond.* Cincinnati: Anderson.

Currie, Elliott. (1985). *Confronting Crime: An American Challenge.* New York: Pantheon Books.

Currie, Elliott, and Jerome Skolnick. (1984). *America's Problems: Social Issues and Public Policy.* Boston: Little, Brown.

Daly, Kathleen. (1989). "Gender and Varieties of White-Collar Crime." *Criminology* 27 (Nov.): 769–794.

Dinitz, Simon. (1982). "Multidisciplinary Approaches to White-Collar Crime." In Herbert Edelhertz and Thomas Overcast, eds., *White-Collar Crime: An Agenda for Research*, 129–152. Lexington, Mass.: Lexington Books.

"Doctors' Dilemma." (1990). *The Economist* 314 (Jan. 27): 69–70.

Donnelly, Patrick G. (1982). "The Origins of the Occupational Safety and Health Act of 1970." *Social Problems* 30 (Oct.): 13–25.

Dowie, Mark. (1977). "Pinto Madness." *Mother Jones* 2 (Sept.-Oct.). In Jerome Skolnick and Elliott Currie, eds., *Crisis in American Institutions*, 22–38. 6th ed. Boston: Little, Brown, 1985.

Durkheim, Emile. (1951). *Suicide.* Glencoe, Ill.: Free Press.

Edelhertz, Herbert. (1970). *The Nature, Impact and Prosecution of White-Collar Crime.* Washington, D.C.: GPO.

Edelhertz, Herbert, and Thomas Overcast, eds. (1982). *White-Collar Crime: An Agenda for Research.* Lexington, Mass.: Lexington Books.

Elliot, Delbert S., and Suzanne Ageton. (1980). "Reconciling Race and Class Differences in Self-Reported and Official Estimates of Delinquency." *American Sociological Review* 45 (Feb.): 95–110.

Empey, LaMar T. (1982). *American Delinquency: Its Meaning and Construction.* Homewood, Ill.: Dorsey Press.

"Employers Found Guilty of Murder." (1985). *New York Times* (June 16): E2.

Ermann, M. David, and Richard J. Lundman, eds. (1992). *Corporate and Governmental Deviance.* 4th ed. New York: Oxford University Press.

———. (1982). *Corporate and Governmental Deviance.* 2d ed. New York: Oxford University Press.

———. (1978a). *Corporate and Governmental Deviance.* New York: Oxford University Press.

———. (1978b). "Deviant Acts by Complex Organizations: Deviance and Social Control at the Organizational Level of Analysis." *Sociological Quarterly* 19 (Winter): 55–67.

Faulkner, Harold U. (1971). *The Quest for Social Justice, 1898–1914.* Chicago: Quadrangle Books.

"Fifty Years Ago . . ." (1986a). *Consumer Reports* 51 (Jan.): 8–10.

"Fifty Years Ago . . ." (1986b). *Consumer Reports* 51 (Feb.): 76–79.

Fisse, Brent, and John Braithwaite. (1983). *The Impact of Publicity on Corporate Offenders.* Albany: State University of New York Press.

Flanagan, Timothy J., and Kathleen Maguire, eds. (1992). *Sourcebook of Criminal Justice Statistics, 1991.* U.S. Department of Justice, Bureau of Justice Statistics. Washington, D.C.: GPO.

Folliard, Edward T. (1970). "When Drinking Was a Federal Crime." *San Francisco Chronicle* (Jan. 18): 2.

Frank, Nancy, and Michael Lombness. (1988). *Controlling Corporate Illegality: The Regulatory Justice System.* Cincinnati: Anderson.

Gardiner, John A. (1977). "Wincanton: The Politics of Corruption." In Jack Douglas and John Johnson, eds., *Official Deviance,* 50–69. Philadelphia: J. B. Lippincott.

Geis, Gilbert. (1988). "From Deuteronomy to Deniability: A Historical Perlustration on White-Collar Crime." *Justice Quarterly* 5 (Mar.): 7–32.

———. (1982). "A Research and Action Agenda with Respect to White-Collar Crime." In Herbert Edelhertz and Thomas Overcast, eds., *White-Collar Crime: An Agenda for Research,* 175–202. Lexington, Mass.: Lexington Books.

———. (1967). "The Heavy Electrical Equipment Antitrust Cases of 1961." In Gilbert Geis and Robert Meier, eds., *White-Collar Crime,* 117–132. New York: Free Press.

———. (1962). "Toward a Delineation of White-Collar Offenses." *Sociological Inquiry* 32 (Spring): 160–171.

Geis, Gilbert, and Robert F. Meier, eds. (1977). *White-Collar Crime: Offenses in Business, Politics, and the Professions,* revised ed. New York: Free Press.

"Generic Drugs: Still Safe?" (1990). *Consumer Reports* 55 (May): 310–313.

Gladwell, Malcolm. (1991). "A Fresh Approach at the FDA." *Washington Post National Weekly* (May 13–19): 32.

Gottfredson, Michael, and Travis Hirschi. (1986). "The True Value of Lambda Would Appear to Be Zero: An Essay on Career Criminals, Criminal Careers, Selective Incapacitation, Cohort Studies, and Related Topics." *Criminology* 24 (May): 213–234.

Graham, James M. (1972). "Amphetamine Politics on Capitol Hill." *Transaction* 9 (Jan.): 14–22, 53.

Green, Gary S. (1990). *Occupational Crime.* Chicago: Nelson-Hall.

Green, Mark, Beverly C. Moore, and Bruce Wasserstein. (1972). *The Closed Enterprise System.* New York: Grossman.

Green, Mark, and Norman Waitzman. (1979). "A Challenge to Murray Weidenbaum." *New York Times* (Oct. 28): 3–18.

Greenhouse, Linda. (1992). "Court Opens Way for Damage Suits Over Cigarettes." *New York Times* (June 25): A1, B10.

Gross, Edward. (1980). "Organizational Structure and Organizational Crime." In Gilbert Geis and Ezra Stotland, eds., *White-Collar Crime: Theory and Research,* 52–76. Beverly Hills, Calif.: Sage.

Hall, Jerome. (1952). *Theft, Law and Society.* 2d ed. Indianapolis: Bobbs-Merrill.

Halperin, Morton H., Jerry J. Berman, Robert L. Borosage, and Christine M. Marwick. (1976). *The Lawless State: The Crimes of the U.S. Intelligence Agencies.* New York: Penguin Books.

Hartung, Frank E. (1950). "White-Collar Offenses in the Wholesale Meat Industry in Detroit." *American Journal of Sociology* 56 (July). In Gilbert Geis and Robert Meier, eds., *White Collar Crime: Offenses in Business, Politics, and the Professions*, 154–167. New York: Free Press, 1977.

Hawkins, Keith. (1991). "Enforcing Regulation: More of the Same from Pearce and Tombs." *British Journal of Criminology* 31 (Autumn): 427–430.

Hindelang, Michael J., Travis Hirschi, and Joseph G. Weis. (1979). "Correlates of Delinquency: The Illusion of Discrepancy Between Self-Report and Official Measures." *American Sociological Review* 44 (Dec.): 995–1014.

Hirschi, Travis, and Michael Gottfredson. (1989). "The Significance of White-Collar Crime for a General Theory of Crime." *Criminology* 27 (May): 359–371.

———. (1987). "Causes of White-Collar Crime." *Criminology* 25 (Nov.): 949–974.

Hofstadter, Richard. (1955). *The Age of Reform*. New York: Alfred A. Knopf.

Horowitz, Lawrence C. (1988). *Taking Charge of Your Medical Fate*. New York: Random House.

"Illinois Court Overturns Conviction in Work Death." (1990). *Wall Street Journal* (Jan. 22): B2.

Inciardi, James A. (1992). *The War on Drugs II*. Mountain View, Calif.: Mayfield.

Isaacson, Walter. (1981). "Let the Buyers Beware." *Time* (Sept. 21): 22–23.

Isikoff, Michael. (1984). "The FTC Throws Away the Old Monopoly Board." *Washington Post National Weekly* (July 2): 33.

James, George. (1993). "Kelly Suggests Hearings' Goal Is a Police-Monitoring Agency." *New York Times* (Sept. 30): B1, B3.

Johns, Christina. (1991). "The War on Drugs: Why the Administration Continues to Pursue a Policy of Criminalization and Enforcement." *Social Justice* 18 (Winter): 147–165.

Johnston, David. (1992). "Prosecutor Shifts Attention to Bush on Iran Arms Deal." *New York Times* (Dec. 26): 1, 6.

Kadish, Sanford. (1963). "Some Observations on the Use of Criminal Sanctions in Enforcing Economic Regulations." *University of Chicago Law Review* 30 (Spring). In Gilbert Geis and Robert Meier, eds., *White-Collar Crime: Offenses in Business, Politics, and the Professions*, 296–317. New York: Free Press, 1977.

Kappeler, Victor E., Mark Blumberg, and Gary W. Potter. (1993). *The Mythology of Crime and Criminal Justice*. Prospect Heights, Ill.: Waveland Press.

Karr, Albert R. (1993). "Administration Raises Request for S&L Bailout." *Wall Street Journal* (Mar. 17): A2, A5.

Katz, Jack. (1980). "The Social Movement Against White-Collar Crime." In Egon Bittner and Sheldon L. Messinger, eds., *Criminology Review Yearbook*, 161–184. No. 2. Beverly Hills, Calif.: Sage.

Kelley, Clarence. (1974). "Message from the Director: 'White-Collar' Crime—A Serious Problem." *FBI Law Enforcement Bulletin* 43 (Sept.): 1.

Kelly, Orr. (1982). "Corporate Crime: The Untold Story." *U.S. News and World Report* (Sept. 6): 25–29.

Kessler, David A. (1991). "Drug Promotion and Scientific Exchange—The Role of the Clinical Investigator." *New England Journal of Medicine* 325 (July 18): 201–203.

Knapp Commission. (1972). *The Knapp Commission Report on Police Corruption*. New York: George Braziller.

Knight, Jerry. (1990). "Let's Keep It Civil." *Washington Post National Weekly* (Aug. 13–19): 34.

Kolko, Gabriel. (1963). *The Triumph of Conservatism*. New York: Free Press.

Kramer, Ronald C. (1989). "Criminologists and the Social Movement Against Corporate Crime." *Social Justice* 16 (Summer): 146–164.

Kuhn, Thomas S. (1962). *The Structure of Scientific Revolutions*. Chicago: University of Chicago Press.

Kurtz, Howard. (1992). "Asleep at the Switch." *Washington Post National Weekly* (Dec. 21–27): 6–9.

Kwitny, Jonathan. (1981). "The Great Transportation Conspiracy." *Harper's* (Feb.): 14–21.

LaFraniere, Sharon. (1990). "When Less Is More: How to Make S&L Charges Stick." *Washington Post National Weekly* (Sept. 17–23): 31–32.

Lane, Robert E. (1953). "Why Businessmen Violate the Law." *Journal of Criminal Law, Criminology and Police Science*. In Gilbert Geis and Robert Meier, eds., *White-Collar Crime: Offenses in Business, Politics, and the Professions*, 102–116. New York: Free Press, 1977.

Leape, Lucian L., Troyen Brennan, Nan Laird, Ann Lawthers, Russell Locallo, Benjamin Barnes, Liesl Hebert, Joseph Newhouse, Paul Weiler, and Howard Hiatt. (1991). "Nature of Adverse Events in Hospitalized Patients—Results of Harvard Medical Practice Study II." *New England Journal of Medicine* 324 (Feb. 7): 377–384.

Lennard, Henry L., Leon Epstein, Arnold Bernstein, and Donald Ransom. (1971). *Mystification and Drug Misuse*. San Francisco: Jossey-Bass, Inc.

Leonard, William N., and Marvin Glenn Weber. (1970). "Auto-Makers and Dealers: A Study of Criminogenic Market Forces." *Law and Society Review* 4 (Feb.). In Gilbert Geis and Robert Meier, eds., *White-Collar Crime: Offenses in Business, Politics, and the Professions*, 133–148. New York: Free Press, 1977.

Levin, Doron P. (1993). "Battle Over GM's Pickup Could Take Years to Settle." *New York Times* (Apr. 12): D1, D5.

Lindesmith, Alfred R. (1965). *The Addict and the Law*. New York: Random House.

Lindesmith, Alfred R. (1947). *Opiate Addiction*. Bloomington, Ind.: Principia Press.

Lipset, S. M., and W. Schneider. (1978). "How's Business: What the Public Thinks." *Public Opinion* 1 (July-Aug.): 41–47.

"Los Angeles Tries Out New Rail Train." (1990). *Antioch Calif. Daily Ledger-Post Dispatch* (Nov. 23): 11.

Madge, John. (1962). *The Origins of Scientific Sociology*. New York: Free Press.

Maguire, Kathleen, and Timothy J. Flanagan, eds. (1991). *Sourcebook of Criminal Justice Statistics, 1990*. U.S. Department of Justice, Bureau of Justice Statistics. Washington, D.C.: GPO.

Mann, Kenneth. (1985). *Defending White-Collar Crime: A Portrait of Attorneys at Work*. New Haven, Conn.: Yale University Press.

Mannheim, Hermann. (1965). *Comparative Criminology*. Boston: Houghton Mifflin.

Manson, Donald A. (1986). *Tracking Offenders: White-Collar Crime*. Bureau of Justice Statistics Special Report No. NCJ-102867. Washington, D.C.: U.S. Department of Justice.

Marcus, Amy D., and Bridget O'Brian. (1990). "Eastern Indicted over Failures in Maintenance." *Wall Street Journal* (July 26): A4.

Margolick, David. (1988). "At the Bar." *New York Times* (Apr. 1): B7.

Martin, Randy, Robert J. Mutchnick, and W. Timothy Austin. (1990). *Criminological Thought: Pioneers Past and Present*. New York: Macmillan.

Matza, David. (1964). *Delinquency and Drift*. New York: John Wiley.

McCormick, Albert E. (1979). "Dominant Class Interests and the Emergence of Antitrust Legislation." *Contemporary Crises* 3: 399–417.

McGrath, Ellie. (1981). "Rumbling Toward Ruin." *Time* (Mar. 30): 11–15.

Merton, Robert K. (1938). "Social Structure and Anomie." *American Sociological Review* 3 (Oct.): 672–682.

Messerschmidt, Jim. (1983). *The Trial of Leonard Peltier*. Boston: South End Press.

Michalowski, Raymond J. (1985). *Order, Law, and Crime*. New York: Random House.

Miliband, Ralph. (1969). *The State in Capitalist Society: The Analysis of the Western System of Power*. London: Quartet Books.

Miller, Judith. (1980). "Congress Reins in Regulatory Authorities." *New York Times* (Jan. 6): Sec. 12, 25.

Miller, Walter B. (1958). "Lower Class Culture as a Generating Milieu of Gang Delinquency." *Journal of Social Issues* 14: 5–19.

Mintz, Morton, and Jerry S. Cohen. (1971). *America, Inc.* New York: Dell.

Molotch, Harvey. (1970). "Oil in Santa Barbara and Power in America." *Sociological Inquiry* 40 (Winter). In R. Serge Denisoff, ed., *The Sociology of Dissent*, 105–127. New York: Harcourt Brace Jovanovich, 1974.

Molotch, Harvey, and Marilyn Lester. (1975). "Accidental News: The Great Oil Spill as Local Occurrence and National Event." *American Journal of Sociology* 81 (Sept.): 235–260.

———. (1974). "News as Purposive Behavior: On the Strategic Use of Routine Events, Accidents, and Scandals." *American Sociological Review* 39 (Feb.): 101–112.

———. (1973). "Accidents, Scandals, and Routines: Resources for Insurgent Methodology." *Insurgent Sociologist* 3 (Summer): 1–11.

"Monopoly on the Cereal Shelves?" (1981). *Consumer Reports* (Feb.): 76–80.

Moran, Leslie J. (1992). "Corporate Criminal Capacity: Nostalgia for Representation." *Social and Legal Studies* 1 (Sept.): 371–391.

Mufson, Steven. (1990). "Taking the Sherman Act Out of Mothballs." *Washington Post National Weekly* (June 25–July 1): 20–21.

Nader, Ralph. (1966). *Unsafe at Any Speed*. New York: Pocket Books.

Naughton, James M. (1971). "President Signs Bill to Cut Auto Fumes 90% by 1977." *New York Times* (Jan. 1): 1, 11.

Newman, Donald J. (1958). "White-Collar Crime: An Overview and Analysis." *Law and Contemporary Problems* 23 (Autumn). In Gilbert Geis and Robert Meier, eds., *White-Collar Crime: Offenses in Business, Politics, and the Professions*, 50–64. New York: Free Press, 1977.

Nye, Ivan F., James Short, Jr., and Virgil J. Olson. (1958). "Socioeconomic Status and Delinquent Behavior." *American Journal of Sociology* 63 (Jan.): 381–389.

Oteri, Joseph S., and Harvey A. Silvergate. (1967). "In the Marketplace of Free Ideas: A Look at the Passage of the Marijuana Tax Act." In J. L. Simmons, ed., *Marijuana: Myths and Realities*, 136–162. North Hollywood, Calif.: Brandon House.

Parks, Evelyn L. (1970). "From Constabulary to Police Society: Implications for Social Control." *Catalyst* 5 (Summer). In William J. Chambliss, ed., *Criminal Law in Action*, 81–93. Santa Barbara, Calif.: Hamilton, 1975.

Patterson, Gregory A. (1992). "Sears Is Dealt a Harsh Lesson by States." *Wall Street Journal* (Oct. 2): A9C.

Pearce, Frank, and Steven Tombs. (1991). "Policing Corporate 'Skid Rows': A Reply to Hawkins." *British Journal of Criminology* 31 (Autumn): 415–426.

Pepinsky, Harold E. (1974). "From White-Collar Crime to Exploitation: Redefinition of a Field." *Journal of Criminal Law and Criminology* 65 (June): 225–233.

Perkus, Cathy, ed. (1975). *COINTELPRO: The FBI's Secret War on Political Freedom.* New York: Monad Press.

Perrow, Charles. (1979). *Complex Organizations: A Critical Essay.* 2d ed. Glenview, Ill.: Scott, Foresman.

Pizzo, Stephen, Mary Fricker, and Paul Muolo. (1991). *Inside Job: The Looting of America's Savings and Loans.* New York: Harper Perennial.

Polsky, Ned. (1967). *Hustlers, Beats, and Others.* New York: Doubleday.

Pope, Carl E., and Lee E. Ross. (1992). "Race, Crime and Justice: The Aftermath of Rodney King." *The Criminologist* 17 (Nov.-Dec.): 1, 7–10.

Potts, Mark. (1991). "What's Gotten into the FTC?" *Washington Post National Weekly* (June 17–23): 32.

Poveda, Tony G. (1992). "White-Collar Crime and the Justice Department: The Institutionalization of a Concept." *Crime, Law and Social Change* 17 (May): 235–252.

———. (1990). *Lawlessness and Reform: The FBI in Transition.* Pacific Grove, Calif.: Brooks/Cole.

———. (1970). "The Image of the Criminal: A Critique of Crime and Delinquency Theories." *Issues in Criminology* 5 (Winter): 59–83.

Presidential Commission on the Space Shuttle Challenger Accident. (1986a). *Report of the Presidential Commission on the Space Shuttle Challenger Accident.* Vol. 1. Washington, D.C.: GPO.

———. (1986b). *Report of the Presidential Commission on the Space Shuttle Challenger Accident.* Vol. 4. Washington, D.C.: GPO.

Quinney, Richard. (1977). *Class, State and Crime: On the Theory and Practice of Criminal Justice.* New York: David McKay.

———. (1964). "The Study of White-Collar Crime: Toward a Reorientation in Theory and Research." In Gilbert Geis and Robert Meier, eds., *White-Collar Crime: Offenses in Business, Politics, and the Professions,* 283–295. New York: Free Press, 1977.

Raab, Selwyn. (1993). "Ex-Rogue Officer Tells Panel of Police Graft in New York." *New York Times* (Sept. 28): A1, B3.

Raynor, Theodore J. (1968). "An Inquiry into the Identification of Opium with the Chinese Minority in the United States During the Nineteenth Century." Master's Thesis, University of California, Berkeley.

Reid, Sue Titus. (1976). *Crime and Criminology.* Hinsdale, Ill.: Dryden Press.

Reiman, Jeffrey H. (1979). *The Rich Get Richer and the Poor Get Prison.* New York: John Wiley.

Reinhold, Robert. (1991). "Violence and Racism Are Routine in Los Angeles Police, Study Says." *New York Times* (July 10): A1, A14.

Reith, Charles. (1952). *The Blind Eye of History: A Study of the Origins of the Present Police Era.* London: Farber and Farber.

Rensberger, Boyce. (1986). "Fire Engulfs Ship with Seven Aboard Soon After Liftoff." *Washington Post* (Jan. 29): A1, A6.

Rosenthal, Andrew. (1992). "Outsider Steals Bush's Rose Garden Scene." *New York Times* (Apr. 30): A18.

Ross, Irwin. (1980). "How Lawless Are Big Companies?" *Fortune* (Dec. 1): 57–64.

Rothman, David J. (1971). *The Discovery of the Asylum: The Social Order and Disorder in the New Republic.* Boston: Little, Brown.

"RTC Asks for Investigation of Its Legal Department." (1992). *Wall Street Journal* (Aug. 13): B3.

"RTC Curbs Aide's Duties." (1992). *New York Times* (June 27): 38.

"S&L's Are Given $26.3 Billion More." (1993). *New York Times* (Nov. 23): B8.

Sarbin, Theodore R. (1969). "The Myth of the Criminal Type." *Monday Evening Papers* (Center for Advanced Studies, Wesleyan University) 18: 1–31.

———. (1967). "The Dangerous Individual: An Outcome of Social Identity Transformations." *British Journal of Criminology* 7 (July): 285–295.

Satin, Joseph, ed. (1960). *The 1950s: America's 'Placid' Decade.* Boston: Houghton Mifflin.

Schrager, Laura, and James F. Short. (1978). "Toward a Sociology of Organizational Crime." *Social Problems* 25 (Apr.): 407–419.

Schur, Edwin M. (1973). *Radical Non-Intervention: Rethinking the Delinquency Problem.* Engelwood Cliffs, N.J.: Prentice-Hall.

———. (1969). *Our Criminal Society: The Social and Legal Sources of Crime in America.* Englewood Cliffs, N.J.: Prentice-Hall.

Schwendinger, Herman, and Julia Schwendinger. (1970). "Defenders of Order or Guardians of Human Rights?" *Issues in Criminology* 5 (Summer): 123–157.

Sellin, Thorsten. (1938). "A Sociological Approach." *Culture Conflict and Crime.* In Marvin Wolfgang, Leonard Savitz, and Norman Johnson, eds., *The Sociology of Crime and Delinquency.* 2d ed., 3–10. New York: John Wiley, 1970.

Shapiro, Susan P. (1990). "Collaring the Crime, Not the Criminal: Reconsidering the Concept of White-Collar Crime." *American Sociological Review* 55 (June): 346–365.

———. (1984). *Wayward Capitalists: Target of the Securities and Exchange Commission.* New Haven, Conn.: Yale University Press.

———. (1983). "The New Moral Entrepreneurs: Corporate Crime Crusaders." *Contemporary Sociology* 12 (May): 304–307.

———. (1980). *Thinking About White-Collar Crime: Matters of Conceptualization and Research.* Washington, D.C.: GPO.

Shenton, James P. (1964). *History of the United States: From 1865 to the Present.* Garden City, N.Y.: Doubleday.

Short, James, Jr., and Ivan Nye. (1957). "Reported Behavior as a Criterion of Deviant Behavior." *Social Problems* 5 (Winter): 207–213.

Simon, David R., and D. Stanley Eitzen. (1993). *Elite Deviance.* 4th ed. Boston: Allyn and Bacon.

Simon, Rita J. (1990). "Women and Crime Revisited." *Criminal Justice Research Bulletin* 5: 1–11.

Simon, William, and John H. Gagnon. (1976). "The Anomie of Affluence: A Post-Mertonian Conception." *American Journal of Sociology* 82 (Sept.): 356–378.

Shah, Angela. (1994). "FDA Cites Evidence of Cigarette Makers Keeping Nicotine at Addictive Levels." *Wall Street Journal* (Feb. 28): B5.

Sims, Calvin. (1993). "Keating Convicted of U.S. Charges." *New York Times* (Jan. 7): D1, D2.

Skolnick, Jerome H. (1969). *The Politics of Protest*. New York: Ballantine Books.

Smith, Richard Austin. (1961). "The Incredible Electrical Conspiracy." *Fortune* (Apr., May): 132–180, 161–224.

Smith, Roger. (1966). "Status Politics and the Image of the Addict." *Issues in Criminology* 2 (Fall): 157–176.

"Snap, Crackle, Flop!" (1982). *Time* (Jan. 25): 58.

Snell, Bradford. (1985). "American Ground Transport." In Jerome Skolnick and Elliott Currie, eds., *Crisis in American Institutions*, 319–342. Boston: Little, Brown.

Snider, Laureen. (1990). "Cooperative Models and Corporate Crime: Panacea or Cop-Out?" *Crime and Delinquency* 36 (July): 373–390.

Steffensmeier, Darrell. (1989). "On the Causes of 'White-Collar' Crime: An Assessment of Hirschi and Gottfredson's Claims." *Criminology* 27 (May): 345–358.

Stevens, Amy. (1993). "Keating Is Given 12.5-Year Sentence for Bank Fraud." *Wall Street Journal* (July 9): B7.

Stevens, William K. (1993). "New Data on Spill Offered by Exxon." *New York Times* (Apr. 30): A18.

Stone, Christopher. (1975). *Where the Law Ends: The Social Control of Corporate Behavior*. New York: Harper and Row.

Stone, I. F. (1963). *The Haunted Fifties*. New York: Vintage Books.

Strum, Charles. (1992). "Major Lawsuit on Smoking Is Dropped." *New York Times* (Nov. 6): B1, B5.

Sulzberger, A., Jr. (1980a). "House, in Compromise, Votes to Restrain FTC." *New York Times* (May 21): D10.

———. (1980b). "Will FTC Battle Inhibit Regulation?" *New York Times* (May 22): D1.

Sutherland, Edwin H. (1983). *White-Collar Crime: The Uncut Version*. New Haven, Conn.: Yale University Press.

———. (1949). *White-Collar Crime*. New York: Holt, Rinehart and Winston.

———. (1945). "Is 'White-Collar Crime' Crime?" *American Sociological Review* 10 (Apr.). In Gilbert Geis and Robert Meier, eds., *White-Collar Crime: Offenses in Business, Politics, and the Professions*, 260–271. New York: Free Press, 1977.

———. (1940). "White-Collar Criminality." *American Sociological Review* 5 (Feb.). In Gilbert Geis and Robert Meier, eds., *White-Collar Crime: Offenses in Business, Politics, and the Professions*, 38–49. New York: Free Press, 1977.

———. (1937). *The Professional Thief*. Chicago: University of Chicago Press.

Sutherland, Edwin H., and Donald R. Cressey. (1960). *Principles of Criminology*. 6th ed. Chicago: J. B. Lippincott.

Swartz, Joel. (1975). "Silent Killers at Work." *Crime and Social Justice* 3 (Spring-Summer): 15–20.

Sykes, Gresham M., and David Matza. (1957). "Techniques of Neutralization: A Theory of Delinquency." *American Sociological Review* 22 (Dec.): 664–670.

Tappan, Paul W. (1947). "Who Is the Criminal?" *American Sociological Review* 12 (Feb.). In Gilbert Geis and Robert Meier, eds., *White-Collar Crime: Offenses in Business, Politics, and the Professions*, 272–282. New York: Free Press, 1977.

Tillman, Robert, and Henry N. Pontell. (1992). "Is Justice 'Collar-Blind?': Punishing Medicaid Provider Fraud." *Criminology* 30 (Nov.): 547–574.

Trebach, Arnold S. (1987). *The Great Drug War*. New York: Macmillan.

U.S. Attorney General. (1974–1976, 1992). *Annual Report of the Attorney General of the United States*. Washington, D.C.: GPO.

U.S. Bureau of the Census. (1991). *Statistical Abstract of the United States: 1991.* Washington, D.C.: GPO.

U.S. Bureau of Labor Statistics. (1992). "BLS 1990 Survey of Occupational Injuries and Illnesses." *Job Safety and Health Quarterly* 3 (Winter): 24–25.

U.S. Department of the Interior. (1989). *Federal Offshore Statistics: 1988.* Washington, D.C.: GPO.

U.S. Department of Justice, Bureau of Justice Statistics. (1992a). *Criminal Victimization in the United States, 1990.* Washington, D.C.: Office of Justice Programs.

———, Bureau of Justice Statistics. (1992b). *Federal Criminal Case Processing, 1980–90.* Washington, D.C.: Office of Justice Programs.

———, Bureau of Justice Statistics. (1992c). *Compendium of Federal Justice Statistics, 1989.* Washington, D.C.: Office of Justice Programs.

———, Federal Bureau of Investigation. (1991). *Crime in the United States, 1990.* Washington, D.C.: GPO.

———, Federal Bureau of Investigation. (1990a). *Crime in the United States, 1989.* Washington, D.C.: GPO.

———, National Institute of Justice. (1990b). *Fiscal Year 1990 Program Plan.* NCJ-119318. Washington, D.C.: Office of Justice Programs.

———, Bureau of Justice Statistics. (1988). *Report to the Nation on Crime and Justice.* 2d ed. Washington, D.C.: Bureau of Justice Statistics.

———, Bureau of Justice Statistics. (1987). *Federal Offenses and Offenders: White-Collar Crime.* NCJ-106876. Washington, D.C.: Bureau of Justice Statistics.

———, Bureau of Justice Statistics. (1986). *Prosecution of Felony Arrests, 1981.* Washington, D.C.: Inslaw.

———, Federal Bureau of Investigation. (1985). *Crime in the United States, 1984.* Washington, D.C.: GPO.

———, Federal Bureau of Investigation. (1982). *Crime in the United States, 1981.* Washington, D.C.: GPO.

———, Bureau of Justice Statistics. (1981). *The Dictionary of Criminal Justice Data Terminology.* 2d ed. NCJ-76939. Washington, D.C.: Bureau of Justice Statistics.

———. (1980). *National Priorities for the Investigation and Prosecution of White-Collar Crime.* Washington, D.C.: GPO.

———, Federal Bureau of Investigation. (1962). *Crime in the United States, 1961.* Washington, D.C.: GPO.

U.S. House of Representatives. (1992). *Why S&L Crooks Have Failed to Pay Millions of Dollars in Court-Ordered Restitution: Nineteen Case Studies.* Staff Report for the Subcommittee on Financial Institutions Supervision, Regulation, and Insurance of the Committee on Banking, Finance, and Urban Affairs. 102d Cong., 2d sess. (Apr.). Washington, D.C.: GPO.

———. (1990). *The U.S. Government's War Against Fraud, Abuse, and Misconduct in Financial Institutions: Winning Some Battles But Losing the War.* Report by the Committee on Government Operations. 101st Cong., 2d sess. (Nov. 15). Washington, D.C.: GPO.

———. (1981). *Hearings Before the Subcommittee on Oversight and Investigations of the Committee on Energy and Commerce.* 97th Cong., 1st sess. (Mar. 12, Apr. 2–3). Washington, D.C.: GPO.

———. (1980a). *Joint Hearings Before the Subcommittee on Energy and Power of the Committee on Interstate and Foreign Commerce and the Subcommittee on Crime of the*

Committee on the Judiciary. 96th Cong., 1st sess. (May 30, June 4, 1979). Washington, D.C.: GPO.

———. (1980b). *Hearings Before a Subcommittee of the Committee on Appropriations (Re: Justice Dept.).* 96th Cong., 1st sess. (March). Washington, D.C.: GPO.

———. (1979). *White-Collar Crime: Hearings Before the Subcommittee on Crime of the Committee on the Judiciary.* 95th Cong., 2d sess. (June 21, July 12, 1978). Washington, D.C.: GPO.

U.S. Senate. (1992). *Civil Litigation Activities of the FDIC and RTC: Hearing Before the Committee on Banking, Housing, and Urban Affairs.* 102d Cong., 2d sess. (June 2). Washington, D.C.: GPO.

———. (1991a). *Examining Practices of U.S. Pharmaceutical Companies and How Drug Prices and Prescriptions Are Affected: Hearings Before the Committee on Labor and Human Resources.* 101st Cong., 2d sess. (Dec. 11, 12, 1990). Washington, D.C.: GPO.

———. (1991b). *Savings and Loan Crisis: Hearing Before the Committee on the Judiciary.* 101st Cong., 2d sess. (Aug. 14, 1990). Washington, D.C.: GPO.

———. (1976). *Final Report of the Select Committee to Study Governmental Operations with Respect to Intelligence Operations.* Book 3. Washington, D.C.: GPO.

U.S. Surgeon General. (1989). *Reducing the Health Consequences of Smoking: 25 Years of Progress.* Rockville, Md.: U.S. Department of Health and Human Services.

———. (1988). *The Health Consequences of Smoking: Nicotine Addiction.* Washington, D.C.: GPO.

Vaughan, Diane. (1983). *Controlling Unlawful Organizational Behavior: Social Structure and Corporate Misconduct.* Chicago: University of Chicago Press.

Vise, David A., and Steve Coll. (1991). "The Two Faces of Greed." *Washington Post National Weekly* (Oct. 7–13): 6–8.

Vold, George B., and Thomas J. Bernard. (1986). *Theoretical Criminology.* 3d ed. New York: Oxford University Press.

Waegel, William B., M. David Ermann, and Alan M. Horowitz. (1981). "Organizational Responses to Imputations of Deviance." *Sociological Quarterly* 22 (Winter): 43–55.

Walker, Samuel. (1989). *Sense and Nonsense About Crime: A Policy Guide.* 2d ed. Pacific Grove, Calif.: Brooks/Cole.

Wallerstein, James, and C. J. Wyle. (1947). "Our Law-Abiding Lawbreakers." *Probation* 25 (Apr.): 107–112.

Walsh, Elsa, and Benjamin Weiser. (1988). "Public Courts, Private Justice." *Washington Post National Weekly* (Nov. 28–Dec. 4): 6–8.

Webster, William H. (1980). "An Examination of FBI Theory and Methodology Regarding White-Collar Crime Investigation and Prevention." *American Criminal Law Review* 17 (Winter): 275–286.

Weisburd, David, Stanton Wheeler, Elin Waring, and Nancy Bode. (1991). *Crimes of the Middle Classes.* New Haven, Conn.: Yale University Press.

Wheeler, Stanton, Kenneth Mann, and Austin Sarat. (1988). *Sitting in Judgment: The Sentencing of White-Collar Criminals.* New Haven, Conn.: Yale University Press.

Wheeler, Stanton, David Weisburd, and Nancy Bode. (1982). "Sentencing the White-Collar Offender: Rhetoric and Reality." *American Sociological Review* 47 (Oct.): 641–659.

Wheeler, Stanton, David Weisburd, Nancy Bode, and Elin Waring. (1988). "White-Collar Crimes and Criminals." *American Criminal Law Review* 25 (Winter): 331–357.

Wilbanks, William. (1987). *The Myth of a Racist Criminal Justice System.* Monterey, Calif.: Brooks/Cole.

Wilcox, Clair, and William Shepherd. (1975). *Public Policies Toward Business.* Homewood, Ill.: Richard Irwin.

Williams, Lena. (1992). "FDA Steps Up Effort to Control Vitamin Claims." *New York Times* (Aug. 9): 1, 34.

Wilson, James Q. (1983). *Thinking About Crime.* Rev. ed. New York: Vintage Books.

Wingersky, Melvin F. (1958). *A Treatise on the Law of Crimes* (Clark and Marshall). 6th ed. Chicago: Callaghan.

Winslow, Ron. (1990). "Safety Group Cites Fatalities Linked to Work." *Wall Street Journal* (Aug. 31): B8.

Wolfe, Sidney M., and Christopher M. Coley. (1981). *Pills That Don't Work.* New York: Farrar Straus Giroux.

Wolfgang, Marvin E. (1974). *Criminology: A Bibliography—Research and Theory in the United States, 1945–1972.* Philadelphia: Center for Studies in Criminology and Criminal Law, University of Pennsylvania.

Wolfgang, Marvin, Robert Figlio, and Thorsten Sellin. (1972). *Delinquency in a Birth Cohort.* Chicago: University of Chicago Press.

Wolfgang, Marvin E., Robert M. Figlio, and Terence P. Thornberry. (1975). *The Criminology Index.* New York: Elsevier.

Wright, J. Patrick. (1979). *On a Clear Day You Can See General Motors.* New York: Avon Books.

Wright, Richard A., and David O. Friedrichs. (1991). "White-Collar Crime in the Criminal Justice Curriculum." *Journal of Criminal Justice Education* 2 (Spring): 95–121.

Yoder, Stephen A. (1978). "Comments: Criminal Sanctions for Corporate Illegality." *Journal of Criminal Law and Criminology* 69, no. 1: 40–58.

Index

About the Author

TONY G. POVEDA is Professor of Sociology at the State University of New York at Plattsburgh. Poveda is the author of numerous articles and professional papers relating to the FBI, organizational crime, and deviance. He is the author of *Lawlessness and Reform: The FBI in Transition*.

ISBN 0-275-94586-3

HARDCOVER BAR CODE